Managing Human Resources in China

China is undergoing a dramatic transition from the old to the new as the country integrates into global product and labour markets. *Managing Human Resources in China* examines the emergence of new and hybrid forms of employment practices within Chinese multinational corporations (MNCs) from the perspective of local stakeholders. These include managers, workers and government officials, who take part in strategic planning and policy implementation whilst coping with the pressure of an ever-changing environment. Working in and observing four foreign-invested manufacturing plants located in one of China's new industrial clusters, Yu Zheng offers a fresh perspective on the management of MNCs. The voices of employees have not been heard before, yet they are the critical actors in China's transformation through foreign direct investment. This book explores the pains and gains, achievements and setbacks of managing the Chinese workforce, which is ever pragmatic, increasingly assertive and constantly evolving.

YU ZHENG is a lecturer in Asian Business and International Human Resource Management at the School of Management, Royal Holloway, University of London. Her research interests are in international human resource management, cross-country transfer of management practices and comparative employment relations. She is currently a member of the Euro-Asia Management Studies Association.

Managing Human Resources in China

The View from Inside Multinationals

YU ZHENG

CAMBRIDGE
UNIVERSITY PRESS

CAMBRIDGE UNIVERSITY PRESS
Cambridge, New York, Melbourne, Madrid, Cape Town,
Singapore, São Paulo, Delhi, Mexico City

Cambridge University Press
The Edinburgh Building, Cambridge CB2 8RU, UK

Published in the United States of America by Cambridge University Press, New York

www.cambridge.org
Information on this title: www.cambridge.org/9781107013551

First published 2013

Printed and bound in the United Kingdom by the MPG Books Group

A catalogue record for this publication is available from the British Library

Library of Congress Cataloguing in Publication data
   Managing human resources in China : the view from inside multinationals /
   Yu Zheng.
      p.   cm.
   Includes bibliographical references and index.
   ISBN 978-1-107-01355-1 (hbk.)
   1. International business enterprises – China – Personnel
   management.   2. Personnel management – China.   I. Zheng, Yu.
   HD2910.M36   2012
   658.300951–dc23
   2012024501

ISBN 978-1-107-01355-1 Hardback

Contents

Figures

Tables

Preface

China is in dramatic transition from an old to a new economy as a consequence of the country's integration into global product and labour markets. Given the scale and spread of foreign direct investment in China, the tensions and triumphs of managing human resources in multinationals have attracted increasing attention from academics and practitioners. However, we still lack a book that tells the story of managing human resources in China from the perspective of "actors" inside multinationals, the people who handle the day-to-day work and cope with the pressures within this ever-changing environment.

In taking an actor-centred approach, I am able to explore the broader meanings of China's country context for managing human resources in multinationals. Instead of interpreting China's immature labour market, non-transparent state–business relations and underdeveloped social infrastructure as *obstacles* to the transfer of more sophisticated management systems, I show China as a site where actors have considerable space for developing alternative management practices that fit organizational needs. In this sense, China's transition allows actors to assess, interpret and negotiate the relevance of the existing management repertoire regardless of origin: whether parent companies, local firms or international business counterparts. New and hybrid forms of human resource management practices are not simply the "adoption", "adaptation" or "re-institutionalization" of established management recipes. Rather, the *emergence* of subsidiary human resource management practices entails workplace-level choices, made through interaction with dynamic local labour markets and changing local institutions.

Adopting an actor-centred approach responds to calls for studies that broaden our understanding of multinationals. This book is based on insiders' views of subsidiaries of multinationals. By examining the process of managing the local workforce, I show subsidiary actors' interests, tactics and restraints in deciding human resource management practices. While the focus here is the subsidary level, I do not, by any means, intend to isolate subsidiaries from the wider corporate and local business networks. The very fact that subsidiaries are both empowered and constrained by international and local stakeholders means actions are often the product of political struggle, with actors contesting different repertoires in the management of local employees.

Finally, by taking an actor-centred approach, I am able to tackle the human resource management implications of the strategic reorientation of multinationals in China. If any conclusion can be drawn about China's economy after the recent global recession, it is that the country's export-oriented growth mode has to change, voluntarily or involuntarily. Being both the major contributors to and beneficiaries of this growth mode, many multinationals in China are now reviewing, or have already reviewed, their local strategy. In this book, I explore the consequences of such strategic reorientation in terms of organizational structure, job design and employment relations in subsidiaries. I show how actors are able to reposition the strategic function of subsidiaries as multinationals review their global and regional strategies.

Acknowledgements

I am grateful to Professor Chris Smith, who inspired me to get over my doubts and fears and put this book forward for publication. His continuous encouragement, constructive comments and whole-hearted support has seen me through this challenging yet fascinating journey.

My sincere thank you goes to Professor Jos Gamble, Professor Fang Lee Cooke and Dr Robert Fitzgerald, who read the first draft of this book and offered generous reviews and valuable suggestions.

I must thank my informants from the companies that participated in my study. To keep their identity confidential, I cannot write down a list of names here. But their insiders' perspectives have tremendously enriched my knowledge of the management practices adopted by Japanese subsidiaries in China. Stories of achievements and setbacks in their daily work as well as managing these subsidiaries are the making of my work.

I am most grateful to the researchers at the Euro-Asia Management Studies Association Conferences, the International Labour Process Conferences and the Critical Management Research Workshop of the Academy of Management Conference. They gave me invaluable feedback on papers, many of which have become chapters or sections in this book.

My research was funded by the Thomas Holloway Scholarship and the School of Management, Royal Holloway, University of London. The Japan Foundation also funded my research trip to Japan. I am very grateful for the generous fellowship these institutions offered.

I would like to say a special thank you to my editor, Paula Parish, assistant editor, Josephine Lane and the reviewers, who gave me kind suggestions and brilliant ideas to improve the quality of this book. I would also like to thank Jessica Main, John Griffiths, Vinti Vaid, Keith Povey and Sue Browning, who helped with proofreading my draft work at different stages. Without their understanding and patience, I would not have been able to improve my academic writing.

I owe much to my family and friends. They laugh with me in the happy days. They console me in my setbacks. Their love and care make life just wonderful.

1 | Introduction: economic transition, multinational corporations and employment practices at workplace level in China

Since China embarked on the journey to economic reform and opened up to foreign investment, the country's industrial landscape has changed significantly. Taking incremental and experimental steps, the Chinese government has re-introduced market competition to the economy, relaxed control over business operations and allowed under-performing state-owned enterprises to go bankrupt. In the northern provinces, the home of large-scale state-owned factories, structural problems have largely restricted the development of the region. While the old factory towns have struggled to regain vitality by restructuring the state-owned enterprises (SOEs), the eastern and southern coastal areas have proven to be more successful in generating industrial output by attracting privately owned, collective-owned and foreign-invested companies. Given the locational advantages and preferential policies offered by the local government, a large number of investors have chosen the coastal regions to set up manufacturing plants. China has thus witnessed a decline of the traditional factory towns in the inner areas and the emergence of new industrial clusters alongside the coastal economic centres.

Structural transitions from a centrally planned economy to a market-oriented economy have been followed by changes in many aspects of employment relations in China as well. Public sector and enterprise reform in the 1990s entailed departure from the dominant *danwei* (or work unit) system, which used to offer employees lifetime employment, healthcare, company accommodation and child care. The government's role has changed from major employer to employment relations regulator. Companies in the non-state sector, including the foreign-invested manufacturers in the new industrial clusters, have increased in importance as employers. Employment contracts have been adopted to specify the rights and responsibilities of employers and employees. A social insurance system, whilst as yet underdeveloped, is expected to provide employees with the social benefits that used to be covered by the *danwei*.

Market-oriented reform has also led to the birth of new employee groups taking jobs at multinational corporations (MNCs). Downsizing of the SOEs created the "40/50" group, who were laid off in their 40s or 50s with some redundancy compensation. This group of employees are trained, well disciplined and keen on finding work again in the rising urban sectors. But given their long years of employment in the SOEs, employers may find it difficult to train them to fit into a different company culture. The second new employee group is the "peasant workers". China has a huge surplus of rural labour. While some of them work in township and village enterprises, many move to the urban areas for jobs. Fast industrialization as a consequence of the economic reform also encourages the move of labour from the agricultural to the industrial sector. With few qualifications, "peasant workers" often take up jobs with low skill requirements in the new industrial clusters. Peasant workers often migrate to cities for work and return to their rural home after a few years and they fill many short-term and temporary jobs. The last group of employees that forms the urban workforce are young students and graduates. The number of university graduates entering the labour market in 2010 was ten times more than that in 1989. The number of vocational school graduates has also increased fourfold during the same period (National Bureau of Statistics of China, 2011). Some secondary school and high school leavers also join the labour market each year. Rapid growth of vocational and higher education reflects the Chinese government's dedication to improving the quality of the local labour force (Cooke, 2005b). However, since the expansion of education has outpaced the demand for students and graduates in urban areas, this group find it hard to secure jobs that match their qualifications and have to take on low-grade jobs. They often aim to advance their career by accumulating work experience which improves their professional skills. This diversity of experience, skills and career perspectives among employees has become an important feature of the emerging labour market in China.

Restructuring of the existing industrial base and development of new manufacturing clusters, changing industrial relations and diversity of employee groups raise questions of how firms can secure and develop the skills for specific jobs, control and direct desirable workplace behaviours, and retain talented employees. This book aims to reveal how different employment practices emerge, become institutionalized and function at MNC subsidiaries in China's new industrial clusters. Here, employment practice is a social construct built by the actors involved in employment relations (Morgan and Kristensen, 2006). Through the stories of managers who have been at the heart of developing appropriate employment practices, the book will be able to offer an actor-centred perspective in understanding how the conflicts and contradictions reflected in managers' actions shape the development of distinctive employment practices at subsidiaries which share similar competitive market pressure, institutional context and corporate strategic orientation.

Three types of managers' actions are considered to be particularly relevant to the development of employment practices: (1) management learning (which means managers can upgrade employment practices through exploring existing knowledge bases and interacting with each other); (2) political networking (which means managers develop employment practices by deploying various bodies that have the power to direct or influence employment-related decision-making); and (3) strategy enactment (which means managers can contextualize corporate human resources (HR) strategies by translating general employment policies into specific measures to manage employees. More detailed discussion of this analytical perspective is included in the following section.

In order to study the actions of managers who enact employment practices at workplace level, I employ an ethnographic approach, a distinctive feature compared with others in this area who have relied mainly on short-term visits and interviews for data collection. By working in, living with, and observing at four foreign-invested manufacturing plants located in one of China's new industrial clusters, I gathered narratives from a wide spectrum of people: expatriate managers, local managers, supervisors, line managers, group leaders, shop-floor workers, inspectors, office clerks, gatekeepers, guards, drivers, cooks and wardens. These voices have not been heard before, yet they are the critical actors in China's transformation through foreign direct investment.

This introductory chapter contains four sections. The first section summarizes the general theoretical background and aims to indicate the gaps in the existing literature on MNCs in China. The second section discusses the possible contributions and limitations of studying employment practices at workplace level (or subsidiary level) by taking an actor-centred approach. The third section considers the possible merits and limitations of using ethnographic methods to research employment practices at workplace level. The last section gives a preview of the structure of this book.

1.1 Employment practices of MNCs in China

There has been extensive debate on how MNCs manage employees in China (Lu and Björkman, 1997; Björkman and Lu, 1999; Björkman, 2002; Cooke, 2004; Gamble, 2003, 2006a, 2006b, 2010; Walsh and Zhu, 2007). Researchers fall into different camps. On the one hand, there are those who endorse the idea of "progressive management transfer" of modern employment/HR practices (Goodall and Warner, 1997; Björkman et al., 2008a). To these authors, MNCs' ownership of capital, technology and managerial expertise and China's lack of an established "local management model" allow MNCs to reproduce some established home-country practices in their Chinese subsidiaries. They argue that the widespread use of information technology in recruitment, training and performance assessment processes, the rise of HR consultant bodies and the growing number of HR professionals in China will make the transfer of standardized employment practices possible. Moreover, the Chinese government's interest in "modernizing" and "upgrading" the country's industry often encourages local firms to adopt established employment practices as well. The problem with this approach is that employment practices are viewed as a set of techniques that are context independent. The underlying assumption is that such techniques can be taken from the social setting where the practices originated and be reproduced in a different social setting. In reality, China's immature labour market, non-transparent state–business relations and underdeveloped social infrastructure often challenge MNCs' attempts to apply some sophisticated management routines and practices, making direct transfer impossible (Gamble, 2000).

Contrary to the "progressive management transfer" thesis, scholars taking an institutionalist perspective emphasize the "strength" of national institutions in shaping management practice within both national and multinational companies (Hall and Soskice, 2001). These

authors argue that different national business systems force companies to adopt employment practices that conform to the host country's institutional settings. For MNCs, organizational structures and
employment relations developed in the home country's institutional
settings cannot be completely transferred to the host countries, where
a different national business system is beyond the control of any single MNC (Whitley, 2005). While recent writings on national business
analysis have started to address the dyadic relation between management practices exercised by MNCs and national institutional changes
(Morgan et al., 2003; Whitley, 2007), they tend to argue for the persistent nature of dominant patterns of management practices embedded in different institutional settings.

If the national institution argument is followed, we should be able to
observe evolving commonalities in the ways employees are managed
in China. However, an increasing number of empirical studies have
unveiled a wide variety of different ways that employees are managed
(see Zheng and Lamond, 2009, for a review). These findings continue
to remind us of the difficulty of generating a single "Chinese model" of
employment practices, if such a model can ever be generalized at all. It
is therefore more important to analyse how and why different employment practices function in MNCs in the Chinese context.

Three theoretical perspectives have often been used by existing studies to explain the different employment practices observed in China: a
contingency approach, a corporate strategic choice perspective and a
political economy analysis.

The contingency argument would suggest that such environmental and organizational contingencies as industry sector, cross-country
institutional differences, corporate structure and strategy, company
size and international experiences, inter- and intra-corporate networks
affect subsidiary employment practices in important ways. For instance,
large-scale firms are more likely to adopt sophisticated employment
practices compared to small ones (Björkman et al., 2008a). Wholly
owned subsidiaries tend to transfer parent practices more than joint
ventures (Ma, 1998). Parent practices are more systematically adopted
in greenfield subsidiaries than in brownfield subsidiaries (Sharpe,
2006). MNCs that intend to develop innovative capacity in China are
more likely to adopt sophisticated employment practices to attract talented locals than those MNCs relocating low-value-added production
to China, where the surplus of unskilled workers allows companies

to use foolproof techniques to control production costs (see Cooke, 2004, for a brief review).

Important as these observations are, the findings of this book reveal a different picture. Contrasting employment practices were observed in foreign-invested companies, despite the fact that these subsidiaries shared established contingencies such as size, age, ownership, international experience, location, production mode and product range, which shows that a simple "contingency-employment practice match" cannot offer sufficient explanation. In order to gain a better understanding of why and how subsidiary employment practices differ, I argue that we need to look beyond the "internal fit" within different employment/HR practices or the "external fit" between employment practices and contingent factors facing subsidiaries. Instead, we should move the research focus on to the process by which subsidiary employment practices are developed. By doing so, the research findings in this book will provide a theoretical corrective to the contingency-based and functionalist thinking reflected in some international human resource management (HRM) literature (Milliman et al., 1991; Schuler et al., 1993; Taylor et al., 1996).

The second strand of research emphasizes firm-specific motivations and choices in shaping different subsidiary employment practices. Extending the strategic choice argument, which suggests that management practices are the bounded and actively constructed choices of organizational actors (Child, 1972, 1997), subsidiary employment practices have often been explained as a planned and rational choice of headquarters in the face of the dual pressures of home-country legacy and host-country locality (Brewster et al., 2008) or the triple imperatives of standardization, differentiation and dominant "best practice" (Pudelko and Harzing, 2007a). MNCs are seen as boundary-spanning actors and hence are not simply tied to national territories. Their international capabilities give them the power to extend their competitive advantage by allocating financial, technical and managerial resources internally so as to take advantage of global-scale operations (Dunning, 2003). MNCs have adopted different international competitive strategies (Porter, 1986; Prahalad and Doz, 1987; Ghoshal and Bartlett, 1994), developed distinctive entry models (Kumar and Subramanian, 1997; Chung and Enderwich, 2001; Nakos and Brouthers, 2002) and assigned different strategic roles to the subsidiaries (Paterson and Brock, 2002). Since MNCs would be able to achieve better performance if employment practices were linked to their corporate strategy (Porter, 1986), subsidiary employment practices are judged to have to serve the needs of different corporate internationalization strategies, rather than simply conform to local settings.

The common ground for many studies following the strategic choice analysis is that the management of MNCs has tended to tackle subsidiary employment practice from the headquarters' perspective. For a long time, studies of MNCs tried to address their capacity to extend their existing competitive advantage by transferring technological and management expertise to overcome the barriers of operating in a foreign country, where the subsidiaries were obliged to comply with local legal codes, labour market conditions and institutions that moderate corporate competitive advantage. However, it is naïve to believe that subsidiary diversity in terms of organizational structure and management practices is merely a planned reaction to institutional differences across countries (Ghoshal and Nohria, 1989). This plays down the capacity and choice of the subsidiaries where the construction of employment practices took place and diverse employment practices evolved. The findings of this book show that the fact that companies had similar employment practices did not mean that management used these practices for the same purpose. This result indicates that the functioning of employment practices is often re-institutionalized at subsidiaries, where subsidiary managers address their needs both in the overall corporate strategies and in locally developed subsidiary-level strategies.

Taking a strategy enactment perspective, which argues that any organization is an open system in which the social construction and interaction of organized actors ratify environmental constraints (Smircich and Stubbart, 1985), this study challenges the assumption that corporate strategies decide subsidiary employment practices. We explore the contextual and historical meaning of employment practices at the workplace level because it is at the workplace level that practices are understood, enacted and institutionalized. Moving from the planning side to the enacting side of the story of how subsidiary employees are managed, this book shows that subsidiaries have developed distinctive employment practices following their parent companies' strategic reorientation in China. As parent companies redirect corporate strategies over time, subsidiary managers are able to reposition their companies within the overall corporate strategy and develop employment practices to address the need for such new subsidiary roles. Findings in this book hence add subsidiary-level dynamics to the corporate strategy–subsidiary management debate by showing the enacted and complex, incremental and political side of subsidiary employment practice development.

The third theoretical perspective, which does take subsidiary actors into account in understanding why subsidiary employment practices differ, is the political economy approach. Unlike the corporate strategic choice perspective that sees subsidiary employment practices as planned and rational choices, the political economy approach suggests that political struggles among organizational actors moderate the market pressure and institutional constraints which shape subsidiary management practices (Quintanilla and Ferner, 2003; Edwards, Colling and Ferner, 2007; Ferner et al., 2012). This approach is very useful in capturing the complexity involved in the development of subsidiary employment practices. However, Edwards, Colling and Ferner's (2007) study was based on a single case of an American company located in the UK. They came to the conclusion that internationalization of MNCs and the institutional transition of the host country has squeezed the scope for workplace-level diversity. This conclusion needs to be tested in different country contexts, because the USA and the UK are both liberal market economies and share important institutions in terms of how firms are governed and organized. Zou and Lansbury's (2009) single case study of a Korean automobile manufacturer in China reconfirms Edwards, Colling and Ferner's conclusion that subsidiary employment practices are constructed through competition between different actors. However, because of the single case-study research design, they were not able to take the argument further in terms of the extent to which actors' choices make a difference to employment practices when the subsidiaries are facing similar environmental and organizational constraints.

Given the transitional nature of the Chinese economy and the scale and economic diversity of China, the country offers a pertinent setting to assess the scope allowed for actors to develop alternative management practices that could conform to organizational needs and compete with their rivals. By locating our multiple case studies in subsidiaries with shared contingencies, this book aims to advance the discussion of how actors' assessment, interpretation and negotiation make sense of the relevance of existing management prescriptions. To this end, the book does not support the view that expatriate managers dispatched from the headquarters to fill management positions in subsidiaries are a homogeneous category of management labour representing the interests of their parent companies and executing parent company decisions at the subsidiary level. The research evidence and argument of this book is that expatriates are more heterogeneous in terms of their interests in the subsidiaries and relationships with the parent companies and hence the actions they take in developing subsidiary employment practices. Nor, and crucially, are local managers viewed as representing merely *local* interests. Rather, both sets of subsidiary managers – expatriates and locals – are considered as actors with competing interests and agendas within and outside a given MNC (Perkins and Shortland, 2006). These political interests and agendas are learned through and embedded in the interaction between subsidiaries, parent companies, sister plants and local business partners, a point that will be further illustrated in the following section.

1.2 Analysing MNCs' subsidiary management in China: an actor-centred approach

As mentioned earlier, the focus of this study is the actors, especially those at workplace level. To assess how actors succeed in developing subsidiary employment practices, three types of subsidiary-level forces are considered: those derived from the composition of the management team, those from the power relations embracing the subsidiaries, and those from the interactions and choices among different parties in the networks where the subsidiaries reside.

Subsidiary actors are important because the composition of the management team sets the physical boundary of the subsidiary knowledge base, which in turn shapes subsidiary management teams' learning capacity to take on management practices adopted elsewhere. "Management learning" is broken down into three categories in this study: cognitive learning, routine-based learning and social learning (Hong et al., 2006). Cognitive learning refers to the capacity of actors who, individually and collectively, acquire, distribute and store knowledge (Huber, 1991). Routine-based learning concerns the behaviour patterns that an organization adopts in the process of obtaining and updating knowledge (Cohen and Bacdayan, 1994). In addition, the book will also show the socialization of subsidiary actors so that particular routines are sustained within the subsidiaries. By locating management learning in the subsidiary context in which employment practices are developed, this book will show the selective and progressive construction of employment practice at workplace level.

If the existing knowledge base is the foundation for subsidiaries to learn from internal or external bodies about how to manage employees, then power relations within the organizational networks allow managers to use their knowledge purposefully in order to achieve particular goals. As discussed earlier, the construction of employment practices at workplace level is an interactive and complex process. Construction here, as conceptualized by Child (1972, 1997), is an ongoing management process, in which structure and environment affect the process not only as external (objective) constraints that the management team deal with, but also as internal (subjective) constraints that managers can rely on to deal with the external constraints encountered. Studies of international HRM often use the headquarters–subsidiary distinction, exploring the roles of expatriates and local managers as representatives of the interests of headquarters and subsidiaries respectively. However, different expatriate managers are from different backgrounds, fulfil different roles, and have various interests and career goals. Likewise, local managers' search for autonomy, their interest in the subsidiaries and their career development strategies will affect their choice of how to develop subsidiary employment practices. Managers do not necessarily need to agree on adopting particular employment practices. Rather, subsidiary employment practices may result from conflicts among managers and be subject to change. Managers may also form alliances with different groups to make changes to or maintain existing subsidiary employment practices. Construction of subsidiary employment practices is often achieved through political networking, where managers collaborate and compete to secure individual or group interests.

Finally, the book incorporates the strategy enactment approach into the analysis. Strategic planning is important. Subsidiaries can take different steps and follow distinctive patterns in implementing corporate strategies. But it is not only the headquarters that can act strategically (Kristensen and Zeitlin, 2005). Subsidiaries have the capacity to learn from, as well as resist the influences of, the parent company and various external bodies. Diverse employment practices at workplace level are here contested processes through which headquarters' strategic decisions are interpreted, evaluated, negotiated and exercised in the subsidiaries. In this way, subsidiary managers take strategic actions to moderate the impact of headquarters' dominance and environmental constraints. Issues of corporate strategy enactment and the possible implications for employment practices at subsidiaries therefore need to be studied in the interaction between headquarters and subsidiaries. In the light of China's transition, many MNCs are reviewing or have already reviewed their China strategy. Strategic reorientation allows subsidiary actors to reposition the subsidiaries within the corporate networks and develop employment practices that support such strategic repositioning.

The actor-centred approach discussed above offers a unique angle to understand the diverse employment practices adopted at workplace level in China. By showing actors' engagement in constructing subsidiary employment practices, the study will be able to explore the meanings of country context, industry sectors and competitive pressures for the particular subsidiary. A subsidiary faces multiple pressures that shape the management of employees. But actors' ability to mediate or moderate these pressures is critical to the actual employment practices adopted at workplace level. Meanwhile, this approach also allows us to assess the activities of MNCs "from the bottom up". Neither subsidiaries nor actors can be divorced from the organizational context they inhabit. However, the pluralist structure within MNCs empowers subsidiary managers to act strategically in an attempt to achieve management goals which may or may not be inconsistent with the overall corporate strategy. An actor-centred approach will therefore reveal the emerging, developmental and political workplace realities that characterize MNCs in China.

1.3 Studying subsidiary management using ethnographic methods

The study adopts a qualitative approach to understanding workplace realities. The book reveals "insider views" of managing subsidiary employment practices (Cooke, 2008b). In reviewing the current approach of theorizing international HRM, De Cieri, Cox and Fenwick (2007: 282) suggested that "the search for an integrative, all-encompassing theoretical base has led to the neglect of diverse voices". They argued that the ethnocentric approach in interpreting the concept of "HRM" risks undermining the explanatory capacity of existing theoretical frameworks and suggested the need for more contextualized research. In particular, by including the voice of subsidiaries, international HRM researchers will be able to "redirect attention to how and why existing practices and discipline are adopted and adapted" (ibid: 293). In contrast to studies based on large-scale surveys or interviews with a few key informants, this book is based on intensive case studies at four Japanese manufacturing plants in China.

Bearing in mind that adopting a qualitative approach will mean some loss of external validity compared with more numerical approaches, this study takes a number of measures to enhance the external validity of the evidence. The first step is to decide the sampling strategy. The sample companies are carefully selected to control the influencing factors such as size, company age, experience in international operations, industry, product range and technology. Multiple case studies were conducted within MNCs from a single home country, Japan. The reason for choosing Japanese MNCs relates to the long-standing reputation of the strong country-of-origin effect of Japanese companies. However, contrary to studies based on the generic "Japan-style HRM" assumption (Matanle and Wim, 2006), which take no account of differences among the Japanese MNCs, this study compares the management practices of the subsidiaries to their parent company to assess differentiation of subsidiary management practices. Interviews with the expatriate managers (both on long-term and short-term assignments) and company documents are mainly used for information concerning the parent employment practices. Interviews with expatriates, local managers and local employees and on-site observation provide additional insights into the local practices.

The second step is to select the different types of subsidiary so that findings gained from one group of companies can be verified by those from another group. This measure aims to achieve triangulation in the information collected. This study also uses different sources of information: descriptive analysis of the company documents and scanning of other accessible written records (such as company data released in the *Toyo Keizai* Data Bank – an annual survey of all Japanese overseas operations); on-site observation of the workplace and attendance at some of the social activities arranged by the companies; interviews with the general managers and HR managers as well as people who work in the subsidiaries in China, where access was permitted. By working in, living with, and observing at the subsidiaries, I was able to gather narratives from a wide spectrum of people, including managers and shop-floor workers, office clerks and guards, whose voices have not been heard before, but who are the critical actors in China's transformation through foreign direct investment.

Finally, spending extensive time at the sample organizations also improved my understanding of the interpretations of concepts and meanings that are used within certain organizational contexts. I worked in the companies as an independent researcher and stayed for several weeks in each plant. The ethnographic method allowed me to participate in the companies' daily routines and engage in informal discussions and conduct formal interviews. I also took part in some managers' after-work activities. This approach helped to develop a holistic view of the multiple realities in the field, as well as to allow new research questions to emerge during the research process (Moore, 2011). Being fluent in both Japanese and Chinese, I was able to immerse myself in the life of the factories in ways that are not possible for researchers without this language facility. As a result of these steps, the cases show particular features as well as general patterns of employment practices at workplace level.

1.4 Outline of the book

This book contains eight chapters. This introduction is followed by a review of existing international business and international HRM literature on MNCs. The chapter evaluates the relevance and limitations of three major streams of studies that are applied in studying subsidiary employment practices: organizational structure and its environment, knowledge transfer and organizational learning, and strategic international human resource management. By addressing gaps in existing literature, the key argument is that other researchers have underestimated the role of subsidiary-level forces in shaping subsidiary employment practices. The chapter proposes that researchers studying subsidiary employment practices need to shift attention from senior management planning at headquarters to the actions of managers at subsidiaries, and from comparing subsidiary employment practices to those of the parent company to understanding the construction of subsidiary employment practices. Chapter 3 follows by explaining the rationale, merits and challenges of doing case studies with mixed research methods.

Chapter 4 provides background information about MNCs in China, a developing economy in rapid transition. The chapter takes a historical look at China's economic reform and maps out the cluster effects that the reform has had on foreign-invested companies. Besides drawing out the wider context of the workplace realities in China, the chapter also argues that China's transition is not merely an objective or environmental force that subsidiary managers face. China's transitional economy has subjective implications for subsidiary managers because changes in the local and international economy can shape managers' ideas and behaviour. Due to China's economic development, traditional Chinese ways of management found in SOEs and family businesses have been challenged or even begun to fade. Also, new business management paradigms have found their position in the economy as new forms of companies arrived in China. In this sense, subsidiaries of foreign-invested companies have brought changes to the environment. In the light of such a dynamic context, the chapter concludes that subsidiary actors' input mediates the impact that environmental and corporate forces have on employment practice at workplace level.

Chapters 5 and 6 aim to reveal the detailed stories of the employment practices at the four Japanese-invested companies that form the case studies for this study. Chapter 5 deals with two subsidiaries in the household white goods industry and Chapter 6 is about subsidiaries in the synthetic fibre manufacturing sector. Both chapters reveal significant subsidiary diversity in terms of the employment practices adopted by the subsidiaries. The chapters show that the subsidiaries are able to develop new forms of employment practices locally and they take different approaches to managing the environmental, corporate and political pressures that influence the construction of employment practices at individual workplaces. In the household white goods industry, the two companies show significantly different employment practices to support *lean production*. In WG-A Co., local managers largely controlled and showed substantial local characteristics in terms of the employment practices applied to the local employees. In sharp contrast, in WG-B Co., the management team is dominated by expatriate managers, where a corporate strategy of restructuring the regional business networks has led to more centralization of the strategic functions of marketing, R&D and HR planning. Subsidiary employment practices showed important parent influence, though critical differences in the functions of certain practices can never be overstated.

Likewise, the two subsidiaries in the synthetic fibre manufacturing sector also make sharp contrasts. SF-A Co. is a case where intensive transfer from the Japanese parent side is observed, whereas subsidiary managers' efforts to use local employment practices are supplementary measures that support the function of parent practices, although such parent practices may not be "fully functioning as they are in Japan", a point that was made constantly by the subsidiary managers during the interviews. The employment practices adopted by SF-B Co. indicate separation of HR policies applied to different employee groups. As in the case of WG-B Co., HR planning became more centralized after SF-B Co.'s headquarters restructured their regional strategy. The senior management group was integrated into the parent HR system while management of the remaining local employees was delegated to individual subsidiaries. A significant observation is the mismatch between what the headquarters international HR strategy intended to achieve and the actual employment practices developed locally, as well as the impact on the attraction, selection, development and retention of local employees. Key arguments developed throughout these two chapters are that subsidiary-level forces exert substantial influence on the direction of subsidiary employment practice development and that such diversity at workplace level will persist.

Chapter 7 takes the discussion in Chapters 5 and 6 further by arguing that diverse employment practices at subsidiary level are an important source of advantage to subsidiaries in competition with their rivals, whether these rivals come from inside or outside the corporate networks. Detailed analysis of the organizational forces was undertaken. The results show how diverse employment practices emerge in the respective subsidiaries, reviewing generalized patterns in the construction of employment practices from the empirical evidence, and how different forces influence the outcomes of subsidiary employment practices. Based on the theoretical framework developed in Chapter 2, three levels of forces have been taken into account: diversity in management team composition, the heterarchical power relations in the organizational networks, and the learning cycle of employment practice development that each of the subsidiaries has followed. The findings suggest that the internal dynamics of subsidiary managers' actions are as important as, if not more important than, the environmental, structural and organizational constraints in shaping the subsidiary employment practices. Such internal dynamics indicate that the meanings of the existing management repertoire could well be detached from their physical forms, and this could entail modified, if not completely new, meanings in the subsidiary context – a result consistent with empirical evidence observed in US MNCs (Edwards and Ferner, 2002). More importantly, the findings also indicate that the capacity of the subsidiary managers to develop new forms of employment practices and to re-assign meanings to existing management practices varies and creates an advantage for subsidiaries competing to attract, develop and retain local employees to fill strategic roles within the corporate networks.

The book concludes by highlighting the value of the actor-centred approach and showing links between various forces that shape subsidiary employment practice development. Existing research suggests that environmental constraints such as the host-country labour market conditions, political economy, institutions and social norms, corporate and local business networks, as well as existing HR strategies and policies, are critical to understanding diverse employment practice at workplace level. This study does not endorse the claim that subsidiary diversity is merely a management construct. Forces beyond the control of subsidiary managers inform and constrain subsidiary actors and drive certain forms of subsidiary employment practices. But what differentiates subsidiaries from each other is that subsidiary management teams enact these environmental, structural and corporate forces in a complex process and subsidiary diversity emerges with subsidiary actors' mediation. The significance of subsidiary diversity lies in the implied advantages over competitors, which existing generic frameworks fail to demonstrate. These research results thus offer critiques to the headquarters-centred approach in studying the transferability of management practices from one country context to another.

2 | *MNCs and management space: a framework to study subsidiary HRM*

The quality of HRM in MNCs is critical to success in international business (Black et al., 1999; Harris et al., 2003). Despite some substantial research that highlights the forces shaping the international HRM strategy, policies and practices of MNCs (e.g. Schuler et al., 1993; Taylor et al., 1996), we do not yet understand how an MNC's international HR strategies relate to different subsidiary HR functions, policies and practices. In this chapter, while acknowledging the achievements of existing international human resource management (IHRM) literature, I contend that the headquarters-centred research approach has jeopardized the validity of the causal relation it proposes between strategic planning at the headquarters and international HR goals achieved at the subsidiaries. In order to better understand the link between an MNC's international HRM strategy and a subsidiary's competence in terms of attracting, developing and retaining competent local employees, attention must be shifted to subsidiaries for a more process-based approach, allowing further investigation into the actors and their actions during the process of subsidiary HR practice development. A more systemic research framework is needed to understand how subsidiary managers' choices will enact international HR strategy, develop subsidiary HR policies and construct subsidiary HR practices.

In four sections, this chapter first summarizes existing research approaches adopted by IHRM scholars. Second, it critiques the lack of attention paid to the actors and action at subsidiaries in IHRM literature, due to the overwhelming focus on strategic planning at headquarters and operational policy implementation at subsidiaries. IHRM researchers predominantly assume that subsidiary management strategies are carried out through managing expatriates. However, we lack conclusive data on the relationship between expatriation and the subsidiary HR outcomes, due in part to headquarters-focused IHRM theory, and in part to a lack of empirical case-study data. The third section discusses this study's research design based on an actor-centred research approach. The final section concludes this chapter.

2.1 Subsidiary HRM top-down: the headquarters-centred approach in studying IHRM

A common element in many existing IHRM research is the underlying assumption that headquarters' strategies decide a subsidiary's organizational structure and management practice. The headquarters' international strategies are executed by a team of expatriate managers. The term IHRM is therefore sometimes used synonymously with expatriate management. When it comes to the question of how international HRM strategies, policies and practices are decided, pluralist paradigms have been proposed to capture the convergent and divergent pressures facing MNCs.

2.1.1 Convergence, divergence and cross-vergence pressures on subsidiary management

The convergence vs. divergence debate concerns many researchers studying international business, MNCs and IHRM, although those taking an eclectic stance view convergence and divergence as the two sides of globalization (Warner, 1997, 2008). The convergence literature predicts a trend of homogenization in management practices as the consequence of fast globalization. The divergence literature, however, argues that national institutions would stand as continuous opposing forces to MNCs' attempts to "standardize" management practice across subsidiaries. As reflected in IHRM studies, the debate is whether companies will eventually implement some HR best practices, or whether different forms of HR hybrids will persist and diversity of HR practice will continue to emerge.

2.1.2 "Best practice", but whose?

Authors promoting "best practice" HR argue that there are some golden rules of HRM or "high performance work practices", which are universally applicable and essential for all organizations to achieve competitiveness (Schuler and Jackson, 1987; Delery and Doty, 1996; Pfeffer, 1994, 1998). The complementary nature of these "best practice"

HR principles means they allow firms to achieve better performance when they are combined in a "bundle". However, the cost of implementing these principles, managers' different perceptions and existing organizational structures are generally viewed as barriers which need to be, and can be, overcome (Pfeffer, 1996).

A universal formula or standardized HRM "best practice" receives as much condemnation as commendation. Advocates of "best practice" argue that good practices work everywhere. Empirical results show a rather mixed picture, however. Those based on developed country data such as the USA and European countries (Huselid, 1995; Hughes, 2002) provide some evidence that companies have increasingly adopted "best practices". Pudelko and Harzing (2007a) conducted a comparative study based on 849 MNCs from the USA, Germany and Japan. Their research findings indicated a trend of convergence to American best practice HRM. Drawing upon Smith and Meiksins' (1995) conceptualization of "dominance effects", they argue that the competitiveness of American MNCs, advisory agents such as consultancies and the business school education based on American experiences made the management practices of the US companies a role model to be copied or acquired. In addition to studies conducted in developed countries, partial evidence that best practice HRM is adopted by MNCs from emerging economies, such as China, is also found (Cooke, 2005a; Edwards and Zhang, 2008).

However, critiques of the best practice principles remain. The key counter-arguments include the ambiguous meaning of "best practice principles" and its relation to specific HRM practices (Marchington and Grugulis, 2000); methodological limitation due to reliance on a single informant – the HR managers (Wright et al., 2001); and excluding the motivation of managers to selectively apply these "best practices" (Truss, 2001). In particular, researchers taking the contingency approach argue that HRM strategies are strongly influenced by national, industrial and organizational factors and any universal formula is not feasible. A large-scale survey based on MNCs in twenty-two European countries found limited evidence that a "global best HR practices" model was emerging (Brewster et al., 2008). Rather, international HRM policies and practices showed considerable diversity, reflecting the multiple pressures of home- and host-country contingencies facing MNCs. Researchers argue that international HRM "best practice" is a relative term (Pudelko and Harzing, 2007a; Smith et al., 2008). Best practice is not a yardstick but is generalized on the basis of practices employed by companies from strong economies such as the USA, Germany or Japan.

2.1.3 Best fit or functional equivalence?

Scholars taking a strategic perspective generally believe that international HRM strategy needs to be allied with a firm's business strategy in order to contribute to the overall corporate performance. This section offers a brief review of the research frameworks that underpin the link between the complex pressures facing MNCs, managing HR globally, and achieving international business goals. This will be followed by a discussion of the debate between the contingency approach, the strategic choice perspective, and the political economy approach in explaining this link.

The contingency approach suggests that organizational properties and differences across countries give rise to different forms of organizational structure and management practices in MNCs. Cross-country differences usually put pressure on structural differentiation and complicate the task of coordinating business activities. To coordinate cross-country operations, managers face competing imperatives of "global integration and local responsiveness" (Bartlett and Ghoshal, 1989). Scholars following the contingency approach suggest environmental changes drive MNCs to find the "best fit" structure in a particular environment (Baird and Meshoulam, 1988; Jackson et al., 1989; Arthur, 1992; Snell and Dean, 1992). Subsidiary differences stem from senior managers identifying structures that coordinate headquarters–subsidiary relations and adapting them to fit into the host country environment. By contrast, scholars adopting the strategic choice perspective in understanding MNC management argue that senior management already knows about local legislation, market conditions and institutional frameworks. These professionals therefore plan out different organizational structures and management practices based on the constraints presented in different societies/countries. Researchers tend to suggest possible functional equivalence (Child, 1972), which means different structures will be equally effective in managing MNCs. The contingency approach focuses on identifying different factors that affect the contingency–structure fit, whereas strategic choice emphasizes the management team's choices and actions as well as the exogenous and endogenous forces that constrain these choices and actions. Some recent studies based on the political economy approach shed light on the influence of subsidiaries on strategic decisions at headquarters (Kristensen and Zeitlin, 2005). In addition, they highlight the ability of subsidiaries to resist the imposition of management policies from headquarters (Ferner et al., 2005). Following this line of research, I argue that such a "bottom-up" perspective will help reveal the dynamics involved in translating corporate HR strategies into HR practices to attract, develop and retain competent employees at the subsidiary level.

Goals and concerns of internationalization

Why do companies internationalize? Depending on the theoretical perspectives taken by researchers, the goals of internationalization may be to safeguard firms from hazards in international trade – transaction-cost analysis (Coase, 1937; Williamson, 1975); to explore firm-specific competitive advantages – the resource-based view (Penrose, 1958; Hoopes et al., 2003), or to exploit cross-country differences – the eclectic paradigm (Dunning, 1980, 1988, 1993, 1995, 1998, 2000, 2003). The transaction-cost economists explain firms' motives for internationalization as a defensive strategy. Williamson (1975) pinpointed the issue of market failure and cost of transactions governing business activities. When the transaction cost governing business exchange in an external market is more than the cost of internal administrative coordination, it is a rational choice for companies looking at international markets to "internalize" this external market (Dunning, 2003). In other words, transaction-cost analysis suggests that companies decide to invest overseas in an attempt to find a cost-effective way to overcome the barriers in cross-country trade.

Transaction-cost analysis does not cause problems in the relationship between headquarters and subsidiaries because it assumes that companies are able to arrange production in the host country the same way as they do in the home country. But empirical studies have revealed that the company is unlikely to achieve this (Dunning, 1980, 1988; Bartlett and Ghoshal, 1989; Nohria and Ghoshal, 1997). In contrast to transaction-cost analysis, the resource-based view highlights the capacity of specific firms to take advantage of economies of scale and scope across different countries. Ownership of financial,

technological and managerial resources gives firms a leading edge
or competitive advantage, which is neither replicable nor replaceable (Hoopes et al., 2003). The knowledge-based view extends the
resource-based view by arguing that competitive advantage lies in a
firm's capacity to create new knowledge. What MNCs actually need
to transfer is the system that creates the core competitive advantage. The research focus here again is on the corporate headquarters, which is deemed to be the holder of resources and knowledge,
and this generates competitive advantage. Although some empirical
works have addressed the innovative capacity of subsidiaries to contribute to an MNC's competitive advantage (Rugman and Verbeke,
1992; Birkinshaw, 1997; Birkinshaw and Hood, 1998), the majority
of studies continue to assume that key competitive advantage comes
from the capacity of MNC headquarters to transfer knowledge internationally across the corporation.

The resource-based view addresses the connection between a firm's
competitive advantage and its management practices. It assumes
that if the parent company transfers its production system or management practices, it will replicate its competitive advantage in the
subsidiary (e.g. Ouchi, 1981; Abo, 1994; Harzing and Sorge, 2003).
However, this assumption may be misleading. Take studies in IHRM,
for example, which assume a connection between a firm's competitive advantage and its HRM practices. Much research has focused
on transfer of home HRM practices overseas, and the factors and
forces that affect the transfer. Very little research has tested differences between parent companies' planned transfer and the actual
HRM practices transferred. Also, not much research has been done
to test how differences in management transfer may contribute to
the overall competitive advantage of the MNC. Despite empirical
evidence that transfer of parent practices is merely "partial" and
productivity of the subsidiaries is varied (Kenney and Florida, 1993,
2003; Elger and Smith, 1994, 2005; Lowe et al., 2000; Morris et
al., 2000), researchers in IHRM reduce competitive advantage to the
influence of parent, host country or best practice HRM (Myloni et
al., 2007; Pudelko and Harzing, 2007a, 2007b). IHRM needs major
empirical studies to establish the relationship between headquarters
HRM strategies and policies and subsidiary management in terms
of: (1) HRM functions and practices, and (2) corporate HRM goals.
For instance, when headquarters and subsidiary HRM goals are

in conflict, IHRM theory is at a loss to explain why (Keenoy and Schwan, 1990; Noon, 1992). This point will be discussed in greater detail in section 3.

The eclectic paradigm (Dunning, 1980, 1988, 1993, 1995, 1998, 2000, 2003), also known as the OLI paradigm, extends transaction-cost analysis and the resource-based view into a more systematic framework, and also deals with host-country competitive advantage in its analysis. In this framework, Dunning argues that three factors will affect competitive advantage in international production: advantages in ownership (O), location (L) and internalization (I). In the first factor, ownership of resources such as capital, technology or management knowledge can provide advantages. In the second factor, location in a particular host country provides an advantageous access to that country's types or factors of production. For example, labour costs for standardized production are much cheaper in China than in Japan. The third element suggests that internalization is a more cost-effective way to organize production than other available ways to explore a foreign market (such as using a sales agent). The eclectic paradigm explains the complexity of internationalization by assessing multiple ways to achieve competitive advantage.

The eclectic paradigm remains one of the leading frameworks for understanding internationalization and has inspired a great deal of theory building in many areas such as IHRM. The eclectic paradigm acknowledges differences between home and host countries and treats these differences as resources that MNCs can explore through internationalization as a growth strategy. Common goals of internationalization include resource exploration, market exploration, production efficiency exploration (Dunning, 1993), or local knowledge acquisition (Archibugi and Lundvall, 2001; Rugman and Verbeke, 2001). In other words, headquarters' rationale for internationalization and transfer of technological and managerial expertise is largely based on a static comparison of the efficiency of production arrangements in different countries and available organizational structures to govern cross-country activities.

Fundamental differences between countries, however, create as much uncertainty and complexity as opportunities in managing MNCs (Chakravarthy and Perlmutter, 1985; Bartlett and Ghoshal, 1989; Whitley, 1992, 1996, 2000, 2005; Hall and Soskice, 2001). MNCs are therefore bounded to and constrained by their corporate capacities to enact the environment (Boisot and Child, 1999). Recent studies of MNCs also revealed that subsidiaries' advantages are often locally embedded rather than transferred from or imposed by the corporate headquarters (Rugman and Verbeke, 2001). These authors, therefore, suggest a federal view of MNCs by emphasizing the contribution of both transferable and non-transferable subsidiary advantages to building firm-specific competence within MNCs. Likewise, seeing increased complexity in the study of MNCs today, Dunning and Lundan (2008) contend that it is inadequate to explain MNCs' activities by applying a static analysis, such as the ownership-based explanation of firm competence. Organizational structure, national institutions and management choice are equally important for the understanding of MNCs' activities, which indicates the need to link the macro-level analysis of international and national institutions with meso-level analysis of functional units of MNCs and micro-level analysis of managers' choices.

Paralleling the developments in international business literature, studies of international HRM also shifted from a more firm-centred static approach to a network-based dynamic analysis of management transfer within MNCs. To understand how international HRM facilitates MNCs in realizing their internationalization goals, many IHRM scholars now use the contingency approach to underpin the relationship between strategic activities of MNCs, corporate structures and transfer of management practices.

The contingency approach
As mentioned earlier, scholars following the contingency theory heavily criticize the "best practice" proposition and argue that different types of international HRM practice will fit the particular strategic, structural and environmental contexts in which MNCs are embedded. Earlier work identified key contingent factors that affect the structure of MNCs. Such contingent factors include: stage of development (Stopford and Wells, 1972; Adler and Ghadar, 1990); size of foreign manufacturing (Egelhoff, 1988); international experiences (Habib and Victor, 1991); senior management international orientation (Perlmutter, 1969); and different integration and differentiation pressures (Porter, 1986; Prahalad and Doz, 1987; Bartlett and Ghoshal, 1989). One of the most widely cited works denoting different types of MNCs is the one developed by Bartlett and Ghoshal (1989).

Stage of internationalization Adler and Ghadar (1990) used the terminology of *domestic, international, multinational* and *global* corporations that was based on product life-cycle theory (Vernon, 1966). This helped them describe four stages of internationalization. In each of the stages, MNCs adopt a different business strategy and have different international HR policies and practices to accommodate the business activities. The authors emphasize that domestic corporations export their products and no international HRM strategy is needed for this type of company. MNCs will expatriate home-country personnel to various branches and offices during the establishment of international operations. When firms become multinational, international HRM strategies are able to assist the companies to attract and retain competent managers, and at the global stage, international HRM strategies are needed to engage appropriate managers.

The suggestion that the global company (the so-called transnational structure as described in Bartlett and Ghoshal's typology) is an ideal type is misleading (Dowling et al., 1999: 53). The authors' use of product life-cycle to denote the life-cycle of international HRM strategies is also problematic. Most MNCs compete on a variety of product lines and provide different services, therefore it is not possible to read strategy from the product life-cycle. Staffing strategies thus need to support the different activities. Also, staffing strategies are contingent on other organizational factors. Availability of competent managers (Scullion, 2001), different control and coordination structures (Harzing, 1999) and knowledge appropriation of the MNCs (Schuler and Jackson, 2001) are just a few factors to be named here. Age and experience in international operations are some of the contingency factors that influence MNCs' international HRM strategy.

Headquarters' international orientation The earliest discussion of the input top managers have in deciding the international HRM strategies of MNCs can be traced back to Perlmutter's (1969) conceptualization of firms' international HRM orientations: ethnocentric, polycentric and geocentric oriented internalization strategies (regiocentric strategy was added later). An ethnocentric MNC will send home-country managers to top positions in all the subsidiaries. MNCs with a polycentric orientation will use local managers to manage the subsidiaries and local managers are seldom promoted to the headquarters. Regiocentric MNCs will use personnel within a particular geographical region.

MNCs taking a geocentric approach will seek competent managers for a position, regardless of nationality. While some scholars predict that the geocentric approach will eventually become the dominant way of international HRM as companies seek effectiveness in utilizing global human resources, no empirical evidence has been found to support this conclusion (O'Hagan et al., 2005).

The ethnocentric, polycentric, geocentric and regiocentric frameworks were developed on the basis of analysing the personality orientation of a group of senior managers from American MNCs. Studies of decision-making processes show that in addition to the characteristics of decision-makers, environment, organizational attributes and the specific decision characteristics also have important implications for strategic decision-making (Pettigrew, 2003). The social process and politics involved also, arguably, affect the outcome of decision-making (Child, 1997). It is not easy to claim that senior management decides subsidiary actions without analysing the specific context. To address the contextual nature of strategic IHRM (SIHRM), later frameworks used the country-of-origin and host-country effects in order to denote the dynamics of management in MNCs (see Brewster et al., 2008, for a review).

Country-of-origin effects/ownership Many studies have addressed the continuing influence of parent company HR practices in shaping the practices adopted at subsidiaries, otherwise known as the country-of-origin effects (see Ferner, 1997, for a review). Country-of-origin effects are a distinctive feature of the home country's national business system (Whitley, 1992, 1996, 1999, 2002, 2005) in shaping MNCs' management practices. Subsidiary HR practices therefore show important parent characteristics, such as American MNCs often taking an adversarial approach towards trade unions, and Japanese MNCs tending to replicate "lean production" and control subsidiaries by extensive use of expatriates. As the centre of many strategic activities, headquarters has unparalleled influence on the formation of MNCs' international HR strategy. Taylor (2006) examined the motivation for MNCs to integrate international HRM and argued that MNCs today are under more pressure to integrate. Such integration pressure comes not only from the traditional incentives of increasing coordination across various subsidiaries, transferring knowledge, exploring firm-specific competence and fostering equality within the organization, but also from

Table 2.1 *Typology of control mechanisms*

	Japan	USA	Germany	Sweden
Personal centralized control	Medium	Medium	Very high	Low
Bureaucratic formalized control	Low	Very high	Medium-high	Medium
Output control	Very low	Medium-high	High	Medium
Control by socialization and networks	Low	Medium	Medium	High
Expatriate control	Very high	Very low	High	Medium

Source: Harzing (1999).

the need to gain corporate competence through developing subsidiaries' capabilities to achieve sustainable development.

Another point worth noting here is that scholars found that the motivation to integrate international HRM varied between MNCs from different countries of origin. Bartlett and Ghoshal (1989) developed the distinction between *decentralized federation*, *coordinated federation* and *centralized hub* models to characterize the different levels of control exercised by American, European and Japanese MNCs. Furthering Bartlett and Ghoshal (1989), Harzing (1999) studied 1,650 subsidiaries of 120 MNCs from Japan, the USA, Germany and Sweden (see Table 2.1). Her findings generally support the proposition that companies from different countries employ different methods to control the subsidiaries.

Country-of-origin effects suggest that headquarters play the dominant role in managing subsidiaries. However, discussions of the country of origin should not play down the political aspect of HR policy and practice formation. The host country's economic, legislative, institutional and social settings are found to present continuous constraints on managers' initial perception of how the parent company management fits in with the host country environment and on their motivation to transfer parent practices (Beechler et al., 1998). Very often an MNC's international HR strategy, policies and practices have to be modified. The embeddedness of subsidiary knowledge allows subsidiary managers to influence the direction of parent HR strategy and advance their own agenda (Ferner and Quintanilla, 1998). Country-of-origin effects are therefore subject to managers' mediation, an aspect this book will explore further.

Host-country effects/locality Host-country effects refer to the pressure on MNCs to behave like companies from the local or host country where subsidiaries are established. MNCs operate in different countries and the economic development, state–business relations, institutional arrangements, education system, labour market conditions and legislation concerning employment relations differ from one country to another. As a result of different research assumptions, host-country effects are studied under the titles of national culture (Hofstede, 1980, 1994, 2001; Laurent, 1986; Schneider, 2000); national business system analysis (Whitley, 1992, 1996, 1999, 2002, 2005); and a variety of capitalism approaches (Hall and Soskice, 2001).

From the culturalist perspective, the way companies are managed is built on shared values and norms that are assumed to be commonly accepted by the majority of people in a particular country (Hofstede, 1980, 1994, 2001; Laurent, 1986; Schneider, 2000). These values are also assumed to come from values shared within countries. Hence countries have particular management cultures based on the diversity of national culture. Scholars following this explanation of cross-country management differentiation tend to argue that the shared belief will impact on managers' perception of the effectiveness of management practices and their decisions as to what management practices to undertake. *Social features* such as language, religion and history, *country conditions* such as laws and regulations, government–business relations and economic conditions, and *"events"* that occur within and outside the boundary of a country will affect the "national culture" and form the "cultural values" which determine what makes effective management in a particular country (Punnett, 1998). However, since cultural values are not directly observable, how far these values affect individual decisions and behaviours is very difficult to study. Furthermore, many studies have shown these cultural forces tend to apply competing or contradictory pressure on firms (see, for example, Smith and Meiksins, 1995; Boisot and Child, 1999). Hence culture is not integrated but differentiated and therefore not a stable influence on organizations. The implications that contextual forces have for management decisions, practices and organizational structure will be clarified when we consider these contextual forces as interdependent, rather than using the heading "national culture value" to explain the behaviours of managers and organizations.

Institutional theory takes a different approach to the effects of cross-country difference on the management of MNCs. This approach views organizations as entities seeking legitimacy of action by conforming to social institutions (Greenwood and Hinings, 1996). Scott (1995) argues that institutions have three aspects: *regulative* (such as laws and government regulations, product and labour markets, and social conventions), *cognitive* (such as individual perceptions, skills and knowledge) and *normative* (such as an accepted way of managing). The analysis of institutions at a national level views organizations as an open system, and makes an important contribution to understanding the competing pressures from home country and host country in shaping the different organizational structures and management practices of MNCs. Some scholars thus use the term "institutional distance" as a means of evaluating and describing the regulatory and normative differences between countries, differences which affect transaction cost, management resources and the transfer of management systems. However, like the criticisms of "cultural distance", there are also accusations that the term "institutional distance" makes a static comparison between some institutional attributes of different countries (Jackson and Deeg, 2008). The criticism of such static comparison is that it underestimates MNCs as global forces that drive changes in national institutions (Strange, 1999) and neglects the presence of powerful economies where dominant or currently assumed best practice prevails, influencing organization in other countries (a common challenge presented by globalization) (Smith and Meiksins, 1995).

In response to these criticisms, researchers within national business system analysis started to address the evolving nature of national and international institutions, admitting the influence of MNCs on host countries' regulative, normative and cognitive institutions. Both national business system analysis and the varieties of capitalism approach argue that the institutional settings of a particular country empower certain organizational forms and management practices. On one hand, researchers using national business systems analysis tend to stress the "resilience" of institutions, arguing that institutional change is largely path-dependent (Deeg, 2005) and that the overall

institutional arrangements of a given national economy are beyond
the control of individual MNCs (Whitley, 2005: 220). On the other
hand, ownership of capital, technology and managerial expertise make
MNCs a powerful interest group in the national and international political economy, generating, contesting and constructing institutions.
MNCs have been the "agents of globalisation" (Kristensen and Zeitlin,
2005: 1), and thus their role in regulatory institutions has long been
recognized. MNCs foster integration of the world economy, stimulate
deregulation of host-country economies (Dunning, 1993) and negotiate for their preferred policies by offering follow-up investments and
technology transfer, particularly in emerging economies (Child and
Tsai, 2005). MNCs also mould the normative and cognitive institutions by disseminating best practice through internal knowledge transfer and the socialization of managers (Boyacigiller, 1997). Any study
of MNCs' management therefore needs to take the dynamics of their
activities and national institutional changes into account.

The logic of global integration and local responsiveness Acknowledging
both country-of-origin effects – pressure to integrate international
HRM – and host-country effects – pressure to localize HR – researchers in international business developed several frameworks to capture
these competing tensions. The logic of "global integration and local
responsiveness" became a core theme in explaining the different organizational structures and management practices adopted by MNCs. For
example, by presenting detailed case studies of nine MNCs, Bartlett
and Ghoshal (1989) identified four types of MNC: global, international, multinational and transnational enterprises. Transnational
enterprises are seen as an evolving "new form" of international operation, which is said to be the most effective structure for companies
that need to accommodate both high levels of local responsiveness and
high levels of global integration.

  Following Bartlett and Ghoshal's typology, Taylor et al. (1996)
developed the *adaptive, exportive* and *integrative* management orientation, which they proposed as the best fit for multi-domestic, global
and transnational MNCs, respectively. An adaptive orientation is to
hire competent human resource specialists or managers to create HR
policies and practices that resemble the local HR policies and practices. An exportive orientation means accomplishing the wholesale
transfer of the parent HR policies and practices. And an integrative

orientation requires senior management to be able to apply best practices from existing management repertoires. This typology itself contains some oversimplification of the host-country effects. For example, they assume that a shared national best practice prevails in various countries. In reality, defining a local HRM system is extremely difficult. Local companies in China, for example, are found to be employing very different HR policies and practices, ranging from those derived from reformed state-owned companies and small and family businesses to various HR practices developed in different international joint ventures. These researchers emphasize that senior management searches for, examines and modifies international corporate HR strategy to fit the context in which they compete. But, as in other studies following the contingency approach, the input of subsidiary actors in this learning process has been underestimated.

Later, Beechler and her colleagues (1998) applied the concept of organizational learning to redefine the adaptive, exportive and integrative distinction by replacing integrative orientation with two approaches of local HR practice formation: the closed hybrid and open hybrid. They presented a model of management transfer following an enactment → selection → retention cycle in which subsidiary managers develop local HR policies and practices. Decisions are tactical, based on the managers' perceived competence in parent HR policies and practices, the perceived fit between the parent management system and the local environment, and feedback gained by applying HRM practices. A closed-hybrid approach refers to the process by which managers refine parent HR practices in order to fit them into the host-country conditions. In contrast, an open-hybrid approach allows HR practices to be developed at subsidiary level to transfer back to the parent company and to guide future parent international HR policies and practices. This distinction is useful in terms of defining the possible trajectories that subsidiaries may take in developing subsidiary diversity. To the authors, a core element in deciding whether subsidiary HR practice development will follow an adaptive, exportive, closed- or open-hybrid approach is the "perceived competitiveness" of managers' existing management practices and "perceived fitness" in the host-country environment. However, a neat distinction between different organizational learning approaches plays down the non-rational, emergent and contested nature of HR policy formation and practice application. To better understand how subsidiary HR practices evolve, we need to look beyond the cognitive aspect of organizational learning and explore the social processes in which managers interact with actors from inside and outside subsidiaries to select, enact and retain subsidiary HR practices. We will come back to this point when discussing the research design later in this chapter.

Industry sector and production strategies In addition to the interplay of home-country and host-country effects, the specific industry sector and the particular production strategy MNCs adopt are found to be relevant to international HR planning and to the transfer of management practices to subsidiaries. The influence of the industry sector is twofold. On one hand, the sector indicates the level of standardization of production, the viable management repertoire performed by competitive peers, and supplier–producer–distributor networks, which restrict both the objective and cognitive capacities of managers to choose management policies and practices (Smith, Child and Rowlinson, 1990). On the other hand, the institutional arrangement of the industry sector may vary across countries, which means that MNCs in a single host country may have to deal with multiple localities.

Many empirical studies indicate the relevance of the industry sector to different HR practices adopted in subsidiaries. Companies in the capital-intensive sectors are observed to be more inclined to conduct systemic transfer of existing parent HR practices than those in the labour-intensive sectors. Comparing automobile and electronic manufacturing subsidiaries of Japanese MNCs in the USA, Milkman (1991) found that the capital-intensive companies tend to transfer more management practices from their parent companies. Whitley et al.'s (2003) study in the UK also found that sector affects Japanese MNCs' manufacturing scale in the host country, hence there is a need for systematic transfer of sophisticated production and management practices from home to host country. The Southeast Asian countries have a social-cultural context similar to that of Japan (Beechler et al., 1998), thus the automobile and electronics assembly plants show significant differences in terms of transfer of production and HR practices (Miah and Bird, 2007; Shibata, 2009). Comparing the manufacturing and financial sectors, Beechler and Yang (1994) found significant differences between Japanese MNCs in the USA in terms of the transfer of HRM practices.

Studies of production strategy followed from the existing analysis of industry sector as a force shaping firm structure and strategies. These studies largely draw upon Porter's (1986) definition of competitive strategies, namely *cost leadership, product-differentiation* and *innovation.* MNCs are selective in terms of how to compete with their rivals and the rationale for investing in a particular host country may vary between these global companies. Schuler (1989) suggests that firms need to develop cost-reduction, quality enhancement and innovation HRM strategies to fit with their specific competitive strategies. For MNCs, Schuler and Jackson (2001) suggest that expatriation policies will have to facilitate the transfer of tacit or explicit knowledge. As transfer and retention of explicit knowledge relies much less on team-based interaction compared with the degree of dependence for transfer and retention of tacit knowledge, MNCs will develop more short-term HRM policies (also see Lam, 1997, 2000).

Empirical studies also provide some evidence of the relevance of production strategies. For example, Kenney (2001) studied Japanese automobile subsidiaries in the USA and found two types of subsidiary – reproductive and learning. Morris, Wilkinson and Gamble (2009) applied commodity-chain analysis and found support for the proposition that a subsidiary's position in the commodity chain indicates its international HR strategy. Based on case studies of twenty-seven MNCs in China, the authors found that the international HRM strategies of these companies fit well with the cost-reduction strategy, a result coinciding with earlier work conducted by Taylor (2001).

Studies of the impact of industry sector and production strategy offer additional insights into differences in subsidiary HR practices. Competitive pressures such as cost control, product turnover and quality standards may be more relevant to MNCs' choice of international HRM strategies than the dual imperatives of global integration and local responsiveness (Taylor et al., 1996) or the triple imperatives of standardization, differentiation and dominant "best practice" (Pudelko and Harzing, 2007a). However, the impact on industry sector and production strategies cannot be exaggerated. "[E]ven when managers are drawing upon a shared repertoire of sector practices, their innovations are marked by the specific contexts and external pressures facing their own enterprise, and that their responses continue to build upon distinctive enterprise traditions and competencies" (Elger and

Smith, 2005: 18). It is exactly this subsidiary diversity and managers'
contributions to it that call for further research attention.

*Integrative frameworks of studying international human resource
management* The contingency approach implies that there is a link
between an MNC's international HRM strategy and the realization
of strategic goals of internationalization. This link is articulated in
Schuler, Dowling and De Cieri's (1993, 1999) *Integrative Framework
of Strategic Human Resource Management in MNCs.* In an attempt
to capture the effect of various contingency factors on MNCs' HRM
strategies and performance, these authors drew a distinction between
"exogenous factors" (defined as variables outside the control of individual companies) and "endogenous factors" (defined as the MNC's
strategy and structure). Industry sector, institutions and society, and
inter-organizational networks are labelled "exogenous factors", and
the MNC's structure (including the structure of international operations, intra-organizational networks, mechanisms of coordination,
organizational and industrial life-cycle, and international entry model)
and its strategy (including corporate strategy, business strategy, experience in managing international operations, and headquarters international orientations) are categorized as "endogenous factors". The
authors argue that MNCs' international HR function, HR strategies
and HR practices need to fit with both these "exogenous factors" and
"endogenous factors" in order to contribute to the overall corporate
performance.

The integrative SIHRM framework is useful in mapping out a list
of factors affecting MNCs' international HR strategy, but the relationship between these factors and the strategy outcomes proposed
in this framework is questionable. This clear-cut distinction between
exogenous and endogenous factors reflects environmental determin-
ist thinking. For example, inter-organizational networks are considered an exogenous factor, while intra-organizational networks are
deemed an endogenous factor, and this may be quite misleading.
Inter- and intra-organizational networks are more than factors that
reside outside or across the boundary of an MNC. Instead, inter-
and intra-organizational networks constitute the arena of power
relations among subsidiaries. By power relations, we mean that the
networks consist of power holders who tend to influence managers'
decisions on maintaining or changing existing management (Clegg,

1998). From the resource-dependence view, the legitimacy of power comes from the ownership of financial, managerial, technological and transactional resources (Bartlett and Ghoshal, 1989). The inter- and intra-organizational networks can thus be viewed as resource-reliance relationships in which agents that provide resources will exert power over those who seek those resources (Geppert and Mayer, 2006). Neither inter- nor intra-organizational networks are able to determine HRM strategy. Take relations with sister subsidiaries, for example; information sharing and learning between sister subsidiaries may reduce the level of resource reliance on the parent companies and thus reduce management transfer from the parent companies. Competition with sister plants also affects the level of management transfer (Elger and Smith, 2005). What organizational networks mean to subsidiary management practices is constructed by managers. In this sense, organizational networks cannot be simply demarcated exogenous or endogenous.

Another problem with this integrative framework of strategic human resource management in MNCs is that the authors seem to promote a formalized process that produces a consensus system of rational decisions. This is not surprising given that their framework is based on the classic HQ-dominant approach. The framework conveys the message that subsidiary HRM is planned at headquarters and executed in the subsidiaries. Internationalization strategy indicates the desirable structure for governing the subsidiary operations. Such consensus rationality has been criticized by scholars taking a heterarchical view of MNCs. As MNCs differentiate their activities, the headquarters is likely to delegate some authority to sub-units, and the degree of centralized coordination may vary across the sub-units. Schutte's (1998: 102) study of thirty MNC regional headquarters (RHQs) concludes that the RHQ plays an important role in shaping the company's regional perspective, developing regional integration, and is more closely linked with HQ than other subsidiaries. Other scholars found that functional centres, such as the R&D centre, assume more power than other operational functions such as sales outlets or manufacturing plants (Hedlund, 1986; Forsgren and Pedersen, 1998).

Subsidiary HR planning is likely to be decentralized as HR policies and practices have to be responsive to the local labour market and local legislation. Furthermore, Edwards, Colling and Ferner's (2007) recent study showed that the HR policies of an MNC were often shaped by organizational conflict. Based on a single case study of an American MNC in the UK, the authors found that subsidiary managers tend to rely on external sources of power to resist headquarters' influence and retain autonomy in determining actual subsidiary HR policies. They therefore suggested a political economy approach in studying international HRM. Such an approach would reflect the competing external and internal forces constraining subsidiaries as well as the actors moderating these forces. By analysing the interplay between international HRM strategy implementation and subsidiary HR practices, researchers are responding to calls for increasing complexity in studies of international HRM (Morgan and Kristensen, 2006). This is especially important in the context of emerging economies, which are characterized by institutional transitions and business complexity.

My research focus is on the subsidiary level and, having seen the limitations of the *Integrative Framework of Strategic Human Resource Management in MNCs*, I chose not to operationalize the proposition in this framework. Instead, the framework was used to help identify the factors that influence subsidiary actors, their actions and the outcome of subsidiary HRM. (This will be discussed in more detail in Chapter 3.)

In summary, the contingency approach is useful in the sense that it reveals the complex environment that MNCs deal with. Its key contribution is the identification of a variety of antecedents that inform international HRM in MNCs. There are also seminal works that explore the dynamics of environment, structure and actors in managing international HRM. Kristensen and Zeitlin's (2005) study of subsidiary actors in shaping headquarters' international strategy, and Edwards et al.'s (2007) study of subsidiary actors in moderating competitive and institutional pressure on HR policy transfer, are some examples. Despite these recent developments, the body of research still suffers from some serious limitations. As reviewed above, a number of studies use static national HRM models and propose a linear relationship between certain contingent factors and particular type(s) of international HRM formulas. Geppert and Mayer (2006: 51) comment on the contingency approach that "divergent interests and local power resources of key subsidiary managers and employee representative bodies are played down or are ignored altogether by this discourse". As reviewed above, some researchers draw attention to multiple power centres within MNCs and the complex process of subsidiary HR practice development. Nevertheless, these studies focused mainly on empirical observations of MNCs located in a mature economy. Less attention was given to transitional or emerging economies, where the host country's lack of established local models could both facilitate and constrain an MNC's attempt to reproduce certain home-country practices. Aiming to address the limitations of the existing body of research following a contingency approach, my study attempts to reveal the role subsidiary managers have in the power play to develop subsidiary HR practices.

Strategic choice and functional equivalence

Originally developed to provide a corrective to the dominant contingency perspective of the 1960s, the strategic choice perspective considers to what extent managers can exert choice despite the environmental constraints (Child, 1972). Child (1997) later developed the strategic choice perspective into a reciprocal framework to highlight the management process. Child suggests that environmental and corporate contingencies have two implications for the management process. On one hand, environmental contingencies indicate the resources available to implement certain management decisions. On the other hand, they also influence managers' knowledge, skills and motivation in making decisions and taking actions. Decision-makers' individual perceptual limitations and environmental constraints are also reflected in the "politics of decision-making", in which managers have to negotiate with relevant parties to reach a decision. Both insiders (managers) and outsiders (clients, customers and government administrators) may be involved when managers develop, implement and modify corporate strategies, policies and practices. The strategic choice perspective suggests that, due to environmental constraints reflected in resources, cognitive ability and interaction, organizations may change their interpretation of certain environmental properties. The implication is that companies will develop different organizational forms or functional equivalence, even though they may be competing in the same segment of the market.

Strategic choice analysis can be very useful in explaining the different organizational structures and management practices employed by companies operating in a similar environment. We must be cautious,

however, not to overstate the capacity of firms and managers in deciding management practices and to what extent these practices can be
"functionally equivalent". As suggested by many scholars, managers'
learning capacity often gives rise to new and hybrid forms of management practice when managers encounter different management
regimes (Kenney and Florida, 1993; Boisot and Child, 1999; Morris
et al., 2000; Pudelko and Harzing, 2007b). Studies of subsidiary HR
practice, therefore, need to highlight managers' choices of engaging
the disengaged, separating compatibilities from clashes, and developing synergies from differences. My own study will extend this perspective by focusing on the learning capacity of subsidiary managers and
its implications for subsidiary HR practice development.

2.2 Reflection on the IHRM frameworks: the headquarters-centred approach and its limitations

Owing partly to influential works by Porter (1986), Prahalad and Doz
(1987) and Bartlett and Ghoshal (1989, 1993), a common assumption
of international HRM is that MNCs succeed when they can "think
globally and act locally". This position, however, obscures our understanding of just how MNCs operate in both home and host countries.
The philosophy behind the statement is that the corporate headquarters of MNCs "thinks", and the rest of it – the subsidiaries – "act". In
other words, MNCs make strategic decisions at home and subsidiaries
undertake the functional tasks abroad. Applying this basic philosoph-
ical orientation, strategic IHRM proposes that MNCs' international
HRM is the combination of "issues, functions and policies and practices" resulting from strategic activities and will influence MNCs'
international goals and concerns (Schuler et al., 1993). This definition
contains three elements: the objectives, planning and content of international HRM. Subsidiaries are excluded from the framework. The
role of subsidiary managers in shaping subsidiary HR practices is considered in a functionalist way as if the goals and concerns of MNCs
will be realized as long as headquarters can plan out the structure and
management practices, based on the nature of their company and the
environment in which they operate.

Empirical research raises questions about the functionalist view
of the impact of subsidiary managers' choice on the HR policies and
practices adopted by subsidiaries. Existing expatriate–centre research

shows expatriates play different roles, have different interests and take different approaches to fulfilling their overseas assignments. For example, Black and Gregersen (1992) use a *dual-allegiance model* to explain differences in managers' personal career expectations. They classified expatriates as *free agents* (those who have low allegiance to both the local operation and parent company); *go native* (those who have high allegiance to the local operation but low allegiance to the parent company); *hearts at home* (those who have high allegiance to the parent company but low allegiance to the local operation); and *dual citizens* (those who have high allegiance to both the parent company and the local operation). Harzing (2001a) distinguished the role of expatriates in management transfer by using the metaphor of bear (pursuing a unified company policy), bumble bee (management development) and spider (socialization of members in the subsidiaries). These findings reveal that expatriates have varied agendas, interests and individual strategies to fulfil their assignments.

Likewise, local managers are from different backgrounds, have different career orientations and motivations at work. Collision between parent companies' and subsidiaries' interests has been highlighted in some recent IHRM studies. Kristensen and Zeitlin's (2005) case studies show that rational strategies can be hazardous for subsidiaries in realizing such organizational objectives as operational efficiency and gaining competitive advantage, due to formalistic business thinking. Their work reveals that headquarters' decisions to reduce the number of employees on economic grounds led to the loss of members who were originally recruited to enhance the HRM competence. Studies of management micro-politics shed light on the interests and actions which directly affect organizational outcomes such as the HR practices adopted (Ferner et al., 2005; Edwards et al., 2007). Headquarters' strategic decisions may cause unexpected results at subsidiaries. To study strategic international HRM, researchers have to view the managers in the subsidiaries (and in the headquarters too) as actors whose actions have a crucial input into the process of forming subsidiary HR practices.

My analysis of subsidiary HR practice development takes the diversity of subsidiary management teams into account. Because subsidiary managers (expatriates and locals) have different interests, concerns and agendas on their assignments, they will engage in purposive actions, exert formal and informal control, and deal

with conflicts to realize corporate, group and individual goals, which
brings into play the politics in managing large-scale organization
(Hardy and Clegg, 1996).

In addition to the undervalued implications of power relations
among different organizational units, the field of IHRM also suffers
from a "paucity" of empirical research (Harzing, 2000). Many studies
have focused on developing typologies and conceptual frameworks to
capture a holistic view of the influence of different factors on MNCs'
international HRM strategy (Schuler, Dowling and De Cieri, 1993,
1999; Taylor et al., 1996). Only a small number of empirical studies
test the propositions of strategy–structure fit and management strategy–performance correlation in different country contexts. Thomas
(1998) reviewed research in international HRM and found studies
in this field were largely descriptive, ethnocentric and centred on
the individual managers. More recently, De Cieri, Cox and Fenwick
(2007) reviewed the current approaches to theorizing international
HRM and observed that the conceptualization of international HRM
remains predominantly ethnocentric, by which they mean a majority
of studies are American company focused. They contended that international HRM researchers need to direct their focus to the pluralist
power structures of MNCs to explain how HR policies and practices are adopted and adapted. Delbridge, Hauptmeier and Sengupta
(2011) shared De Cieri, Cox and Fenwick's views. In reviewing the
latest developments in studies of MNCs, they suggested that researchers need to conduct multi-level analysis to make sense of the institutional, industrial and organizational context of international HRM.
These researchers also called for more research that incorporates the
actors and voices from different levels of MNCs, and this is the focus
of this book.

In summary, while studies using the contingency approach and
those following a strategic choice perspective have different research
focuses, they share some common research concerns. These studies
include questions of how MNCs can transfer management practices
developed in one national context to another; how far cross-country
differences will endorse or constrain such transfer; and how subsidiary actors and their actions will affect the corporate international
HR strategy concerning transfer as well as the development of subsidiary HR practices. In this book, my main objective is to address the
last question, although we cannot completely rule out the first two

questions from the discussion. To this end, subsidiary actions need to be studied from three angles. The first is a political economy angle and this is directed at understanding the social processes and the power struggles that subsidiary managers have to negotiate to develop subsidiary HR practices. The second is an extended strategic HRM angle, which allows us to build the link between subsidiary managers' interests in developing subsidiary-specific advantages and HR policies and practices. The third angle is that of management learning cycles, which offers a perspective for understanding subsidiary managers' choices as constrained by the environment in which subsidiaries are embedded. The next section provides more detailed discussion of these three angles.

2.3 Developing an actor-centred approach to studying subsidiary HRM

This section presents a framework for studying the implementation of corporate international HR strategy and the development of HR practices at the subsidiary level. As noted above, the structure of the prevailing frameworks in the IHRM area is not conducive to investigation of the complexity surrounding strategy implementation and subsidiary HR practice development. Specifically, these prevailing frameworks are not able to take account of subsidiary actors' choices and the way they execute these choices. Contrary to a functionalist view of the environment–organization relationship, which considers the exogenous and endogenous impact on MNCs' strategy, structure and organizational outcomes, this study investigates the scope for subsidiary actors to mediate or moderate the influence of these environmental, structural and organizational constraints on the development of subsidiary HR practices, which in turn will contribute to achieving subsidiary management goals. The actor-centred approach draws upon the political economy analysis of MNCs (Edwards, Colling and Ferner, 2007), the strategy enactment view (Pettigrew, 1992), as well as the concept of management learning (Cohen and Bacdayan, 1994). The study views managers' choices as contextual and are shaped in a contested terrain where environmental complexity, organizational networks and interactions between relevant actors (inside and outside the organization) form the resources of, and constraints on, subsidiary managers' choices.

2.3.1 Managers' choice: power struggles, strategy enactment and management learning

In order to gain an in-depth and refined understanding of the management of HR at subsidiaries, "managers' actions" will be put at the centre of our inquiry. The key actors in the development of subsidiary HR practices include the expatriate managers and local managers in a given subsidiary, the HRM experts, if any, expatriated in the short or longer term to the subsidiaries and the local employees. The composition of the management team varies in terms of number of management posts, the demography of managers and the career path each manager experienced to be appointed to these posts. In what way do such differences affect the development of subsidiary HR practices?

The headquarters–subsidiary distinction has long been used to explore the roles of expatriates and local managers as representatives of the interests of headquarters and subsidiaries respectively. However, expatriate managers are from different backgrounds, fulfil different roles, and have various interests and career goals. Likewise, local managers' search for autonomy, their interest in the subsidiaries and their career development strategies will affect their choice of how to develop subsidiary HR practices. A simple dichotomy between expatriates as executives implementing the strategies decided at the headquarters and local managers forging alliances for autonomy is divorced from the reality of organizational life. In this study, I adopt a pluralist view of what affects subsidiary managers' actions and choices in developing subsidiary HR practices. The following section explains a theoretical framework that underpins how managers make sense of subsidiary HRM politically, enact HRM strategies and accumulate HRM techniques/know-how through individual and collective learning.

When developing subsidiary HR policies and practices, managers face conflicting demands from members from within and outside the MNC. Earlier research on subsidiary management often focused on the bilateral power struggle between the headquarters and the subsidiaries. Given that corporate headquarters is the primary financial, technological, business and managerial resource holder, many studies of power relations in MNCs tend to agree on the superiority of headquarters power and the restraints it imposes on subsidiary autonomy. Subsidiaries have only bounded autonomy to make decisions related to the subsidiary matters (Child, 1997). This partly explains why IHRM authors tend to view the presence of parent company personnel in subsidiaries as a key indicator of headquarters power. However, the power relations in which subsidiaries are embedded are far more complex than a two-way battle between central control and local autonomy.

In contrast to the hierarchical view of headquarters–subsidiary relations, studies of the pluralist power structure suggest that the empowerment of and constraints on subsidiary managers come from various resource holders. The organization-as-networks perspective and the political economy perspective both suggest that subsidiaries should be analysed in their own right rather than as functional spin-offs of the headquarters. The organization-as-networks perspective explores the implications of MNCs' heterarchical power structure for the autonomy allowed at subsidiary level. The political economy approach, in contrast, considers the power struggle between managers in shaping management policies and practices.

The organization-as-networks perspective suggests that regional headquarters, strategic and functional centres and the subsidiaries all represent different power centres within MNCs (Hedlund, 1986; Schutte, 1998). By exploring the attributes of different subsidiaries, researchers argue that the autonomy of subsidiaries varies according to their function (Forsgren and Pedersen, 1998), relationship to other units within MNCs (Nohria and Ghoshal, 1997; Birkinshaw and Ridderstrale, 1999; Elger and Smith, 2005) and the activities undertaken within the value chain (Rugman, Verbeke and Yuan, 2011). By applying the concept of embeddedness, researchers are able to map out subsidiaries' relative interdependence between different units of MNCs. They argue that interdependence is critical to a given subsidiary in developing management policies and practices.

While acknowledging that subsidiary embeddedness means that subsidiary managers face competing resource holders and conflicting interests within MNCs, the organization-as-networks approach holds a rather ethnocentric view of headquarters–subsidiary relations. The key concerns are to explore the leverage of subsidiaries within the MNCs and the autonomy allowed by the headquarters. In contrast, the political economy approach takes a pluralist view of the source of subsidiary power. This approach emphasizes the capacity of managers to mediate the economic, institutional and corporate pressures that constitute and shape workplace relations. Managers are actors who are agents of corporate institutions. Agents of national and industrial institutions, such as government, trade unions, industrial and professional bodies, are also actors who hold critical management resources and intend to influence the direction of management policies and practices. The impacts of national, industrial and corporate institutions on management policies and practices are filtered by these actors. In the studies of international HRM, researchers following the political economy approach argue that HR practice development is a political struggle, where managers collaborate or compete with agents of institutions to advance individual or group interests (Edwards, Colling and Ferner, 2007). Subsidiary managers, being agents of subsidiaries, have the ability to make choices in terms of how to access and deploy various agents of institutions in order to mitigate their impact on the institutionalization of HR policies and practices at the subsidiary.

While the political economy approach helps to explain the constitution of subsidiary power bases, the perspective remains rather ambiguous as to the structural implications of internal division of production functions (or service provisions) within MNCs for the development of subsidiary HR. Sector characteristics sometimes transcend national institutions in shaping firm HRM (Hauptmeier, 2011). The implication of sector characteristics for international HRM has been examined under the concept of the new international division of labour (Frobel et al., 1980) and global commodity-chain analysis (Gereffi, 1999). These researchers argue that MNCs run a chain of functional units in order to effectively coordinate productions and service provisions to consumers worldwide. How MNCs coordinate these functional units varies in different types of commodity chain. The researchers also mapped out a hierarchy of various functions according to the technological complexity and labour intensity required for performing the specific functions. They further contend that firms performing the lower end functions need to develop the capability to move up the hierarchy (or "upgrade") by accumulating necessary capital, knowledge and human resource.

In this book, I explore the implications of upgrading subsidiary function to subsidiary HRM from a strategy enactment perspective. As discussed earlier, the development of subsidiary HR practices is an interactive and complex process. For years, scholars in IHRM have followed the "strategy as a plan" approach, viewing the parent company as the centre of decision-making and subsidiaries as the loci where corporate HR policies are implemented. However, recent studies suggest that not only are MNCs' production and service units locally embedded but also subsidiaries develop local strategies, advantages and functions (Brewster et al., 2003). Subsidiary managers can also influence the direction of corporate policies by utilizing external pressure (Kristensen and Zeitlin, 2005; Edwards et al., 2007). Since subsidiary managers' actions are purposeful, their strategy of upgrading production or service provision within MNCs makes institutionalization of HR practices in subsidiaries a selective, political and emergent process (Gamble, 2010). In other words, subsidiary managers face the strategic choice to position (and reposition) the subsidiary within the functional division of production and service provisions within the MNC, which will in turn shape subsidiary HR practices. I therefore argue for an extended SIHRM approach incorporating subsidiary-level strategies with subsidiary HR outcomes.

The political economy approach and the extended SIHRM approach, however, do not go far enough to explain the developmental nature of subsidiary HRM. Apart from the politics of managing people, subsidiary HR practice development is also a progressive process – subsidiary managers explore the existing organizational knowledge base and *learn* from their experience through trial and error. Management learning may be broken down into three types: cognitive learning, routine-based learning and social learning (Hong et al., 2006).

Cognitive learning refers to the capacity of actors who, individually and collectively, acquire, distribute and store knowledge (Huber, 1991). For the purpose of this study, the focus is on how subsidiary managers as organizational actors accumulate, share and disseminate HR knowledge that presumably functions to attract, develop and retain competent employees. I am interested in discovering both the formal and informal sources used by subsidiary managers to acquire relevant knowledge, how relevance of HRM knowledge is understood and interpreted by subsidiary managers, as well as the socialization of managers to pass existing knowledge on to the next generation.

Routine-based learning concerns the behaviour patterns that an organization adopts in the process of obtaining and updating knowledge (Cohen and Bacdayan, 1994). In this study, I will consider how subsidiary HR practices reflect management know-how and techniques, as well as their contribution to attracting, developing and retaining competent local employees. Here, two sets of routines will be considered: job design (which is seen as formalized routines through which employees are organized around tasks) and HR practices (which can be viewed as institutionalized routines through which employees are bound to the subsidiaries). Unlike studies that compare subsidiary HR practices to a "check-list" of "Japanese-style HRM practices" (e.g. Itagaki, 1997), comparison in this study is based on both the forms and functions of the HR practices employed by subsidiaries in contrast to those of their Japanese parent companies.

And finally, social learning in subsidiary HR practices will be explored by considering the context and development of HRM knowledge. Here, subsidiary managers are viewed as cohorts of purposeful actors from diverse backgrounds undertaking managerial functions to address the concerns of various stakeholders, including parent companies, subsidiaries, local and international suppliers and clients as well as local government agents. Any HRM practice developed through this social process of learning will not simply be the direct reflection of environmental or organizational contingency. Rather, subsidiary managers evaluate the situation, negotiate decisions, make choices, take action, gain feedback and then proceed to modify their perceptions, choices and actions. A cycle of learning is embedded in the social interactions between managers (Beechler et al., 1998). How subsidiary managers' backgrounds, roles and strategies affect this cycle needs to be explored to better understand the influence of managers' action in developing subsidiary HR practices. Since subsidiary managers' action is purposeful, their view on the relevance of existing management practices to the development of subsidiary competitive advantage is crucial to the outcomes of subsidiary HR practice development (Gamble, 2010). By considering the actual learning process that subsidiary managers undertake, I intend to show the selective and progressive nature of HR practice development.

2.3.2 *Subsidiary managers as informed and constrained actors*

MNCs operate in a complex environment, which is reflected in the interplay of standardization (best practice), integration (parent company dominance) and differentiation (local responsiveness) that sets the scene for IHRM (Harzing and Sorge, 2003). The complex environment of MNCs is also reflected in the pressures of competition from industry sectors, product and labour markets. The increasing influence of standardized technology, economic dependency between countries, and prevailing market principles seem to be producing a convergence of organizational forms. At the same time, institutional, societal and historical differences between countries constantly remind us of the resilience of locality and the differentiation of organizational forms. Observing MNCs operating across national and institutional boundaries, researchers in SIHRM often use the term "hybridization" to indicate that subsidiary HRM combines contrasting traits of home country, host country and best practices (Harzing and Sorge, 2003). However, environmental constraints, as Ferner and his colleagues (2006: 3) suggest:

leave 'space' for actors to contest the nature and meaning of the institutional framework they inhabit. Even the most highly regulated systems leave such space, and MNCs, as powerful actors, have the capacity to exert a strong influence over the evolution of institutions.

"MNCs" in this quote are an ambiguous unit, referring to headquarters, subsidiaries or maybe both. However, it is not companies but managers that make or act on decisions. To resolve the question of how differentiation emerges in the development of subsidiary HR practices, we need to move the focus to the micro-level to analyse the dynamics of environmental constraints and management outcomes.

The system, society and dominance effects framework provides a corrective to the polarization of contingent forces by suggesting that competing and contradicting forces continue to shape national institutions, organizational forms and managerial choices. In this framework, *system effects* refers to forces that transcend country borders and have universal implications, such as market-based competition and science and technology development. *Society effects* refers to the inheritance and institutions within a given society that call for conformity. *Dominance effects* refers to the influence of best practice exercised in a leading economy at a particular time. The transfer of Japanese production systems overseas and the diffusion of HRM best practices reflect such dominance effects.

More importantly, the framework views organizations as game players that follow the rules set by principles of political economy, national institutions and the dominant economies. Managers cannot ignore the rules set by the capitalist system, the state and institutional settings of a given society or the dominant players in the market. Nevertheless, the competing nature of these rules allows some degree of freedom for assessment, interpretation and negotiation by managers. "Actors operate within and outside the organisation, and ensure that any common structural pressures are mediated and negotiated in divergent ways that reflect actor interest and not straightforwardly local institutional rules" (Smith, 2008: 40). The subsidiary HR practices, therefore, are not a simple hybridization of practices from different systems, societies or transnational models, but emerge from the interplay between systems, society and dominance pressures, and are mediated by the management process.

Following this line of argument, I view cross-country and cross-industry sector differences both as constraints and as the origins of managers' power in constructing and executing management choices in international HRM strategy implementation and the development of subsidiary HR practices. The key environmental forces to be considered in this study include: structural differences between home and host countries; the economic, legislative and institutional setting of the host country; international competition surrounding subsidiaries as well as their headquarters; and factors specific to the industry sector and product market where the subsidiaries compete. This environmental amalgam is subject to MNCs' active construction. For example, the leverage of MNCs in national economies is used as a source of power through which subsidiaries negotiate favourable policies with the state, particularly states in developing countries. In this sense, we understand the subsidiary environment as both the cause and the consequence of negotiation between subsidiary managers and relevant actors.

2.4 Key learning points

This chapter has reviewed the literature on strategic IHRM. Given the dominant influence of the contingency approach on most SIHRM authors, many studies seem to follow the functionalist link between environment, international HRM strategy and organizational outcomes, without questioning the potential disruptions and conflicts in the achievement of these strategies. A range of factors affect firms' international HRM strategy: individual expectations and performance, ownership, size, international experience, inter- and intra-organizational networks, home-country and host-country effects, industry sector and production strategies, politics and the learning cycles of the management process. The fragmented nature of the research body indicates the difficulties of establishing an integrated theoretical framework, if such a theory is ever possible. How these forces shape subsidiary HR practice development, and whether any causal chain operates to link them, remain open questions that case-study research can usefully explore. Some scholars support a contingency–structure–strategy match (the integrative framework of human resource management of MNCs is one of many examples). However, within the debate, what is striking is the lack of attention to how international HRM strategy, planned on the basis of these factors, actually works (or does not work) at the subsidiary level and how subsidiary actors' input shapes or influences the outcome of subsidiary HR practice development.

To address this gap, I proposed that research attention should be moved from addressing the questions of "how headquarters decides the HRM strategy" to "what happens during the process of international HR enactment within subsidiaries". If the strategic planning of international HRM is based on economic, institutional and organizational factors, it does not guarantee that subsidiaries will achieve the goals set by headquarters. Nor will finding the "right" managers or designing appropriate supporting systems ensure the implementation of headquarters practices, whether these are for HR transfer or the localization of HR practices. We need to understand the social process of subsidiary HR practice development and the interactions between subsidiary managers within and across the boundaries of subsidiaries.

I set out to study the subsidiary level in order to analyse how subsidiary managers make decisions and take actions to develop subsidiary HR practices and to achieve a particular international HRM strategy. I specifically wanted to investigate how the composition of the management team, the micro-politics in the management process and the actual learning cycle affect the subsidiary management system. However, I understand that subsidiaries cannot be divorced from the environment and organizational networks they inhabit. I see subsidiary actors as engaging with organizational networks and the environment and mediating or moderating their effects on subsidiary HR practice development.

In terms of research methodology, I argued that international HRM strategy design and implementation is not about finding the best combination of home, host and best practices but is a contested process in which the subsidiary managers interact with the environment, the organizational networks and each other. Given the fragmented nature of the body of literature and because the nature of my research subject is highly embedded, I have not developed a set of testable hypotheses. A qualitative research approach will be more promising as regards empirical insights, which will later inform the conceptualization of theories. The following chapter considers the research methodology of this study.

3 | Doing case studies with mixed research methods

This chapter focuses on the research design and the data collection process. I compare the strengths and limitations of the two major social science methodologies – the quantitative and qualitative approaches. This chapter suggests that a qualitative approach will best accomplish the objective of investigating interaction between expatriate and local managers in the process of international HRM strategy implementation and the development of subsidiary HR practices. The rationale for conducting multiple case studies will follow Yin's (2003) guidebook of research design. Sample selection, information sources and the methods used for data collection and analysis will be elaborated in support of the proposed case studies. By explicitly detailing the research methodology for this project, this chapter aims to discuss the methodological principles (McNulty and Ferlie, 2002) and provide precise and consistent guidelines for researchers when conducting fieldwork and analysing research findings.

The chapter is divided into five sections. The first section explains the rationale for conducting multiple case studies based on the research questions and the objectives set out for the study. Quantitative data will be added to support the research design. The second section comprises a detailed discussion of research validity issues. Although the qualitative approach is often criticized in terms of the generalizability of its research findings, this section describes some concrete measures I used to tackle validity issues. The third section evaluates the reliability of this study. The main focus of this section is on how I collected, stored and analysed the data collected at the site of the sample companies. It also deals with the ethical issues associated with a qualitative research methodology. The fourth section concentrates on the data collection process. It explains how the study was conducted, including how I gained access to each sample company, the conduct of observations and interviews, and the scanning of company documentation. The final section summarizes the key learning points of the chapter.

3.1 Quantitative vs. qualitative approaches

Previous studies outlining the differences between quantitative and qualitative approaches appear to draw a clear-cut boundary between the two. However, there is more overlap than is often admitted by researchers. For this study, I am inclined to endorse a pluralistic approach of methodological theorizing (Clegg, Hardy and Nord, 1996) and show the feasibility of engaging in qualitative research supplemented by quantitative data (as demonstrated in the field of organizational process studies; see Pettigrew, 1992; McNulty and Ferlie, 2002).

The fundamental difference between the quantitative and qualitative approaches lies in how variables are codified and how research findings emerge. Developed from methods used in physical sciences, the quantitative approach has its strength in producing numerical, reliable results regarding the interrelationship between certain variables (Creswell, 2003). A typical quantitative approach in social sciences selects samples randomly and then applies statistical tests to data collected through questionnaires or experiments. The interrelationship between the variables is tested through statistical regression. The major weaknesses with this approach are that it often divorces the research objects from their context and has limited capacity to dig out "unknown" variables, which can emerge when using a qualitative approach (Neuman, 1997). The qualitative approach, by contrast, allows researchers to access the rich context of the research object. It can provide a wealth of detail about, for example, consumer behaviour, organizational processes, or the effects of public policy (Yin, 1994). Patterns or trends are summarized through observing a relatively small number of cases. Because researchers interact directly with the research "object" during the course of study, the objectivity and generalizability of research findings are often questioned. Meanwhile, the question of researchers' bias arises, as the qualitative approach relies on the skill of the researchers in crafting and posing questions, a skill that may vary considerably (Creswell, 2003). These fundamental differences between quantitative and qualitative approaches suggest that both are able to produce results if they are applied to appropriate research questions (Silverman, 2000).

Quantitative and qualitative approaches are not incompatible research paradigms although they are based on different assumptions, fieldwork procedure and academic language (Bryman, 1988; McNulty and Ferlie, 2002). There has been constant debate among researchers about the possibility of bringing the two approaches together to create a new methodology, one which is able to bring different perspectives to the research "object" (Bryman, 1988). In fact, in fields such as organizational process studies and social marketing research, a combined approach has already generated important results: the findings from relatively independent projects that used alternative methodological approaches have corroborated each other (for example, McNulty and Ferlie, 2002: 83). This study acknowledges the limitations of the qualitative approach in establishing research objectivity, generalizability and reliability, and thus follows Yin's (1994, 2003) suggestions for carefully designed research protocol and data analysis measures. The study indicates the need to include supplementary quantitative information at the research design stage to support selection of sample companies, interview questioning techniques and data analysis methods.

This supplemented approach will be elaborated in the following two sub-sections. The first sub-section will describe the advantages of using the qualitative approach as the fundamental research approach in studying contextual and longitudinal phenomena. In the second sub-section, I will describe how aspects of a quantitative approach can be added to form a combined paradigm.

3.1.1 Multiple case study with a mixture of qualitative research methods: exploring a contextual and longitudinal process of subsidiary HR practice development

Taking a case-study approach with a mixture of qualitative research methods, I aim to develop a comprehensive understanding of how and why subsidiary employment practices are formed, as well as the role of actors in the formation of subsidiary HR practices. As previously stated, the aim of this study is to compare the international HRM strategy and the development of HR practices across subsidiaries. It seeks to understand how organizational networks and the micro-politics of organizations cause variations in the subsidiary HR practices. Comparison is a key term for this study. Multiple case studies will provide data for comparison and thus reveal insights into subsidiary-level forces and the reasons they differ. Data is collected

qualitatively using structured and informal interviews, on-site observations, and from an examination of company documents and archive
materials, where these are available.

I endorse the ideas of research methodologists, particularly the
suggestion that *why* and *how* questions are better explored through
a qualitative approach (Pettigrew, 1992; Yin, 1994). However, as a
practitioner in the field, I hold that it is always constructive to consider what might be added with alternative approaches. Quantitative
approaches tackle the *why* and *how* questions as well. Earlier research
findings, for example, have focused on the causal relations between
new policies and their various effects, which depend on variables
such as size, company age, technology, and the environmental factors
of the broader political, economic and social context. As discussed
in Chapter 2, these findings assume a structural and environmental
determinism that neglects the subsidiary input – which is precisely
where environmental factors are processed and organizational outcomes emerge. The *why* and *how* questions in this study are directed
towards a twofold understanding of the environment in terms of
outer context and towards organization in terms of inner constraints
that produce varied organizational outcomes. By outer context, I refer
to the interplay among the economic, institutional and industrial
forces that shape subsidiary HR development. By internal context I
mean the coalitions, conflicts and compromises within the organizational processes that shape HR strategy, policies and practices. I hold
that the complexity involved in the development of subsidiary HR
practices cannot be measured merely by causal quantitative formulas
(McNulty and Ferlie, 2002), and thus a basically qualitative method
is required.

The desire to allow unexpected insights to emerge from the context of the research object suggests case studies with mixed qualitative methods (Holdaway, 2000; Moore, 2011). Given the paucity
of research on the subsidiary level, I do not intend to test existing
theories, although they do serve as the background for this study. As
illustrated in the previous chapter, this study is about subsidiary HR
practice development. The book incorporates multi-level analysis,
which explores the political economy of subsidiary HR development,
the strategy enactment of global industrial structure and the management learning process. What it adds to micro-level dynamics is the
macro-level dynamics which highlight the interaction between agents

and institutions in shaping management and workplace relations. These theoretical approaches play an important role in guiding this study but do not serve as a foundation for developing hypotheses to be tested empirically. Rather, they give an inductive, qualitative approach to the study of organizations, one which promises to suggest improved or novel theoretical paradigms.

Another important consideration for this study's research approach is a focus on the day-to-day management process, which again is the strength of case studies (Elger and Smith, 2005). The basic assumption of this study is that organizations are "open systems" (French et al., 1985). The various independent actors within organizations interact with one another and with the environment in which the organizations are embedded. As mentioned earlier, the qualitative approach does not remove the research object from its context. Rather, researchers approach the research object either by entering that context or by consulting people who have experienced that context, or both. Researchers spend time within the context of the research object engaging in direct observation or speaking with those who have. This has enabled researchers to improve their understanding, to reach underneath the surface of the phenomenon and gain valuable insights (McNulty and Ferlie, 2002). For this study, the qualitative approach provides the practical instruments that allow me to become immersed in the workplace realities so that I can build knowledge of the subsidiary HR practice development process as well as locate the meanings attributed to phenomena by the organizational actors in the inner and outer context.

The third important consideration is to determine whether extensive control can be exerted over the research object (Yin, 1994). This study investigates international HRM strategy implementation and subsidiary HR practice development to find out how the outcomes of certain strategies vary across companies and how the functioning of the management team accounts for such variation. As such, the level of control over the research object is limited. In fact, control is impossible during the data collection stage. A better strategy in this case is for the researcher to be immersed in the organization and to gather information by watching people as they work together, by talking to people about their work and by "non-participant observation".

As regards the time period, this research examines a contemporary phenomenon – the overseas subsidiaries of MNCs. The variables to be examined suggest a synchronic approach with exhaustive description of phenomena during a single time period. However, when it comes to the question of international HRM strategy implementation and the development of subsidiary HR practices, the focus is definitely not static. The research has to explore the diachronic dimension that connects the implementation of corporate international HRM strategy and development of subsidiary HR practices. It is hence critical to place the analysis in the time stream that links the organization's past, present and future. This suggests the inclusion of diachronic considerations into a mainly synchronic study. Again, qualitative approaches are an improvement on quantitative approaches in accessing the diachronic aspect (Yin, 1994) of the research subject of this study.

Lastly, multiple case studies with mixed qualitative methods allow me to deal with subjective elements without abstracting them from the context where they were developed (Creswell, 2003). The study collects voices of subsidiary actors. A variety of subjective, individual elements play a role in how these teams implement policy. These managers might be expatriate, local, senior or junior, experienced or newly promoted. Moreover, these management teams are made up of individuals with various backgrounds, expectations and vested interests in the organization. Encountering the subjective elements of individual members in the context of the function and environment of the management team in each case site is indispensable for interpreting their meaning for certain HR issues. For example, different companies may have conceptualized the meaning of "localization" in different ways. It is also possible that the expatriate and local managers may have different interpretations of "localization", especially when this term is not defined and disseminated in the subsidiaries. These interpretations may be based on subjective considerations related to managers' individual career goals, their interest and concerns in developing certain forms of HR practice, and their relationship with the parent company. Again, a senior manager may not share the same evaluation of the effect of certain HR policies or practices with a junior manager, given the different positions they have in the management hierarchy, their different roles in the organization or the different kinds of information disclosed to them. It is thus important for researchers to link the individual's interpretation to his or her educational background, work experience and stake in international HRM strategy implementation and developing subsidiary HR practices. By adopting qualitative methods, I was able to interact face-to-face with these individuals, probe the meanings of their actions and understandings, and connect these meanings to the circumstances within which they developed.

3.1.2 Sampling strategy: using quantitative data for case selection

Sampling strategy is critical to addressing the research validity and reliability of qualitative studies and often involves a series of decisions (Fletcher and Plakoyiannaki, 2011). This may be either a statistical approach, such as random sampling in studies following a quantitative approach, or a theoretical approach to identify diverse cases to extend a theory (Eisenhardt, 1991; Buck, 2011). Ideally, by selecting the theoretical approach of sampling, the cases selected will serve to enhance "replicative reliability", which occurs "if similar results are obtained from all selected cases, replication is said to have taken place" (Yin, 1994: 55). This means that researchers must choose a rationale made up of individual criteria for sample selection which they believe will result in replication, and they need to screen all possible candidate cases before commencing the study properly. All these reasons made the quantitative data relevant in providing supplementary information to screen and select the appropriate cases.

The first and foremost criterion for sample selection is to ensure that an individual researcher is able to collect sufficient information from the cases without sacrificing validity and reliability. Thus for this study, I chose to integrate two sets of companies with two cases in each set. Further criteria for sample selection are consistent with the general assumptions of the study: (1) preference for cases where a company's global and competitive strategies affect the HRM strategy at their overseas subsidiaries (in ways consistent with strategic IHRM assumptions); and (2) preference for cases where the effects of structural features and environmental factors on the micro-political internal context of an organization are observable, since these shape organizational outcomes (Child, 1997) including HR practices. Following these criteria, the two sets of companies represent subsidiaries that are serving different roles in the parent companies' competitive strategy in the host country. Additionally, the sample companies (especially the ones in the same set) share some similar structural characteristics and outer contextual (environmental) dynamics, which are important factors that lead to variations in the HRM outcomes across organizations.

I undertook three rounds of selection and finally screened out all but the four samples studied here. The first round of selection was made based on the home country of the MNCs and the host country of their subsidiaries. For this study, I selected Japanese MNCs with subsidiaries in China. The second round of selection was made based on the role of the MNCs. For the study, MNCs that play different roles were selected so that the study would cover at least two types of subsidiary – thus contributing to the replicative reliability. The third round of selection was made based on company size, company age, international experience, ownership structure, product range and so on. Two similar companies were chosen on the assumption that this would facilitate the comparison of qualitative data on internal context. All of these selections were made with the aim of reducing the number of uncontrolled variables, which would have been labelled "control variables" in a quantitative study.

In the case of the first selection round, variables associated with parent companies and host countries were considered. An overseas subsidiary's management philosophy, policy and practices will be shaped by the management norms that are prevalent in their parent companies, otherwise known as the country-of-origin effect (Rosenzweig and Nohria, 1994). To control for the influence of country of origin on international HRM strategy implementation and subsidiary HR practice development at the subsidiary level, I decided to select sample MNCs from a single home country. Furthermore, parent MNCs from some countries display convergent management practices whereas MNCs from other countries diverge. I understand how difficult it is to distinguish between variations (if detected in the empirical study) in the process of developing subsidiary HR practices originating at the subsidiary level or at the parent companies. Therefore I determined that the selected MNCs ought to share similar HRM philosophies, policies and practices in their home country. This selection criterion made the Japanese companies stand out as relevant cases. Japanese companies have long been studied as a group whose members share common HRM practices (Kopp, 1984; Kawakami, 1996; Harzing, 1999; Legewie, 2002). As Japanese MNCs establish operations overseas, they tend to export some HRM practices – that is, they have a consistent country-of-origin effect. As a result, their subsidiaries also show similarity in terms of HRM policies and practices. This similarity is reflected in many ways, such as the integration of local managers (Yoshihara, 2001). The scope of sample selection was thus scaled down to the Japanese MNCs.

The extent to which the country-of-origin effect occurs in a specific host country is another critical factor that I sought to bring under control. Scholars have found that a host country's economic, business, political, legal and social environment would influence the HRM approach of MNCs (McGaughey et al., 1997; Dowling et al., 1999). The scale of a host country's economy and performance will affect the extent to which an MNC transfers its parent company's operation system to its subsidiaries, as, for example, in HRM practice regarding expatriation (Abo, 1994). In addition, when MNCs establish operations in a host country, they come under pressure to comply with local laws that regulate workplace practice. As Dowling and his colleagues have argued, countries having rigid legislative regulation regarding the workplace leave little room for organizations to apply HRM practices that deviate from the locally accepted HRM models (Dowling et al., 1999). However, in countries with looser legal systems or a less institutionalized workforce, organizations can impose their own HRM policies and practice. These policies can mimic those in the home country, be in conformity with the country-of-origin effect or depart from home-country models. Studies also show that developing countries generally provide a less disciplined or a less institutionalized labour force and a more flexible legal and regulatory environment than developed countries. Such empirical findings prompted me to restrict this study to a single host country, China – a major developing country that has attracted a large volume of foreign direct investment (FDI), especially from Japan (JETRO, 2005).

While the environment of China as an FDI host country will be further illustrated in the following chapter, it is worth noting here the symbolic implications of this selection. China was selected because of its potential as a source of variation in terms of HRM policies and practices. It is a developing country undergoing major systemic reforms. The old planned economy system has already been demolished but a mature market economy system has still not been established. This transitional state is reflected in its labour market. China has a large supply of relatively low-cost labour composed of young graduates, unemployed workers formerly employed in SOEs, and migrant workers from rural areas. At the same time, labour laws in China are at a legislative stage that encourages enterprise reform and seeks to establish a social security system (Kwong and Qui, 2003). National and local laws and regulations concerning workplace practice are provisional and subject to revision from time to time (Luo, 1998). The labour markets in China are in transition. State trade unions and enterprise unions in general are not formally involved in collective bargaining and balloting on industrial action (Clarke, 2005), although some spontaneous forms of industrial action are widely reported (Lee, 2007). This transitional environment between developing and developed economy can accommodate organizations with a variety of management and HRM strategies. A number of empirical studies have demonstrated this variety. For example, low investment in HR, low-trust employment relations and tight managerial control over an unskilled local workforce are found to be prevalent in some foreign-invested manufacturing plants (Gamble et al., 2004). Partial transfer of Japanese-style management is also observed in some Japanese-invested enterprises (Zhu and Warner, 2000) (though there are arguments that those practices are not transferred to but originated in China; Taylor, 1999). Also, companies house workers to deal with problems associated with their migrant workers (Pun and Smith, 2007). Given the nature of China's labour market, its loosely regulated legal system and weak industrial institutions, it is possible to accommodate companies with divergent HRM policies.

After selecting Japan as the home country and China as the host country based on a desire to reduce the country-of-origin effect and host-country environment effects while still allowing variation in HRM policy, I began to screen Japanese subsidiaries in China for those with comparable features. Ideally, the four intensive case studies, two sets with two subsidiaries each, would display contrast and variation between the two sets, and easily comparable cases within each set. The companies in each set thus share strategic, structural and environmental contexts. This allows me to rule out the largest possible number of variables that might lead to variation in HRM policy and complicate the study of the micro-political inner context of each case.

The first important difference considered in determining the contrasting sets was the industry sector of the sample companies. Based on the earlier-established contingency approach, Smith, Child and Rowlinson (1990) argue that sector is an arena where companies compete for resources and target product markets. The industry sector also places limits on technology, an area where companies gain their competitive advantage. As a result, competition within a single industry sector tends to reduce variation in management practice for companies within that sector. Consequently, companies vary more across sectors than within one sector. Abo's (1994) empirical study of Japanese subsidiaries in the USA seems to go a step further. They found that the intentions of parent companies with regard to implementation of home-country practices in the subsidiaries also varied across sectors. For example, companies in capital-intensive sectors are more inclined to transfer some home-country operational systems to their subsidiaries than those in labour-intensive sectors. Thus the internal dynamics of a single sector, as well as parent company strategy that varies by sector, can increase the variation observed between companies in different sectors. Following these arguments, I decided to select two sample companies in labour-intensive sectors and two from capital-intensive sectors.

Uncontrolled variation is limited as much as possible within each sample set. The selected sample MNCs are comparable in terms of company size, years of operation, years of experience in international operations and product range. At the subsidiary level, they are also similar in terms of subsidiary size, years of operation in the host country, scale of investment, ownership structure, competitive strategies and product range. As for environmental factors and local influences in the host country, the selected sample subsidiaries are close together. This limits differences in labour market conditions as well as local legal, institutional and social arrangements. In a country as geographically diverse as China, the subsidiaries must be relatively close together to ensure comparability. The list of possible case studies was narrowed down according to these criteria.

The database used was *Japanese-invested companies overseas: sorted by destination countries* [*Kaigai Shinshutsu Kigyo Soran: Kokubetsu Hen 2006 nen han*] (2006 edition), published by Toyo Keizai Inc. This database has been published annually since 1989. The 2006 edition listed over 4,200 Japanese MNCs investing in 21,000 overseas subsidiaries, excluding those subsidiaries having less than 5 per cent Japanese investment. For each of the subsidiaries, the database listed fourteen basic types of information about the Japanese parent companies with particular attention to company name, capital and sector. The total number of the overseas subsidiaries of a particular Japanese

MNC was used to indicate the scale of international operations. In addition, this database provides a profile for each subsidiary including company name, location, year of establishment, investment scale, ownership structure, number of employees, product and service range. Grouping subsidiaries by industry sector, I narrowed down the list of possible sample subsidiaries by excluding firms according to the following criteria: (1) the parent company has fewer than five overseas subsidiaries; (2) the parent company employs fewer than 800 employees; (3) the Japanese side's investment is less than 50 per cent; (4) the subsidiary recruits fewer than 200 employees; (5) the subsidiary has been established within the past five years; or (6) key company profile data is missing from the database.

From this round of selection, I found that the top three industry sectors that attracted Japanese investment in China are the electronic assembly, the automobile and the textile sectors. After researching these sectors, I decided to exclude the automobile industry because it is a newly deregulated sector and the Japanese car manufacturers are located in relatively dispersed areas in China. Since differences in regional governments' policies and regulations may affect employment issues, samples from this sector would not have been comparable. Within the textile sector, capital-intensive synthetic fibre manufacturing companies display the greatest comparability. By contrast, the large number of small-scale, labour-intensive garment manufacturers showed more diversity in terms of size, company age and international experience. Capital-intensive synthetic fibre manufacturers were therefore a logical choice for selection as a sample set. Within this set, two major rivals with comparable structural characteristics were selected as the sample cases.

Narrowing down a potential set in the electronics sector took considerably more time. There were many similar subsidiaries; however, these showed large variation in product range. Thus similar subsidiaries that produce a similar product in the electronics sector were chosen as the basis for the second set.

Unfortunately information about the competitive strategies of each of the subsidiaries was not included in the database initially consulted. To identify this important information, I turned to the Ministry of Economy, Trade and Industry of Japan's (METI) *Basic Survey on Overseas Business Activities* (2005). This survey is conducted every two years to identify patterns in Japanese international investments and includes a section where Japanese MNCs are asked to identify their rationale in choosing China as an investment destination. More than fifteen reasons were listed in the survey and the MNCs had the option of choosing multiple responses. The results show that there are two main reasons why Japanese companies establish subsidiaries in China: first, to gain a source of low-cost manufactured products which are then re-exported to Japan; and second, to target the local consumer market. (These two motives are not necessarily mutually exclusive. In fact, the case studies show that subsidiaries' products serve both international and local markets.) The same survey result also revealed the companies' reliance on the home country for sourcing raw materials for production. For the two selected sectors, the capital-intensive synthetic fibre textile sector and the electronics sector subsidiaries showed roughly equal reliance on home- and host-country markets for raw material procurement and product sales. Most synthetic fibre manufacturers in the Chinese market have a relatively homogeneous strategic orientation, and they specifically aim to seek a low-cost production base. The electronics manufacturers, by contrast, vary between the two main investment strategies for Japanese MNCs in China. Some are engaged in low-cost production for re-export while others are targeting the local consumer market. Thus, in the case of the electronics sector, I decided to limit possible sample cases to those companies that are local-market oriented. Ultimately the textile sector set is focused on the re-export strategy, and the electronics sector set on selling to local markets. I reconfirmed the competitive strategy with the sample companies selected when conducting the fieldwork. It turned out that the companies' actual competitive strategies are consistent with METI's survey results, which helped to validate the selection.

Potential sample subsidiaries in the electronics sector were limited to those focused on selling to the local market. But the number remained very large. I did not have concrete empirical data on each subsidiary's sales record pattern and thus I further limited the number of sample subsidiaries to those located in a single city. Manufacturers of household white goods fit all of these criteria, and thus two possible cases of household white goods manufacturers in the city of Shanghai reflecting similarity in local environment and in their competitive strategy were identified. This was confirmed when I directly approached these companies. The two synthetic fibre manufacturing subsidiaries also reflect similarity in local environment as they are

Table 3.1 *Company profiles of the sample cases*

	WG-A Co.	WG-B Co.	SF-A Co.	SF-B Co.
Incorporation	1995	1995	1994	1996
Location	Shanghai	Shanghai	Nantong	Nantong
No. of employees	600 (+800 temporary)	1,300	1,500	1,800
Investment	US$58 million	US$42 million	US$340 million	US$507 million
Ownership	Japan (52.4%) China (47.6%)	Japan (70%) China (30%)	Japan 100%	Japan 100%
Products	Household white goods	Household white goods	Polyester garments	Polyester garments
Market	China (95%) Other Asian countries (5%)	China (80%) US (20%)	Japan (33%) China (33%) Others (33%)	Japan (40%) China (60%)
No. of managers	18	32	19	24
No. of expatriates	6	11	8	4

located adjacent to each other in an industrial zone close to Shanghai. Table 3.1 shows the company profiles of the sample subsidiaries. (The names of the sample companies have been changed for reasons of confidentiality.)

To summarize, I have described above the process of choosing a basically qualitative research approach, supplemented with quantitative data. The combined approach is reflected in the process of narrowing down sample companies to two sets, with two companies in each, including the rationale for selection and exclusion of sample subsidiaries. It is necessary now to consider the possible implications of these choices for research findings, especially in relation to issues of validity and reliability.

3.2 The research design: constructing validity

The aim of this study is not to establish a causal correlation but to show the importance of the causal relationship between subsidiary HR

practices, the social process of HR practice development and environmental contexts that support the methodological implications of the
study. The process of narrowing down and choosing specific sample
subsidiaries described in the previous section was undertaken with a
view to enhancing causal internal validity. By picking samples that are
similar in key ways, I intended to ensure that the relationship between
organizational context and subsidiary HR practice development is at
the centre of observation and analysis. This means the possible causes
of variation in policy have been limited. In addition to the problem of
"spurious relationships" – that is, a non-causal relation mistaken for a
causal one – researchers must also be aware of the dangers of "infer-
ence" (Yin, 2003). To address the problems inherent in inferring from
any set of data, this study uses the strategy of "triangulation" to further
enhance internal validity (ibid.). To achieve triangulation in the data
collection process, the research used different sources of information.
In all four sample companies, data were collected through interviewing people at different levels: managers at the Chinese headquarters
and subsidiaries, expatriates and locals, senior managers, mid-level
managers, workshop supervisors and workers. Company documentation was used to reflect on information collected through interviews.
These data were also compared to published information from the
respective companies.

The final implication for internal validity is related to manipulating
the data collection process and the result to be achieved. I designed
and applied a research protocol to enhance internal validity. The
research protocol specifies scheduling the order of visits to the sample
companies, contact with major interviewees in each of the companies,
the structure of the interview questions, and planning of data analysis
procedures.

When attempting to obtain rich and detailed data from a single site,
it is important to note the length of time spent at the site. I conducted
intensive fieldwork by spending thirty to forty days in each of the
targeted sample companies and living in some company dormitories.
I did not expect to be able to detect all the subsidiary HR practices
within such a limited time. The period spent at the sample sites was
in fact aimed at becoming familiar with the internal, micro-political
organizational context and the people that are its members. This close-
ness to the subsidiaries and their employees, in turn, led to a rewarding interview process as I was able to get to know and get along with

people in different positions. I am aware that international HRM strategy implementation and subsidiary HR practice development is a long-term process and the time needed for policy changes in practice varies significantly across companies. I thus supplemented observations and synchronic data with diachronic data gained by interviewing people about their experiences. While key informants are considered as a major source of information, staying on site also allowed me to encounter a broader range of people and incorporate different perspectives. Moreover, staying in the company accommodation enabled me to deepen the level of observation, and served as material for comparison and confirmation of data gained through interviews and company documents.

I decided on a protocol of addressing each set of companies separately, completing one before beginning the next. The sequence settled on was to visit the synthetic fibre group first and wrap up the two cases before moving on to investigate the electronics group. Although each intensive case study involved roughly one month spent on site, I maintained communication with the company after the period of intensive study had ended through telephone and email contact with the interviewees. The continuing communication provided the opportunity for follow-ups to address areas where more information was needed as well as for obtaining important new information, both of which supplemented the final results.

The key informants in the study of international HRM strategy implementation and subsidiary HR practice development are the decision-makers in the management team of each case, including both expatriate and local managers. Aiming to gain a more holistic view of the outcome of international HRM strategy implementation in each of the subsidiaries, I did not limit the range of interviewees to the key informants only. Junior managers, team leaders or supervisors, managerial trainees and some workers were also invited to comment on the HRM policies and practices at their workplace. Information was gained through semi-structured interviews, informal discussions at the offices, smoking cubes, canteens, dormitories, and sometimes after-work dinner gatherings. Table 3.2 summarizes the demographic information about the people approached for interviews and discussions and shows the number of interviews and discussions conducted in each company.

Table 3.2 *Number of informants*

	WG-A Co.	WG-B Co.	SF-A Co.	SF-B Co.
Semi-structured interviews	45 (5 Japanese)	48 (12 Japanese)	54 (9 Japanese)	62 (6 Japanese)
Informal discussions	122	156	246	213

There may be concerns over consistency in a research model where a single researcher travels around to stay at and visit four Japanese subsidiaries in China. I chose to conduct the case studies consecutively and was thus immersed in each sample company as well as conducting an intensive, centralized study sequentially. One effective and practical measure for maintaining consistency across cases is to use a research protocol (Yin, 1994; Ferlie and McNulty, 1997) prior to the data collection stage. The open-ended structure of the interview questions allows for an individual response from interviewees which is nevertheless within the range of issues that I was focusing on.

Another possible reason for inconsistency is the potential improvement in questioning techniques, the discovery of new problems, or the realization, during the course of the study, that important variables were missing in the original research design. This causes a situation where richer data are collected from the later sites. It is crucial for researchers to reflect in the field and conduct follow-up studies where necessary.

Before beginning fieldwork at the four case-study subsidiaries, I conducted a pilot study at a subsidiary that is invested by the same Japanese parent company as one of the four selected cases in the main study. The pilot aimed to test the research approach and methods. Pilot data were used to modify the research approach before proceeding to the main study. One major modification of the research approach was to move from taking on a role within the companies to a more detached method of non-participant observation. My original plan was to become part of the company and to be involved in developing subsidiary HR practices. This did not accord with the company's expectations in the pilot study. The company was unable to accommodate me by providing a position in the HRM division. The time period of each intensive study also ruled out the possibility of acting as an intern. However, I was given a desk in the office, allowed to utilize the office resources, and given physical access to the HRM division. I was also free to move within the company and ask questions. After encountering difficulties in the pilot study with "becoming an employee", I decided to focus on gaining the same level of physical access and mobility at each of the four main sample sites.

Another major change was the decision not to use written consent forms for the main study. During the pilot, I found that the pressure of signing a document "raised the concern of obligation to the answers given", as it was put by the director of the pilot company's Chinese headquarters. The same person expressed similar resistance to his employees being tape-recorded:

it is more important to get information rather than asking people to take responsibility for what they had said. I will suggest tape-recording not to be used and you take a note with doing the interview. This makes the interviewees more relaxed and would be easy for you to ask questions freely. (Head of SF-A Co. Beijing Representative Office, Japanese, 55, male)

As a result of this reluctance, I switched to a style of oral consent, where the rights of the interviewer and interviewee were communicated verbally during the session. I felt this would allow access to more information and wished to respect the opinion of the company in this matter. In addition to oral communication of information required for consent, a *Confidentiality Agreement* was signed by me at the company's Chinese headquarters. This document contained clauses regarding research ethics.

I also faced the critical question of how a study based on Japanese MNCs in China could be generalized to inform the wider field of SIHRM. In other words, how are we to demonstrate that findings based on a small number of samples are applicable to the larger community of MNCs' overseas subsidiaries? There is no need here to elaborate on how case studies have contributed to theory building. Rather, I am concerned with developing a sophisticated research design to build upon the existing research agenda and explore the implications of the research findings for relationship studies conducted in different country contexts.

3.3 The research design: constructing reliability

It is difficult to judge the reliability of a qualitative study based on criteria for establishing reliability in quantitative approaches (Ferlie and McNulty, 1997). In quantitative research, reliability means that different researchers will obtain similar, if not identical, results by following the same research procedure. However, for qualitative research using case studies based on interviews and observations, the researchers themselves, and their skills in data collection and analysis, will affect the results they obtain (Kirk and Miller, 1986). This does not mean that researchers should abandon the goal of reliability in conducting case studies. However, it does mean that the techniques used to enhance the reliability of qualitative research would be different from those in the quantitative studies, particularly in terms of research design.

As outlined in the sample selection section, I used multiple case studies to investigate international HRM strategy implementation and development of subsidiary HR practices. The sample selection process was carefully designed to incorporate two contrasting sets with the aim of replicative reliability. The two sets of sample companies represented Japanese-invested subsidiaries, manufacturing two different types of product: synthetic fibre and household white goods. Moreover, they were from two types of industry with different competitive strategies: the capital-intensive sector and the labour-intensive sector. There is also a contrast between the internationalization strategies of the two sets, with one set seeking to re-export their products and the other to target the local consumer market. The contrasting nature of the sample sets served to test whether results were replicable; if they were, they represent a means of reducing the effect of the researchers themselves, and other uncontrolled variables, on results.

The method of storing the information collected is also a major concern in the construction of reliability and the maintenance of accuracy. Considering the exploratory nature of this study, I believed that tape-recording was the best way to save the insights delivered by the interviewees. However, when I approached the sample companies, the managers tended to be unwilling to accept tape-recorded interviews. This might be largely due to the interviewees' perception that I would stay in the companies for an extended period and possibly reveal the contents of the interview to others, even though they were assured that

their responses would be kept completely confidential. It is also difficult to tape-record the conversation when the interview is conducted
in an informal way such as in the smoking cube in the workshops, in
the employees' canteen, employees' dormitory or at evening gatherings. An equally effective method of recording the interviewees' narrative is manual recording or note-taking (Hayes and Mattimoe, 2004).
This method relieves the interviewees' sense of anxiety over their voice
being recorded by a digital device.

Another way I stored information was in my field notes. Besides
conducting interviews with people from different positions within the
companies, I had the opportunity to accompany managers on their
daily routines, attend different kinds of meetings, tour around the
workplace, and join employees for lunch and sometimes dinner. My
observations at each occasion and the questions these observations
raised also comprised an important source of information.

With so much information collected on site, I was at risk of drown-
ing in information and hence not being able to abstract concepts, patterns or theories from the data. It was very important to be organized
with the data, especially since the research involved four cases with
a large number of interviews at each site. In this study, I decided to
use NVivo, a qualitative data analysis software program that helped
to organize and code the data collected. An advantage of using qualitative data analysis software is that it enhances the structure of the
data analysis process (Poole et al., 2000). However, as a large amount
of my record at the sample sites was recorded manually, retyping the
data was laborious and time-consuming, and this prolonged the data
analysis process.

3.4 Data collection

As mentioned in the previous section, I have relied on the idea of triangulation, using various sources of information to increase reliability.
The sources include company documentation (published and internal),
on-site observations and individual interviews. I kept field notes of
the observations and interviews conducted. A diary recorded happenings in the organization, whereas interview notes were intended to
record the interpretations and explanations of particular individuals.
The type and amount of documentation differed across companies.
Although I got some chances to read through company documentation

(for example, the managers' appraisal forms), this material could not be reproduced due to its confidential nature. As an additional source of information, I also conducted interviews with some government administrators and members of industry associations to gather third-party views. Such information was used to supplement the data collected from the sample companies.

The major information collection measure was interviews. In all four sample companies, a wide range of employees were interviewed, including general managers, senior managers, HR managers, junior managers, managerial trainees, production line supervisors, group leaders and workers. Due to the constraints of time and research resources, I was not able to approach the HQs of the companies selected for this study. Managers from the Chinese HQs or Chinese representative offices (for those without Chinese HQs) were also interviewed. Interviews were aimed at establishing abstract patterns regarding the managers' subjective perspectives, and these were compared with patterns drawn from other selected interviewees in the company, local government administrative authorities and some industry associations.

Most of the semi-structured interviews with managers were conducted at the office, normally in meeting rooms with no third party present. I began each interview with a general introduction of the research project and some key issues that would be included in the interview. This introduction gave interviewees an idea about the objectives of the interview and a preview of the interview questions. I was also allowed to move freely within the companies and to raise questions on site. Within this access I endeavoured to arrange informal interviews with people while they were working. Other informal interviews with key informants were conducted at off-work venues. Regardless of the venue where the interview took place, the interviewees were informed that the research project was for academic purposes and that any information provided would be kept strictly confidential. They were also informed that they could choose not to answer any of the questions. I also gave the interviewees the option to withdraw from the interview if they felt uncomfortable either about the questions or the way they were delivered. The length of the interviews varied depending on the interviewees' timetable and availability. The planned time for the interview questions to be covered was between one and a half and two hours. However, a single interview with the key informants sometimes lasted for three to four hours. As I had mobility inside the company and access to its employees, some of the key informants were revisited for follow-up questions. These informal follow-up interviews were usually short, either because the interviewee had fewer comments about the issues involved or was unable to talk at length with me.

The language used in the interviews was the interviewees' native language. Japanese managers were interviewed in Japanese and notes recorded in Japanese initially. Similarly, Chinese managers were interviewed and recorded in Chinese. The reason I did not adopt a single research language was that the interviewees had different levels of proficiency in English. Another important reason was that using the interviewees' native language created a relaxed environment and allowed them to give precise answers to the questions raised by me. However, it is possible that the findings might be distorted by factors related to translation, culture and use of language. For example, the original meanings could have been misinterpreted in the translation process. To avoid such technical errors, I, being familiar with the research subject and fluent in Japanese and Chinese, conducted the translation in person. The translations have also been proofread by a native speaker to make sure that meanings are correctly conveyed in this process.

All interview notes were treated equally and reviewed by the end of the day on which the interview took place. I typed the interview notes and emailed the interviewees for confirmation. This was routine unless the interviewees stated that there was no need or time for confirmation. The confirmed interview notes were normally returned to me within one or two days and I reviewed the changes, if any, and reconfirmed these with the interviewees. The notes were collected either in electronic or printed form, according to the preference of the interviewee. With unreturned interview notes, I followed up by phone with offers to collect the reconfirmation. Feedback and changes, as well as the original interview notes, were stored for analysis.

The period of intensive fieldwork was from February to July 2007 and I revisited the case sites in August 2010. During this period I travelled around the case-study sites and stayed either in the dormitory of the company (for the synthetic fibre manufacturers as they are located in an industrial zone with no guest accommodation), or at home with an employee's family. This also allowed time for me to discuss some issues in a more casual way with non-decision-makers and understand their concerns and evaluations of HRM policies and practices in their companies. After concluding the intensive fieldwork, I maintained regular email contact with the interviewees.

The data collection process went smoothly. I did not encounter any difficulties, such as being refused an interview or a refusal to answer particular interview questions. It was often necessary to negotiate for access and scheduling of interviews, a time- and energy-consuming task. It turned out, however, that effort spent on the negotiation process greatly enhanced the efficiency of the fieldwork. The general manager of one case company refused to be interviewed as the study was HRM-centred, and the general manager claimed to have no familiarity with the issues. I was directed to the HR manager in their Chinese headquarters, where HRM strategy in China is designed. This HR manager accepted the interview.

3.5 Key learning points

In this chapter, I have compared the quantitative and qualitative approaches, and found that the most suitable for the current study was a qualitative approach supplemented by quantitative methods. Upon critical review, the qualitative approach was found to be a more powerful way to investigate the complex process of international HRM strategy implementation and emergent subsidiary HR practices. Within this study, the quantitative approach served as an indispensable methodological yardstick. It guided research design, especially the sample selection process. I acknowledge the limitations of generalizability and reliability of research findings based on the qualitative approach, but have endeavoured to extend the broader theoretical implications of the study through a carefully plotted and adaptively implemented research design.

Considering the possible trade-offs between internal validity, external validity and the reliability of the research findings, the foremost task for me became pursuing high internal validity. Careful sample selection served to increase internal validity before each sample case was examined in depth. Database screening helped identify two contrasting groups of samples as well as disentangling the environmental and structural factors that affect organizational outcomes. This brought internal forces to the forefront of the analysis. Also, the research framework discussed in the previous chapter offered a guide to the data collection and analysis process. These measures allowed me to get as close as possible to the phenomenon being studied but at the same time avoid being overwhelmed by information or becoming "native" to any of the cases studied. To address external validity, I used triangulation, relying on many different sources of information. For further reliability, the study aimed to replicate results in two sets of samples.

This study aimed to conduct an investigation within the micro-political corporate context in order to discover the interplay between relevant actors in that context as well as its implications for organizational outcomes. An important aspect of the study was to eliminate the influence of contingency factors, that is, the size, age, years of experience, host-country effect, home-country effect, sector effect and location effect. It was impossible for me to move the organizations away from their environment or to change their structural characteristics, but one way to eliminate the influence of contingent factors was to place the study in companies that share similar contingency factors as much as possible. Selecting Japan as the home country and China as the host country both aimed to serve this research purpose. However, as long as the study is conducted within such a context, the selection of home country and host country is not a major issue. The research design is sophisticated and it is possible to conduct follow-up studies in a different setting, such as US-invested companies in Japan. While it is not my objective to replicate the cases in this particular study, it could be extended by this researcher or others in follow-up studies.

In summary, analysis and theory are generated on the basis of narrative evidence provided by insiders. I took the stance of a detached observer to interpret behaviour in the interaction between expatriate and local managers within the organizational context, the synchronic and diachronic aspects of international HRM strategy implementation and the development of subsidiary HR practices. The study has been designed based on refined theoretical and methodological frameworks, which increase confidence that the study is replicable to organizations from different home countries or for those investing in different host countries.

4 | *Multinationals in China: an overview*

This chapter will discuss the research site – the rising industrial clusters in China and the inflow of MNCs into these areas. Special attention will be given to Japanese MNCs, whose investment in China parallels the formation of new industrial clusters. In view of the structural differences between China and Japan, some studies predict progressive transfer from the Japanese parent plants and systemic learning in the Chinese subsidiaries (Campbell, 1994; Ma, 1998; Hong et al., 2006). Critiques of the "progressive transfer" arguments arise from both the national business system (NBS) and production strategy analysis. Scholars following the NBS approach have explained the difficulty of transfer by stressing the uniqueness of the Chinese context (Goodall and Warner, 1998; Warner and Zhu, 1998; Ip, 1999). They also suggest the inability to extract the socialization and network-based control mechanisms from Japanese society and transfer these to another space (Legewie, 2002: 906). After examining the production strategy of Japanese FDI in China, other scholars argue that shifting routinized and low-skill production from Japan to China indicates simplification or "Taylorist" job design and employment relations, and therefore limited transfer of HR practices from the parent company (Taylor 1999, 2001; Gamble et al., 2004; Morris et al., 2009). In this chapter, I intend to revisit these arguments by analysing the changing pattern of Japanese FDI in China over the past twenty years and to explore the implications of multiple realities of locality for developing HR practices in the Chinese subsidiaries of Japanese MNCs.

The chapter is divided into four major parts. I will first provide an overview of China's economic reform, in particular the Reform and Opening-up Policy and FDI inflow that followed. I will discuss the transition of the key legislation governing FDI inflow to China. The second part discusses trends in Japanese FDI inflow to China over time and the changing motivations of Japanese MNCs in selecting China as a host country. Specifically, the discussion explores the influences on the management and organization of Japanese MNCs brought about by China's economic development and policy changes. At the same time, I will also consider the economic transition in other Asian countries and its implications for Japanese FDI to China. In the third part, there will be further discussion of China's transition from a micro-economic perspective. I will then look at change of ownership and management in the local companies and rising consumer power, as well as labour market mobility and institutions, which are of particular importance to Japanese-invested companies' operations in China. The fourth part analyses the effects of sectors – another important element in the context of Japanese FDI in China. This section will analyse the industry background of the case companies: the household white goods and synthetic fibres clothing industry. I argue that the internationalization of these two industries is driven by different forces, and this indicates the different roles of the Chinese subsidiaries in the parent companies' global production network. I assume industry sector might be a key indicator of managers' choice of whether to transfer management practices from the parent companies. Finally, the chapter concludes by summarizing the dynamic locality that Japanese foreign-invested enterprises face in China and the possible implications for the development of subsidiary HR practices.

4.1 Foreign direct investment inflow to China

China embarked on the journey to economic reform after the 3rd Central Meeting of the 11th Representative Committee of the Chinese Communist Party. One of the most significant steps of reform was the launching of the Reform and Opening-up Policy and the authorization of FDI inflow to China. Subsequently, the Chinese government promulgated three general laws to regulate FDI inflow: the *Law of the People's Republic of China on Chinese–Foreign Equity Joint Ventures* (enacted on 1 July 1979), the *Law of the People's Republic of China on Chinese–Foreign Cooperative Joint Ventures* (enacted on 13 April 1988) and the *Law of the People's Republic of China on Wholly Foreign-Owned Enterprises* (enacted on 12 April 1986). These legal frameworks had authorized three forms of foreign investment enterprise by the end of the 1980s: Chinese–Foreign Equity Joint Ventures (CFEJV), Chinese–Foreign Cooperative Joint Ventures (CFCJV) and Wholly Foreign-Owned Enterprises (WFOE).

In addition, supplementary and provisional legislation and policies are often promulgated to attract, redirect or inhibit FDI to certain sectors or regions (Child, 1994).

The Reform and Opening-up Policy was implemented at a gradual and experimental pace. First, four southern coastal cities, *Shenzhen*, *Shandou*, *Zhuhai* and *Xiamen*, were named special economic zones (SEZ). These served as pilot locations where foreign companies could establish their operations. With successful experiences in the SEZs, eastern and northern coastal areas were opened up for FDI, and they were closely followed by the opening of the interior regions. Since China's Reformist Deng Xiaoping's speech upon his return from a tour of the southern provinces in 1992, the central government has been determined to promote nationwide reform targeted towards a market-oriented economy, setting the guiding principles for long-term FDI. In December 2001, China joined the World Trade Organization (WTO) and this was followed by a timetable to further deregulate FDI in China (JETRO, 2002).

China has witnessed a precipitous surge of FDI inflow during the past fifteen years and foreign-invested enterprises (FIEs) have occupied a considerable segment of the economy in terms of their contributions to GDP, employment and increased wage levels, as well as wage gaps across regions within China (Wu, 2000), and technology transfer and development (OECD, 2002). Table 4.1 shows the share of FDI in FIEs' contribution to China's export-led economic growth since 1992.

The consistent increase in both the amount of FDI-led exports and their proportion of China's total exports indicates that standardized production has characterized a large proportion of FDI inflow to China. The geographic distribution of FIEs in China follows the track set by the Reform and Opening-up Policy and most FIEs are clustered in the coastal areas. I will illustrate some characteristics of FDI in China with the case of Japanese investments.

4.2 Japanese investments in China

Japanese FDI forms one of the leading sources of world FDI. Many Japanese manufacturers rely on exports to the developed economies and relocation of production is market driven. Japanese FDI to the USA represents the biggest share of Japanese FDI outflow, followed

Table 4.1 *FDI and its contribution to China's exports (US$m),*
1992–2009

Year	FDI	Exports	Exports led by foreign-invested enterprises (FIEs)	Contribution of exports to GDP growth (%)
1992	110.07	–	–	–
1993	275.15	917.4	252.4	27.47
1994	337.67	1,210.1	347.1	28.68
1995	375.21	1,487.8	488.8	31.50
1996	417.25	1,510.5	615.1	40.72
1997	452.57	1,827.9	749.0	40.98
1998	454.63	1,837.1	809.6	44.07
1999	403.19	1,949.3	886.3	45.47
2000	407.15	2,492.0	1,194.4	47.93
2001	468.78	2,661.0	1,332.4	50.07
2002	527.43	3,256.0	1,699.9	52.21
2003	535.05	4,382.3	2,403.1	54.84
2004	606.30	5,933.3	3,385.9	57.07
2005	603.25	7,619.5	4,441.8	58.30
2006	630.21	9,689.4	5,637.8	58.19
2007	747.68	12,177.8	6,953.7	57.10
2008	923.95	14,306.9	7,904.9	55.25
2009	900.33	12,016.1	6,720.7	55.93

Source: National Bureau of Statistics of China, *China Statistical Yearbook* (1996 to 2010).

by the European Union. Japanese FDI in Asia, by contrast, is largely driven by cost considerations, shifting from seeking low-cost production resources to low-skilled, low-cost labour. For Japanese companies, the economic recession in Japan, rising domestic production costs and appreciation of the Japanese yen all account for outward investment. At the same time, lower labour costs, the preferential policies of host countries to attract FDI, a currency pegged to the US dollar (before the Asian financial crisis in 1997) and potential market growth (after 2000) also contributed to the concentration of Japanese FDI inflow since 2005 to the newly industrialized economies (NIEs), ASEAN4 (Indonesia, Malaysia, the Philippines and Thailand), China, and later, India (see Figure 4.1).

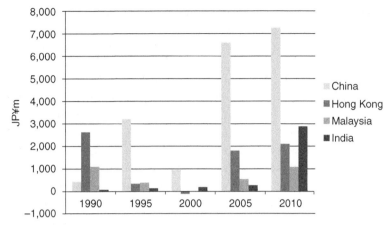

Figure 4.1 Japanese FDI to Asia

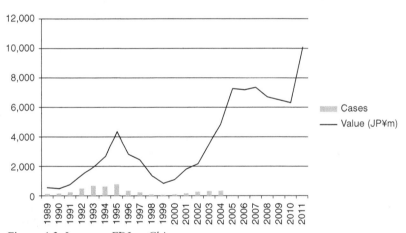

Figure 4.2 Japanese FDI to China

In China's case, three surges of Japanese FDI inflow since the promulgation of the Reform and Opening-up Policy can be observed: early to mid 1990s, 2000 to 2005, and 2010 onwards (see Figure 4.2).

Early Japanese FDI inflow to China was closely related to resumption of diplomatic relations. A pattern of "economic diplomacy" dominated business relations between the two countries and a handful of large-scale projects sponsored by the governments were established before the end of the 1980s (Ritchie, 1998: 138). Both the Chinese government and the Japanese companies were very cautious about selecting companies to take part in such bilateral cooperative projects. The Chinese government announced several large-scale SOEs called "window companies". Foreign companies were restricted to trading with or setting up joint ventures with the nominated SOEs. There was some Japanese private investment in China's old industrial bases centred in Dalian, which used to be a colony during the Japanese occupation before 1945 (Guan and Fan, 2003). But overall, Japanese FDI remained at a low level because many Japanese MNCs were unfamiliar with the Chinese market and had difficulty in finding suitable local partners. The majority of companies chose to channel business through Japanese trading houses, which set up representative offices in major Chinese cities as early as 1979–80 to assist the less experienced Japanese companies to develop business channels in China (Dicken and Miyamachi, 1998; Kawamura and Hayashikawa, 1998).

The first half of the 1990s witnessed the first surge of Japanese FDI inflow to Asia, including China. In general, the scale of investment was small. A large number of the investors were medium- and small-scale manufacturers in labour-intensive industries such as clothing manufacturers and household white goods assembly plants. This indicated that the Japanese MNCs were driven more by cost reduction than political reasons (Inagaki, 2003). Many smaller sub-contractors or parts suppliers also eventually decided to move production centres to China as a measure to reduce production and transportation costs (JETRO, 2002). This surge of Japanese FDI inflow to China was supplementary to the investment in Southeast Asian countries, which explains the downturn of Japanese FDI inflow to China after 1995 and the rise of FDI to some NIEs and ASEAN (Association of Southeast Asian Nations) countries till the outbreak of the Asian financial crisis in 1997. The fall of Guangdong International Trust & Investment Corporation (GITIC) in 1999, which remains the largest case of SOE bankruptcy in China to date, revealed serious problems with China's financial system for monitoring foreign capital flow (Toyo Keizai, 2000). The Foreign Exchange Control Bureau of China therefore launched new policies to regulate the domestic financial market and new procedures for establishing FIEs to tighten control over foreign currency flow. Establishing an FIE became more time consuming and involved more paperwork, which discouraged the Japanese from investing in China and caused them to shift back to the Southeast Asian countries for

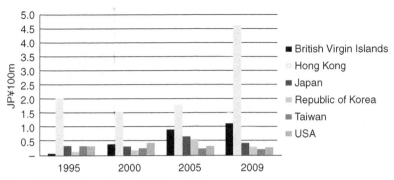

Figure 4.3 Major sources of FDI to China

low-cost production bases. The Asian financial crisis of 1997 and its aftermath forced Japanese MNCs to re-evaluate the risk of investing in the region, which led to a slowdown of Japanese FDI and a restructuring of existing manufacturing plants. The restructuring thus involved some closure of plants in Thailand, Malaysia, Singapore and China. This result is reflected in Carver's (1996) observation that China was a less important investment destination for Japanese MNCs and the Japanese subsidiaries generally acted in an opportunistic, experimental and footloose manner during this stage.

China's entry into the WTO in 2001 stimulated the second round of FDI inflow in China. By the end of 2005, there were in total 5,020 Japanese subsidiaries in China (Toyo Keizai, 2006) and the net Japanese FDI inflow to China was US$7,251.69 million by the end of 2010 (JETRO, 2011), making Japan the third largest source of FDI to China after Hong Kong and the British Virgin Islands. If the round-trip FDI is excluded, Japan is virtually the largest source of FDI (Figure 4.3).

METI's (2006) analysis showed that an important characteristic of Japanese FDI after 2000 is the higher average investment value per project than in the first surge. This is because Japanese FDI inflow was led by a number of large-scale companies that sought to establish capital-intensive projects in newly deregulated sectors. For example, the automobile and transportation machinery industry has attracted all the major Japanese manufacturers in the sector. For these companies, the target has been mainly the local market rather than reverse-exports to Japan (Inagaki, 2003). Toyota, for example, enlarged investment in automobile assembly networks in Tianjin and Guangdong in order to reach the local sales target of 1 million cars by the end of 2010.

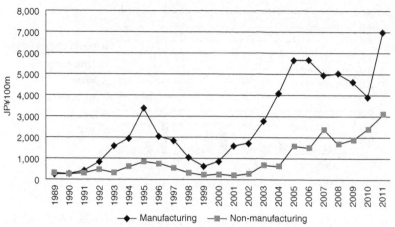

Figure 4.4 Trends in Japanese FDI to China

Since 2005, an increasing amount of Japanese FDI has also gone to non-manufacturing sectors such as financing and insurance, logistics and warehousing, distribution chains, retailing, information services, leasing, hotel and real-estate management (Figure 4.4). The targets of these MNCs are again local companies and consumers.

During this stage, Shanghai acted as the economic centre with the highest GDP per capita among all cities in China (CSYB, 2011) and attracted more non-manufacturers than any other area. Surrounded by several industrial bases, having a more flexible policy granted by the central government, and with higher household income level, Shanghai remains an ideal location for Japanese MNCs to access the local market.

We can also see the change of Japanese FDI in China in terms of industry sectors (Figure 4.5). In the first surge of FDI inflow into China, the largest investment was in the textile and electrical machinery industries. FDI in the textile industry quickly declined from 1995 whereas electrical machinery and general machinery remained the key sectors for Japanese FDI. After 2002, Japanese FDI in the transportation machinery sector surged, reflecting the Chinese government's deregulation in the automobile sector, a sector in which Japanese companies have shown continuous competitive advantage around the world (JETRO, 2005). There was a resurgence of Japanese FDI in both the textile and general machinery sectors since 2010, which marked China becoming the Asian centre to many Japanese MNCs.

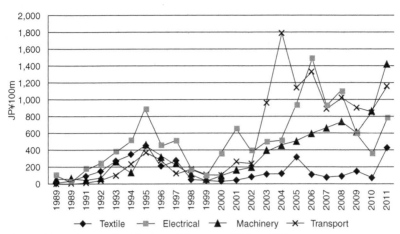

Figure 4.5 Industry distribution of Japanese FDI to China

The motivations for investing in China also changed over time. Toyo Keizai Press has conducted surveys about the overseas investment motivation among Japanese manufacturers every year since 2000. Figure 4.6 illustrates the shifts in motivation between 2001 and 2006.

For the Japanese MNCs invested in China by the end of 2001 and 2006, the three most important investment motivations were "to build an international manufacturing and logistics chain" (26.1% and 29.5%), "to explore the local market" (24.1% and 26.5%) and "to access low-cost labour" (14.7% and 12.9%). During this five-year period, the proportion of Japanese-invested companies motivated by the first two reasons slightly increased by 3.4% and 2.4%, respectively. In comparison, the motivations "to export back to Japan" and "to re-export to third country" went down by 4.2% and 0.4%. These figures indicate that, while China remained a relatively low-cost production base, many manufacturers were attempting to integrate the production locations in China into their international production networks, and to sell their products in the local market. Many companies chose to create systems to coordinate production, which explains the increase in companies motivated "to build international logistic and manufacturing chains". As reverse-exports and exports to third countries shrank and local trade grew, the number of Japanese-invested companies which chose to set up logistics, information collection and R&D in China to

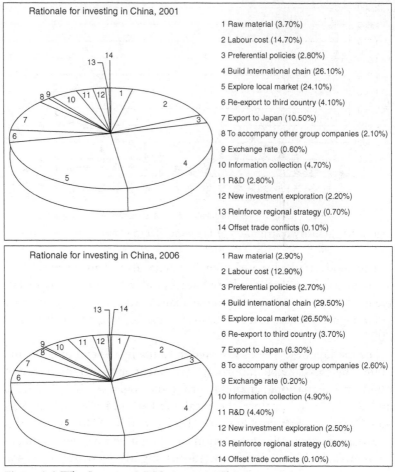

Figure 4.6 Why Japanese MNCs invest in China

facilitate production also grew. Meanwhile, the number of companies motivated by low-cost labour and raw materials decreased slightly by 1.8% and 0.8%, respectively. This result resonates with the trend of increasing investment in more capital-intensive sectors, where labour cost is less critical. The diverse investment motivations show that Japanese MNCs intended to reinforce their production centres in China with supportive functional networks. Distribution of the Chinese products may increase and diversify further in the near future with such networks in place.

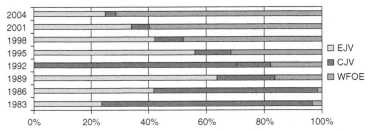

Figure 4.7 Proportion of EJVs, CJVs and WFOEs of Japanese-invested companies in China

The entry mode of Japanese MNCs has shifted from seeking joint ventures to setting up wholly owned subsidiaries (Figure 4.7).

During the early stages, Japanese subsidiaries that chose a contractual joint venture (CJV) ownership structure outnumbered the other two forms of investment. This was mainly due to a lack of capital and technology among the Chinese companies. CJV ownership allowed the Chinese side to provide land and workers as a form of investment while the Japanese side brought in capital and technology. Meanwhile, the Japanese investors were cautious and the CJV ownership structure was seen as a more flexible form of investment than the long-term partnership of Equity Joint Ventures (EJV). More EJVs were set up during the late 1980s and the proportion of EJVs exceeded that of CJVs. Although this proportion started to drop in 1992, it remained the largest form of Japanese FDI until 1998, when the Chinese government liberalized WFOEs in more industrial, financial, and other service sectors, causing the number of WFOEs to rise. Since 2001, the dominant form of Japanese-invested companies is the WFOE, representing 59.8 per cent of Japanese subsidiaries. While the change from EJV to WFOE can be interpreted as an expansion strategy in a gradually opened-up market like China, it is also the case that many Japanese-invested companies attempted to resolve conflicts in their subsidiary management teams and aimed to enhance their control over the policies and practices implemented in the subsidiaries (Inagaki, 2003). This will be further explored in Chapter 5, in which two cases of joint ventures will be studied.

Like most MNCs, these Japanese-invested companies are concentrated in the coastal clusters (see Figure 4.8). Shanghai, the frontier of China's economic reform and gateway of internationalization,

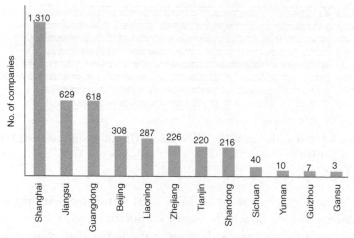

Figure 4.8 Distribution of Japanese subsidiaries in China

attracted the largest number of Japanese-invested companies, followed by its neighbouring province, Jiangsu. The two sets of case studies are based on companies located in Shanghai and Jiangsu. Third and fifth places are taken by Guangdong and Liaoning, which were among the earliest regions opened up, becoming preferred FDI destinations in south and north China respectively. In contrast, there is only limited investment in the interior of China. The largest western province, Sichuan, has forty Japanese subsidiaries.

As mentioned above, this trend of geographic concentration among Japanese-invested companies is consistent with China's experimental and multi-phased scheme for liberalizing foreign investment. Although the central government has promulgated preferential policies in recent years to encourage investment in the interior provinces, coastal areas remain the focus of FDI. Better infrastructure, faster economic growth rates and an enlarging local consumer market all make the coastal areas more attractive investment destinations for Japanese MNCs.

Accumulation of Japanese manufacturing plants is sometimes interpreted by Japanese companies as an intention to replicate the production networks in China and the possible transfer of management practices (Fukuda, 1995; Penga et al., 2001). However, this cluster effect may vary across sectors. The relationship between the key manufacturers and their sub-contractors varies significantly across, and within, industry sectors (Guillot and Lincoln, 2004; Hoetker, 2004). Competition from local and other foreign-invested spare-parts manufacturers may weaken the relationship between the manufacturers and existing sub-contractors. Furthermore, whether parent HR practices can be transferred or not depends on the local labour market and local institutional setting. The profile of the workforce varies across regions. In the Liaoning area, the main workforce is formed by the workers laid off by the SOEs. The industrial new towns in the Guangdong area rely heavily on migrant workers. The workforce in Shanghai is formed by more diverse groups, constituting rural and urban migrants, young graduates and ex-SOE employees. Ownership of the subsidiaries affects management transfer as well. Wholly owned subsidiaries are more likely to employ parent practices than the joint ventures (Fukuda, 1995). However, as Taylor (2001) commented in his review, very limited empirical research has been done to study Chinese subsidiaries of Japanese MNCs and these studies lack a systemic research design. Even Taylor's own work included only one wholly owned subsidiary, which weakens the conclusion that management transfer is not happening. Morris et al.'s (2009) study includes a larger pool (27 companies) of Japanese MNCs in China. The research findings suggest that a cost-reduction strategy is one of the key reasons for non-transfer of parent practices to the Chinese subsidiaries. Both studies focus on the workers, whereas HR practices concerning the local managers have not been included in the discussion. We still lack a holistic view of the HR practices employed in Chinese subsidiaries and do not know how different HR practices developed.

The analysis above suggests changing patterns of Japanese FDI and increasing demand for local employees. The shift from seeing China as a supplementary regional production base to integrating the Chinese market into a global or regional strategy also indicates the Japanese subsidiary may need more sophisticated HR practices to attract, develop and retain local employees. The observation that Japanese MNCs lack a consistent strategy for managing the HRM function in their Chinese subsidiaries may be true for the time being (Guan and Fan, 2003). The question yet to be explored is how these subsidiaries develop HR practices, and this may involve transfer of parent practices, adopting local practices, learning from best practices or perhaps integrating all of these in a hybrid pattern.

4.3 Something called "local": China in transition

China's transition is the result of interplay between multiple forces ranging from the central government's planned restructuring to outer pressure from the international community (Child and Tse, 2001). The previous section concentrated on the companies' economic rationale and a government-directed economic liberalization that has led to geographic centralization of subsidiaries, surge over time in investment, and changes in the entry mode among Japanese MNCs. In this section, the focus is on China's market-economy-oriented reform and how it has interacted with the rest of the world. This interaction caused enormous changes in Chinese society, and the influence of Western countries cannot be overestimated. At the micro-economic level, these changes are mirrored in the reform paradigm that local enterprises are based on. From the macro-economic perspective, they are reflected in increasing deregulation, declining government intervention in corporate management, and legal system reform. In the social-economic arena, they have had wide implications for local people's perception of their jobs, working life and relationship with the company – all of which underpin the distinctive institutions emerging in the local labour market. Japanese-invested companies are embedded within a transitional host country, where local institutions continue to emerge as the society voluntarily integrates liberal market elements developed in Western countries, and replaces features inherited from a centrally planned economy. Some of these features, however, remain and show the dominance of central planning in the past.

4.3.1 Laws vs. policies: legislative institutions in China

China's transition is often seen as a centrally planned process of economic restructuring, policy reorientation and institutional reform (Child and Tse, 2001). After more than three decades of reform, the Chinese state's intervention in regulating firms' activities remains strong. As explained earlier, the country has gradually opened up all regions for FDI. Deregulation of foreign investment has also extended the entry mode of FDI. The barriers for FDI in most industry sectors have been gradually removed as well. The *Catalogue for the Guidance of Foreign Investment Industries* divides industry sectors into four categories: sectors prohibiting foreign investment, sectors restricting foreign investment, sectors allowing foreign investment and sectors encouraging foreign investment. These new guidelines expanded both the sectors that *encourage* foreign investment and the sectors that *allow* foreign investments. Sectors that *restrict* foreign investment are shrinking. Only a few sectors with a high involvement in national security concerns continue to *prohibit* foreign investment. FIEs therefore have gained considerable freedom to decide on their ownership structure, subsidiary locations and market strategies. Along with deregulation, the central government is planning to promulgate a unified enterprise law to govern local and foreign-invested companies. One of the implications of this legislation is that many preferential policies towards FIEs will have to be withdrawn.

In terms of labour market regulations, the Chinese state has transformed its role from a major employer to a labour market regulator that promulgates employment laws, interprets employment regulations and administers legal enforcement. Employment legislation is aimed at setting up national standards such as wage levels, overtime, holiday, insurance, workplace safety and employee rights and welfare. The Chinese government is actively promoting long-term and commitment-based employment relations through restructuring the SOEs, giving preferential industrial policies to the high-tech and electronics sectors, introducing statutory employment regulations and setting up a supportive social security system (Cooke, 2003; Kwong and Qui, 2003; Lee, 2007). Evidence of more positive intervention by the Chinese state, such as an increase in employment tribunals in recent years and the new Employment Contract Law introduced in 2008, are seen by some as the government intervening to manage social disorder in response to considerable labour protests (Silver and Zhang, 2009). In particular, promulgation of the Employment Contract Law can be interpreted as an attempt by the government to create some common standards of employment practices (Friedman and Lee, 2010).

While FIEs are pressured to conform to the expectations set by local law, they are far more than passive recipients of these standards. With their stake in the national economy, FIEs can exert considerable leverage in negotiations with the Chinese central government regarding potential policy changes, either individually or collectively through industry associations. One of the most recent cases of collective negotiation between FIEs and the Chinese government involved the appeal of American and European industry associations, representing hundreds of MNCs, to the Chinese government in order to filibuster legislation of the new Labour Law (Brown, 2006). The central government was under great pressure to give serious consideration to this appeal as it came from major foreign investors, despite the fact that local labour, their representative associations, international human rights organizations and some other MNCs were in favour of the Chinese government's proposed reform (Global Labour Strategies, 2007). This kind of direct MNC–state confrontation, however, is infrequent in China. More often, companies prefer entering legislative consultations through the mediation of industry associations. For example, the Japan–China Trade Promotion Organization (JCTPO) is one organization that arranges regular consultation sessions, bringing administrative officials and Japanese investment companies together for discussion about policy issues. The concerns of Japanese investors have been changing over the years, but a major theme is to work for fewer policy changes and for advance warning if there is to be one (my own interview with JCTPO, 2005).

China is undergoing incremental political reform. The legal framework has been changed to delegate more autonomy to the firm level and to enhance fair competition. Although this process is far from straightforward, it is likely that a disorganized legal system, ad hoc policies and different regional policy interpretation will continue to characterize the country's legislative institutions for some time. Negotiating and navigating in this complex situation will remain essential for FIEs in order to realize business strategies set in China.

4.3.2 Local enterprises: the diversity of "local practices"

While operating in China, foreign-invested companies have to deal with many types of local enterprise: SOEs, privately owned companies and FIEs from different countries of origin. In terms of the HR practices adopted by these companies, a mixed picture has been reported (Rowley et al., 2004; Zhu, 2005; Björkman et al., 2008a; Warner, 2009). On the one hand, China's integration into the global economic networks has encouraged systemic learning, which directs local companies to best practices that originated in established economies. Voluntarily or involuntarily, many local companies have experienced organizational reorientation based on established HR models that are designed to enhance organizational efficiency. On

the other hand, local institutions, especially the labour market institutions, have forced the FIEs to deviate from best practice developed
in their home countries and to develop practices appropriate to the
local institutions.

When the Chinese government launched a series of systematic reforms
to break the "iron rice bowl" model ([*tie fan wan*], characterized by
life-long employment, centrally planned work allocation, managerial
positions appointed by government, in-house training and egalitarian
pay schemes) of SOEs in the mid 1990s, the large-scale SOEs represented the dominant form of business organization and practice in
China. SOEs comprised more than 50 per cent of the country's fixed
assets, recruited more than 70 per cent of the urban working population and accounted for approximately 28 per cent of the gross industrial output by the end of 1999 (National Bureau of Statistics of China,
2000). Despite taking up such a large proportion of China's resources,
many SOEs performed poorly in the 1990s. They experienced economic stagnation, financial losses and lay-offs. But this was not all: in
addition to poor financial performance, the SOEs were also entangled
in credit crisis, which is reflected in the problem of "triangle debts"
where inter-firm debts resulted in the overall financial stagnation of the
companies involved. It is generally agreed by analysts that inefficiency
in management led to this poor performance (Nakagane, 2000).

As part of its market-oriented reform, the Chinese central government initiated reform of SOEs in order to restructure them based
on the convergent modern enterprise system (CES) and group company system (GCS) models, which were believed to be more efficient
and competitive forms of organization. The CES and GCS models
were developed on the basis of organization and management practices prevalent in developed Western countries (Hassard et al., 2006;
Hassard, 2007). These models were polished and promoted by a government think-tank, which mainly consisted of management and social
science specialists trained (and sometimes based) in US or UK business
schools. The central government also subsidized the setting up of business schools and management training programmes (Cooke, 2011).
In addition to the Chinese central government's continuous effort to
reform SOEs, the United Nations Development Programme and the
World Bank also sponsored projects to assist reform of SOEs by establishing several model companies with consultants such as McKinsey
(Carver, 1996). While the task of SOE reform is far from completed,

the direction is quite clear: to learn from the advanced economies and develop efficient management models among Chinese enterprises.

Reforms of Chinese SOEs show how some hybrid forms of HR emerge (Zhu and Warner, 2000; Zhou et al., 2002; Zhu, 2005; Li et al., 2008). Empirical studies that compare HRM in the Chinese SOEs to the "best practice HRM" seem to indicate a moderate trend of convergence, although some *Chinese characteristics* are predicted to remain strong. Warner's (1997, 1999, 2000, 2008, 2009) series of studies suggests that, in stages, China's SOEs have moved away from the "iron rice bowl". Zhu (2005: 17) summarizes the change of employment practices in the SOEs as follows:

Old HR practices have undergone unprecedented changes: the responsibility for labour allocation has shifted from a centralized planning authority to forecasting and planning departments within enterprises; a contract labour system has replaced traditional lifetime employment; open competition replaced authority-nominated cadre appointments for managerial positions; and production and reward systems moved from emphasizing egalitarianism to rewarding efficiency and performance. Managers in China have started to show an increased interest in using HR practices, such as compensation and motivational systems, to increase productivity at the individual, group and enterprise level.

Meanwhile, most SOEs stopped offering company accommodation, medical care or in-house social services. External bodies started to assume the provision of social welfare and healthcare. While reform has effectively improved SOEs' performance, the consequent large-scale lay-offs, inadequate compensation and lack of re-employment opportunities have triggered spontaneous collective actions, though in contained ways (Lee, 2007).

Another important group of local enterprises is the privately owned companies. With the promotion of a market economy countrywide, the leverage of privately owned companies in the economy has risen quickly during the past fifteen years. According to the *China Statistical Year Book*, privately owned companies accounted for 27.9 per cent of GDP and 20.4 per cent of the national taxation revenue in 1992 (CNSYB, 1996). By the end of 2005, the number of privatized companies exceeded 50 per cent in both categories (National Bureau of Statistics of China, 2006). Compared to the government-led reform and collective learning sponsored by some international organizations, private companies are market driven. Without government subsidy, Chinese privately owned enterprises are under more pressure than the SOEs to search for adequate management systems in order to improve productivity and quality of products and services.

The privately owned companies display significant differences in terms of their possession of management resources, production technologies and management approaches. Some of the most successful ones such as Hair, Lenovo and Huawei have developed sophisticated management systems and employment practices (Wu, 2007). Others, set up by overseas returnees [*haigui*] and listed on foreign stock markets, have adopted HR policies and practices that develop long-term employment relations, encourage employee commitment and link individual rewards with organizational performance. A large majority of the privately owned companies, such as family businesses and the township and village enterprises (TVEs), however, have continued to be organized in a paternalistic manner. They rely on the exploitation of low-cost labour to survive amidst severe competition. Despite the influence of Western organizational and management strategies, the traditional reliance on the founder's charisma in decision-making, short-term oriented business goals, family-member-centred promotion and succession, and lack of HR planning still dominate local privately owned companies (Chen, 2004; Zhu, 2005; Cooke 2005c, 2012). These companies merely apply rudimentary techniques in sourcing, developing and retaining labour. Terms of employment are often ambiguous. Labour protection is rather inadequate. Apart from some HR policies attempting to reward individual performance, the privately owned companies have lagged behind in terms of HR planning, employee retention, and training and development.

FIEs form the third group of local companies. This group consists of subsidiaries of MNCs from different countries of origin. Chronological comparison of the HR practices adopted by the MNCs' Chinese subsidiaries seems to indicate a trend of convergence. Björkman and his colleagues (2008a) surveyed fifty-seven European MNCs in China in 1996 and eighty-seven in 2006, and found that those companies had embraced more HR policies and practices adopted by the parent companies back in the home country. The extent to which subsidiary HR policies and practices *resemble* those of the parent companies is dependent on subsidiaries' ownership structure, company size and experiences in China (Björkman et al., 2008b). FIEs' local strategy in China is also found to be relevant to the adoption of parent HR policies and practices. In their study of Japanese subsidiaries, Takeuchi, Chen and Lam's (2009) case study of five Japanese manufacturing plants in China showed that subsidiaries that compete by "product quality" are more inclined to transfer the parent company HR policies and practices to support the quality cycles, facilitate team-building and encourage employee involvement. In subsidiaries that undertake a "cost leadership" strategy, however, employment relations were found to be based on short- and fixed-term labour contracts, pay was contingent on daily output, training was restricted to a limited range of tasks, and welfare was limited or not offered to the majority of employees.

Other researchers, however, are more cautious about such simplistic comparison between parent and subsidiary HR practices. They argue that HR practices adopted at subsidiaries often take "hybrid" forms, which means that subsidiary HR practices can assume functions that differ from both the parent management practices and local ones (Child, 1994; Warner, 1995, 2005, 2008, 2009; Zhu, 2005; Zhang and Edwards, 2007). Assessing the impact of the global economic crisis and the launch of the new employment law in 2008, Jaussaud and Liu (2011) argue that significant variations exist between FIEs in terms of the implementation of HR practices. Gamble's (2006a, 2010) case studies of British and Japanese MNCs in China reveal the ongoing re-institutionalization of HR practices at subsidiaries. This result suggests that HRM can be applied in different ways, even within the same MNCs.

Overall, widening economic reform has enabled significant transformation of management in the local companies. Management issues such as "clarification of individual responsibility", "establishing merit-based appraisal" and "recruiting employees on a contract basis" have become the centre of local enterprise reform. HR practices exercised in more advanced economies have gained wider recognition and have been applied in various forms in local companies. However, some features of the old-style management still have their influence, such as the *danwei* developed in the 1950s or family business styles that go back even earlier in Chinese history (Chen, 2004; Cooke, 2005a, 2008a, 2012). The defining feature of China's transition is this dyadic locality: *old* and *new*, *established* and *emergent*, *sophisticated* and *pre-mature*, and HR practices parallel this opposition.

Table 4.2 *Employment by enterprise ownership, net (10,000 people),*
2001, 2005 and 2010

	2001	2005	2010
Economically active population	74,432	77,877	78,388
Total number of employed population	73,025	75,825	76,105
Urban employed persons	23,940	27,331	34,687
State-owned units	7,640	6,488	6,516
Urban collective-owned units	1,291	810	597
Cooperative units	153	188	156
Joint ownership units	45	45	36
Limited liability corporations	841	1,750	2,613
Share-holding corporations Ltd.	483	699	1,024
Private enterprises	1,527	3,458	6,071
Units with funds from Hong Kong, Macao & Taiwan	326	557	770
Foreign-funded units	345	688	1,053
Self-employed individuals	2,131	2,778	4,467
Rural employed persons	49,085	48,494	41,418
Township and village enterprises	13,086	14,272	15,893
Private enterprises	1,187	2,366	3,347
Self-employed individuals	2,629	2,123	2,540
Number of registered unemployed persons	681	839	908
Registered unemployment rate in urban areas	3.6%	4.2%	4.1%

Source: *China Statistical Year Book*, 2002, 2006 and 2011.

4.3.3 *Rising labour costs and mobility of the local workforce*

The implications of China's transitional labour markets on managing HR in MNCs' subsidiaries cannot be overstated. This transition is characterized by (1) economic disparity in different regions of the country and labour migration; (2) an increased demand for and increased turnover among skilled labour and managerial personnel; and (3) inadequate laws and institutions to protect and to facilitate the establishment of stable employment relations. Since I have discussed these three points in the previous section, here I will focus on the labour supply and turnover of the workforce. Table 4.2 shows the statistics of employment in China.

Chinese workers were often seen as victims of the country's rapid industrialization (Chan, 2001; Perry and Selden, 2010). Some independent research shows that unemployment in China is much higher than the officially published 4 per cent. Downsizing of SOEs has created large surpluses of labour in urban areas. This surplus has not been absorbed by emerging companies, whether these are privately owned, jointly owned or foreign-owned enterprises (Brooks and Tao, 2003). The economy also has to deal with a large surplus of rural labour. Some of this surplus rural labour is employed in TVEs, and some migrates to the cities for jobs. A large proportion, however, remains unemployed. While the new industrial clusters have absorbed some urban and rural migrants, the global economic crisis in 2008 brought bankruptcy, restructuring and withdrawal of privately owned enterprises. Employees made redundant were forced to seek re-employment opportunities.

Despite urban and rural labour surpluses and unemployment, labour turnover concerns many FIEs in China. The *China Labour Statistics Bureau* announces that labour turnover in China is lower than the OECD standard. But these numbers may not reflect what is happening in many manufacturing firms as the figures exclude migrant workers, who make up an important proportion of the shop-floor workforce (Reutersward, 2005). More importantly, skilled workers and managerial personnel are in short supply. It is difficult to predict an increase in this supply, and thus the problem of how to attract and retain potential managers will be a major issue confronting companies in China (Cooke, 2005a, 2008c).

In fact, MNCs in China are reporting labour shortages, which means difficulty in retaining "good quality and loyal" employees. A survey conducted by Development Dimensions International Inc. (Howard et al., 2008) indicates that employee turnover in mainland China is higher than in other countries in Asia. Short-term career orientation among many migrant workers may be a key reason for the observed high employee turnover, but one has to note that an equally important cause is the economic boom and massive FDI inflow that has led to a shortage of technical and managerial personnel. As a short-term solution, some companies "poach" groups of managers and skilled workers from other employers, and this is a new challenge that FIEs have to deal with in some of the new industrial clusters in east China (Li and Sheldon, 2010).

Table 4.3 *Average age and average tenure of employees in the subsidiaries of Japanese MNCs, 2003 and 2005*

Place of work	Average age		Years of tenure	
	2005	2003	2005	2003
Asia	32.1	32.1	6.7	6.9
China	29.9	29.1	5.0	4.4
Other Asian countries	33.3	33.1	7.7	7.8
Middle and Near East	40.3	36.8	11.3	8.0
Europe	37.0	37.4	8.9	8.2
North America	39.4	38.9	7.7	8.2
Central and South America	36.4	36.0	8.0	7.7
Africa	41.4	37.0	13.0	11.5
Oceania	39.0	38.5	7.4	6.3

Source: 4th Survey of Human Resource Management in Japanese MNCs conducted by The Japan Institute for Labour Policy and Training, 2005.

As far as the Japanese-invested companies are concerned, they tend to use a younger workforce when compared with their peers in other regions. It is interesting to note that Chinese employees have a higher turnover at Japanese-invested companies than in the rest of the world (Table 4.3).

In terms of the subsidiary senior management team, the proportion of expatriate managers has increased and that of local managers decreased since 2003. More senior managers have been expatriated to Chinese subsidiaries since 2003, and this trend is consistent with Japanese MNCs around the world as the companies started to reinforce their regional strategies. An increase in the proportion of expatriate managers in middle-level managerial positions is significant in China. This jump in numbers contradicts the trends in Japanese subsidiaries elsewhere (JILPT, 2006). Since there is no indication of differences between regions in terms of opportunities for promotion, we can assume that the increase in expatriate managers was largely due to difficulty in securing local potential managers. Many Japanese companies believe that employee turnover has increased the HR costs associated with sourcing, selecting, training and replacing managers (Guan and Fan, 2003). Deploying more expatriate managers in

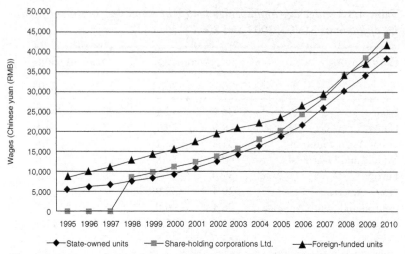

Figure 4.9 Average annual wages of employees in SOEs, private enterprises and FIEs

managerial positions may be a temporary solution. Some Japanese companies have started to review HR practices at the subsidiary level in an attempt to solve this problem. All four subsidiaries studied for this research were facing problems of not being able to retain employees compared with their Western competitors in China. Details of how individual companies deal with the issue of turnover in the workplace will be reported in the following chapters.

In addition to the increased HR costs of sourcing and replacement associated with labour turnover, real labour costs are also rising in China. Figure 4.9 shows that wage levels at FIEs went up approximately two-and-a-half times from 1995 to 2005. The wage gap between FIEs and local Chinese companies has decreased. In particular, the share-holding corporate Ltd. has overtaken FIEs in terms of average annual pay.

Very limited statistical data can be found to compare wage levels within MNCs' subsidiaries from different countries of origin. Zhongzhi (2008), a Chinese consultancy company, conducted a large-scale survey in Shanghai to find the wage differences between FIEs. The results of the survey showed that the wage gap between workers and managers is smaller in the subsidiaries of the Japanese MNCs compared with those of US and European MNCs. The same survey also showed that the

Japanese subsidiaries pay higher wages to fresh graduates (15% more than FIEs from the USA and European countries), whereas the wage for experienced managers is much lower (25% less than FIEs from the USA and European countries). The authors of the survey inferred that the reason for such wage differences is that Japanese MNCs tend to transfer an *egalitarian* HR approach. However, as I will show later in the case studies, such a generalization glosses over the fact that local factors and the subsidiary management process shape compensation practice much of the time. I will discuss this point further in Chapter 7.

Local legislation and provisional policies, developing various hybrid forms of HR practices among local companies, rising labour costs and high mobility of the local workforce have affected HR management of FIEs in China. However, competition for skilled workers, junior and senior managers and engineering personnel may be the direct cause of revision of the subsidiary HR system among Japanese FIEs. Japanese subsidiaries may not experience difficulty in attracting young unskilled workers; the critical task is to establish an effective local HR policy, one that focuses on retaining competent employees.

4.4 The new industrial clusters: exploring textile and household white goods commodity chains in China

Most FIEs are clustered in the coastal areas and special economic zones. After considering the general issues encountered by FIEs in China, it is important to go into more detail regarding the effect that industry clusters have on company organization and management. In this section, special attention is given to the newly industrialized clusters that have attracted significant FDI since the early 1990s. This is aimed at assessing the impact of industrial sector on management (Smith et al., 1990). The two sectors studied are the synthetic fibre clothing and household white goods sectors. Both have attracted a large number of Japanese MNCs.

With its lower labour costs, China has become an important production base in the global textile industry. China's textile and clothing exports account for a quarter of the total textile trade worldwide. The upstream sector, synthetic fibre manufacturing for the clothing industry, has grown dramatically, especially in the Yangtze delta area. A large number of the local synthetic fibre manufacturers rely on economies of scale to earn their competitive advantage. As a result of these

efforts, the output of synthetic fibre manufacturing in China has accel-
erated since the mid 1990s. By the end of 2006, China contributed
more than half of the total output of textile synthetic fibre worldwide
(HighBeam, 2009). But handling explosive growth is not easy and two
of the problems associated with fast expansion are excessive production and price competition in the local market. This becomes especially
acute for the low value-added synthetic fibre industry. The Chinese
government has launched measures to regulate the establishment of
new textile fibre manufacturing plants and has imposed a high import
tax (from 70% to 130%) for these low value-added products (Custom
House of China, 2007).

Compared to China, Japan seems to have lost competitive advantage
in the labour-intensive textile industry. To compete with the Chinese
clothing manufacturers, many Japanese manufacturers chose to set up
subsidiaries in China. Commodity-chain analysis (Gereffi, 1994) suggests that many companies relocated the labour-intensive part of their
operations to China, seeking lower production costs, while the parent
companies focused on designing, branding, marketing and channel-
ling the products made in China to consumers. The companies making
such changes are normally small to medium-sized enterprises (SMEs)
and their products are mainly re-exported to the Japanese market.
Compared to the clothing manufacturers, the upstream fibre manufacturers have large-scale production yet their product scope extends
to non-textile fibre such as recyclable fibre, semi-synthetic fibre and
non-bio-fibre. As major garment manufacturers moved to developing
countries, production of synthetic fibre for clothing began shrinking in
Japan (JCFA, 2007). Relocation of fibre manufacturers to China was
driven by the need to serve domestic clients, and the majority of the
production in Chinese subsidiaries is either exported directly as material or indirectly as finished garments.

Unlike the clothing synthetic fibre industry, internalization of household white goods manufacturers is producer directed. Japanese manufacturers are the dominant actors in the international market and
many Japanese-branded electronic products enjoy a good reputation
among Chinese consumers. Chinese government policy in the household white goods sector is to direct foreign companies to establish
operations and encourage knowledge transfer through joint venture
projects. Because of this policy, deregulation for wholly owned foreign
companies in the household white goods industry was delayed and did

not occur until the late 1990s. Most Japanese-invested companies in the early and mid 1990s were joint ventures.

Lower production costs were not the only reason that Japanese household white goods manufacturers decided to establish operations in China. As labour costs went up drastically in Japan, many chose to automate their plants in Japan and moved assembly lines to developing countries, especially to Southeast Asia in the mid 1980s. Setting up Chinese subsidiaries a decade later did not replace production in most Southeast Asian assembly plants. Harwit (1996) thus argued that many household white goods manufacturers saw China as a potential market and concentrated on products that catered for local consumers. Constraints on managers' choice, however, come from both the instability of local policies and the imbalance in economic development.

The above analysis presents the distinctive nature of the synthetic fibre and household white goods sectors in Japan and China. Manufacturers in these two sectors therefore show different characteristics in terms of competitive advantage, internationalization strategy, and competitive strategy in both their home country and host market. We thus assume that the level of transfer of parent practices may show some distinct patterns. The larger investment scale and client-driven exports-oriented production strategy of the fibre manufacturers suggests that the parent companies will exert a higher level of control and coordination. This factor clearly suggests a more active transfer of the production system and maybe the HR system as well. On the other hand, the household white goods manufacturers need more local resources to explore the Chinese market. Their subsidiaries therefore may show more local characteristics as local managers are able to control these local resources and use them to their advantage in the subsidiaries.

4.5 Key learning points

In this chapter, I have shown the possible implications of China's transition on the managers' perception of HR policies and practices. I suggest that "local practice" in China consists of many hybrid forms of management practices and China's emerging economy has fostered further hybridization. The reformed SOEs and some large-scale private companies show some sign of incorporating "best practice" HRM.

Some collectively owned companies are also found to be experiment-
ing with HRM, though paternalism remains strong in many TVEs
and family businesses (Warner, 1993, 1997; Zhu and Warner, 2000).
FIEs develop management practices that diverge from their home
practice yet show qualitative difference from the management practices adopted by most local companies (Cooke, 2004; Gamble, 2006a,
2006b). We cannot easily generalize a dominant local management
model. This means empirical research is more important than would
be the case in more settled institutional environments where it might
be possible to "read off" internal firm HR arrangements from external structures. Such possibilities are not available in the dynamic and
transitional world of firm development in China, and direct fieldwork
is essential to understand how HR is operational at the workplace
level.

Several features make the Chinese context a very significant site for
this study. But what does China's transition mean to individual subsidiaries of MNCs? The key debate of "Japanization" is mainly based
on studies of Japanese subsidiaries in the USA and Europe, principally
the UK (Kenney and Florida, 1993; Abo, 1994; Beechler and Yang,
1994; Graham, 1995; Beechler, Bird and Taylor, 1995; Danford, 1998;
Elger and Smith, 1994, 2005; Kenney et al., 1998; Morris et al., 2000;
Morgan et al., 2003; Sharpe, 2006). As China has gradually become an
important recipient of Japanese FDI, there has been growing research
interest in examining the similarities or particularities of management
of Japanese subsidiaries in China and comparing the research results
to studies conducted elsewhere (Taylor, 1999, 2001; Gamble, 2010).
However, problematic research design has limited our understanding of how Japanese MNCs manage their subsidiaries in China. In
particular, limited attention has been paid to how local management
engages with or works alongside expatriates to develop subsidiary HR
practices.

I have presented a dynamic picture of Japanese FDI in China and
argued that the observation of varied subsidiary management practices reflects the transitional nature of both locality and the changing
internationalization strategy of many Japanese MNCs. China has
changed its policy and shifted from providing preferential policies to
attract MNCs to directing MNCs as local firms. Rising costs may have
different implications for Japanese MNCs applying a "race-to-the-
bottom" production strategy in China. Some companies seeking the

export business strategy may have chosen to relocate to countries or areas with lower labour costs. An example may be the companies from the clothing manufacturing industry. Other companies, however, may choose to reinforce their strategy in the Chinese market. Cost pressure can therefore be a driving force for developing more sophisticated management systems to enhance production efficiency and to compete locally. In the following chapters, I will investigate how Japanese subsidiaries may (or may not) be able to achieve these goals.

5 | Household white goods manufacturing plants: targeting an emerging consumer market

This chapter discusses two household white goods manufacturers, WG-A Co. and WG-B Co. Both these companies are located in suburban Shanghai – China's economic centre that hosts the largest number of FIEs in the country. Questioning Guan and Fan's (2003: 68) argument that lacking a systemically designed internal promotion route for local employees is the major barrier to localization, I will examine the HR practices employed in the sample companies in the coming two chapters. The focus is on three major HRM issues concerning the local employees: (1) overall corporate HRM strategies; (2) HRM policies of integrating local managers; and (3) HRM practices in recruitment and selection, training and development, reward and compensation, appraisal and promotion, retention and dismissal. A comparison is drawn between the subsidiaries and their parent plants. The evaluation of transformation of management practices in Japan is beyond the scope of this study, and I want to emphasize that the study of subsidiary HRM development has to take into consideration a dynamic parent HR practice back home.

Both WG-A Co. and WG-B Co. had announced a strategy of "localizing" subsidiary management and had adopted complex HR practices to implement this strategy. However, a closer examination of the management system revealed that the subsidiary HR practices did not follow the track of a "progressive transfer". Also, the locals failed to gain full control over managing the local employees, as described by the "race-to-the-bottom" thesis. Variation in HR practices is actually a result of ongoing negotiation for change and struggles for control among the managers. Such struggle is most evident in the realm of subsidiary HR practice development: local managers claimed that they were familiar with the local institutions and had expertise in dealing with the local workforce, whereas expatriates emphasized the efficiency or "the internal consistency of a superb management system" – a common observation in studies of transferability of HR practices across country borders (Beechler et al., 1998; Elger and Smith, 2005). To understand how "localization" strategy translates into various subsidiary HR functions, policies and practices, I examined the process by which subsidiary managers de-codify the meaning of "localization", negotiate for subsidiary HR policies, design management practices, evaluate the effect of HR practices, and modify relevant policies and practices. Managers' input into this process greatly influences the HR practices employed in subsidiaries. There are many reasons for this. First, the interpretation of "localization" is highly contextual and subsidiary-specific. Second, differences between the two subsidiaries reflect managers' active construction of subsidiary competitive strategies and hence I observed varied degrees of embeddedness in the locality. Finally, besides the micro-politics within the subsidiaries, I also found that managers interact with the stakeholders in the organizational networks and agents of the local environment in order to exert external pressure to influence management decisions.

The chapter contains four major parts. The first part is a general introduction to how the two companies operate in China. The second and third parts report detailed information on employment relations for each case study. The focus will be on the interplay among the internal and external forces that shape employment relations and on where subsidiary deviation emerges. The final part summarizes the two cases.

5.1 White goods manufacturers: ownership restructuring, price competition and product upgrading

WG-A Co. and WG-B Co. were both established in 1995 as Japanese–Chinese joint ventures with Japanese investment of 51 per cent and Chinese investment of 49 per cent. This ownership structure was a result of the foreign ownership restrictions in the general electrical industries, which were withdrawn in the late 1990s. Both companies have reviewed their ownership structure several times during the past ten years and the share of Japanese investment has gradually increased. As to the parent companies, the Japanese sides are dominant household white goods manufacturers in Japan and worldwide. They offer a wide range of household electrical products and are similar in terms of their annual production output and sales revenue. The Chinese sides were state-owned white goods manufacturers, but were much smaller in both production scale and product range. Setting up joint ventures was part of the government-led SOE reform. Production in Japan is highly automated and assembly plants use a limited number of shop-floor workers. In sharp contrast, production by subsidiaries is semi-automated. The assembly lines of WG-A Co. and WG-B Co. rely heavily on shop-floor workers to conduct unskilled or semi-skilled tasks.

In terms of the local market, China is both the largest producer and consumer of household white goods (BZERC, 2007). Household white goods producers face severe competition in China. By the end of 2002, there were approximately 400 household white goods manufacturers, which included Japanese manufacturers like WG-A Co. and WG-B Co., as well as Korean, Taiwanese and local manufacturers. In addition to pressure from rival producers, the specialized electronics superstores have had a significant impact on price. These stores further boosted price competition because they normally negotiate directly with the manufacturers, and are successful in achieving low prices through economies of scale and by offering special promotions. Additionally, the physical layout of electronic superstores has a large impact on consumer choice as it makes price comparison very straightforward. When manufacturers face this kind of price competition, they come under pressure to provide more competitive products to the consumers.

After facing a growing number of competitors and pressure to provide more competitive products, both the Japanese parent companies adopted strategies to reinforce local responsibility of the subsidiaries. Both WG-A Co. and WG-B Co. announced mid-term plans to provide products with reliable quality and hoped to lower production costs and provide better customer services by localizing customer-service facilities. The central issues involved in this localization were to source manufacturing material from local suppliers, transfer some R&D function, strengthen sales and customer services and take steps to integrate more local managers into the engineering and management teams. While the subsidiary goal of localization was similar, the management policies and practices developed to serve localization and its effect on employment relations differed significantly between the two companies.

5.2 WG-A Co.'s struggle to upgrade

Among the twenty-eight subsidiaries in China, WG-A Co. was one of the earliest manufacturing plants to produce models designed and developed in Japan. The factory faced drastic structural changes in the household electrical white goods industry and subsequent price competition in the local market during the late 1990s, and was ultimately forced to cut production costs. In order to enhance the products' quality-to-price ratio to cater to the rising middle class and provide some luxury products to the new upper class in China, the factory moved away from products generally accepted in Japan to those that are designed specifically for the Chinese market. WG-A also expanded its production scope to include new product lines that experienced less competition in the Chinese consumer market. In the words of a local senior manager, these changes were to "strive towards local-market oriented competitive strategy" or localization. However, as I will show later, the central debate among the managers was how to consolidate WG-A Co.'s market position and provide an organizational structure that would facilitate production and market expansion.

These localization measures suggest that the factory intended to gain more autonomy from both its parent companies. While WG-A Co. was set up as a joint venture, the Chinese parent company was seldom directly involved in its decision-making processes, and the subsidiary was always the centre of decision-making concerning production, sales, customer services and HR. The Japanese parent company continued to control strategic planning of R&D and to coordinate marketing and offer technical support and quality control. The Japanese side also maintained its influence by providing technical support to the organization of production and sometimes sales of products. More importantly, the Japanese parent company centralized product model design, which many local managers saw as a restriction on the upgrading of WG-A Co.

5.2.1 Building up a local business network

WG-A Co.'s initial investment strategy was to replace high-price, imported goods with locally manufactured products in reaction to the import barriers imposed by the Chinese government.

We chose China as we foresee a potential market for household electrical products. Consumption of electronic goods in China has moved up steadily as people's living standard increased during the late 1980s to early 1990s.

However, when we compare the quantity and quality of the electronic devices used by the Chinese household and those in Japan, we see a huge gap and there lies our potential market. (General Manager, Japanese, 56, male)

Our company used to export a small number of products to China in the early 1990s. However, China's importation tax used to be 15% for household white goods, plus a 40% luxury goods tax. Production costs in Japan and the importation taxes added up to a high price for these products, which is hardly affordable for the normal household. But the demand for household white goods and a lack of supply capacity on the part of local manufacturers created a big market gap. What we found was that some smuggled products filled in this gap. (Chief Accountant, Japanese, 52, male)

WG-A Co. did not enter China seeking a low-cost production base for re-exports. The company was sensitive to local product prices when entering the Chinese market and thus prioritized the creation of a local sales network.

Judging from WG-A Co.'s financial performance, the company has successfully achieved its original objectives. On one hand, the factory reduced manufacturing costs by sourcing from local suppliers, though some key parts continue to be purchased from Japan via the Japanese parent company. On the other hand, the factory built up a local sales network and gradually their market share in China increased to reach 15 per cent by the end of 2006. In terms of product market, 95 per cent of products are sold locally to specialized electronic superstores (55%), local real-estate project organizers (25%) and local wholesale merchant houses (20%). Although the managers generally agreed that efficient factory-centred production, sales and customer service had effectively contributed to the company's success in the local market in the past, they had specific concerns over the future of their local service and sales network. The Chinese management of the company, in general, seemed confident about the efficiency of the localized factory whereas the Japanese management of the company saw the need for further specialization. A Chinese management representative stated:

Our factory is not just an assembly plant like the other Japanese electronics manufacturers here. We are the only one among all the Japanese joint ventures in China that centralized the functions of manufacturing, sales, and customer services. These functions are effectively connected and coordinated here. There is not much time wasted with communication. This gives our factory a major [competitive] advantage. (Head of the Department of Sales, Chinese, 42, male)

In contrast, more Japanese managers saw the need to specialize these functions along with the expansion of the factory's production scale and scope.

We are a manufacturing plant without a marketing function. The [Japanese] headquarters handles product design, development, and marketing functions. That is why we would prefer to use a specialized trading company – a wholly owned subsidiary of our parent company – to extend our market share in China. Meanwhile, the factory can concentrate on centralizing production-related functions. (Chief Accounting Officer, Japanese, 52, male)

The WG-A Co. factory contracted with a group trading company for marketing and sales for one series of products in 2006 and, according to the Japanese managers, this reflected a pro-specialization approach. Many of the Chinese managers, however, seem to have reacted to this decision negatively. The R&D had not been moved to the subsidiary, yet control over sales of some products was taken away, upsetting many of the local managers. Some of the locals considered it a group *teikei* [support], which is a common practice among Japanese companies (Gerlach, 1992). Others interpreted the move of site control of product sales to the trading company as a way for the Japanese parent company to distribute profit among its subsidiaries and avoid local income tax.

Each subsidiary is an independent fiscal entity, and thus it is not difficult to understand the local managers' doubts about using a foreign-invested trading company to handle certain local sales, especially since the existing supply–production–sales–customer-service network was functioning well. WG-A Co.'s mainstream products had a good local reputation among Chinese consumers and its factory has also enjoyed sound financial performance since 2002 despite strong competition. Unfortunately, the new sales route did not bring immediate improvement in the sales record. Most Chinese managers assumed that in exchange for moving sales of some profit-making products to the parent companies' direct subsidiary (the trading company), the factory would gain an advantage in negotiating for local R&D functions. However, the expatriate managers expressed a rather ambiguous

attitude on the rationale for integrating R&D at WG-A Co. This could be interpreted as a message from the Japanese parent company that R&D functions would not be established at the factory, at least in the near future. Chinese management chose to interpret the movement of certain sales to the trading company as a "stake" to trade with the Japanese side for internalizing R&D at the factory level. Management had already initiated several rounds of negotiation to this end since 2004. Negotiations, however, did not go smoothly, because the parent company's criteria for evaluating subsidiary qualification for product design was far more complicated and time consuming than managers at the factory had assumed.

At the centre of the debate was the subsidiary's pursuit of becoming a fully functional unit and the parent company's intention to coordinate and control production functions among its subsidiaries. This eventually led to contradictory interpretations of "localization" between local and expatriate managers. As discussed above, the local managers saw the factory as the centre of its business network and tended to agree that localization of sales was where the factory gained a competitive advantage in the local market, especially in competition with other Japanese manufacturers. The local managers intended, therefore, to negotiate for more strategic functions to be localized, and prioritized R&D. The Japanese parent company still questioned the ability of the factory to maintain quality for the brand. But it is worth noting that the factory also coordinates business activities among different subsidiaries invested by their Japanese parent company, and it is thus in a better position to promote "localization" in a broader sense, that is, to promote specialization among its different functional subsidiaries in China – not only at the factory.

When the factory was revisited in 2010, it was still unclear whether the parent company intends to delegate R&D to the factory or to establish a more specialized R&D centre elsewhere. A major gap remained in the understanding of the relationship between the factory and their sister subsidiary companies in China and this created conflict related to localization strategies. The Chinese parent company took a passive role in supporting the subsidiary's proposal. This passive role might be explained by the worry that localization strategies might eventually marginalize the Chinese parent company.

While negotiations for a local R&D function had not reached a mutually acceptable conclusion, the factory did start producing higher grade models. The general manager explained that producing this type of product was critical for survival in the Chinese market:

Competition among the household white goods manufacturers is ridiculous here, especially after the year 2000. The number of companies producing similar products increased to more than 400 by the end of 2001. It is definitely a buyer's market and there will be vicious price competition. We know many of the other Japanese companies who are dedicated, or maybe forced by the retailers, to join in the price competition with their best effort. They may have won market share but their profit has been seriously limited, and some have even ended up with a deficit and had to seek further investment from Japan. However, this is not what our factory is planning to do. Our company has long been competitive with superior technology and product quality. Buyers of our products are less sensitive to price than consumers of, for example, CRT TVs. This has offered us some leeway to explore the market with new and high value-added products. (General Manager, Japanese, 56, male)

Statistical data partially support the above statements. WG-A Co.'s products began to be sold at the highest retail price in the Chinese market, and their mainstream products were at least 25 per cent higher than most (only one Korean-invested brand has comparable retail pricing). However, compared to early 2000, price competition in the local market forced the average price of most of these products to go down approximately 200 per cent (BZERC, 2007). WG-A Co. was affected, too, and its pricing dropped about 100 per cent. Given this aggressive price dropping, cost reduction remained a critical issue for the factory to survive in the local market.

5.2.2 *Job design and HRM routines*

The Japanese side had exerted a strong influence on many areas such as shop-floor job design, production management and product storage. The shop-floor layout was very similar to that in Japan. The assembly line and automatic control system were imported directly from the Japanese parent company. Most subsidiary managers acknowledged that the Japanese production system had demonstrated its efficiency in controlling production costs. The Japanese had superb control over the manufacturing process and their technical know-how had developed over the years. As a result, implementation of the Japanese parent company production system had encountered less resistance from the local people. Many of the interviewees, who were familiar with the work culture of both the parent company plant and the local factories, commented that there were many similarities in the way production was organized.

The setting of assembly lines, production process and procedures, job design and skills are very like those in Japan. The only difference is the degree of automation. Many jobs that are done by workers here are accomplished by machines in the Japanese plants. (Head, Division of Production, Japanese, 53, male)

The Japanese plants are advanced in automation compared with our factory. But this is not because we cannot implement automation in our plant. It is not necessary. The cost of labour is much higher than investing in machines in Japan but it is definitely not the case in China. Other than that, on-site production management [seisan genba kanri] is very similar. (Deputy Head, Division of Production, Chinese, 40, male)

Workshop jobs were highly routinized with rather limited skill requirements from the workers. This was reflected in the detailed division of labour, precise position allocation to each worker, accurate calculation of the standard time to finish the particular job at each position and the standard time to produce one unit, as well as specified and written working procedures in manufacturing manuals. Some specific techniques were also transferred from Japan. For example, in order to connect different parts of the shop floor, a whiteboard was prominently displayed in the workshop and this facilitated communication with workers. The whiteboard exhibited diagrams of manufacturing processes, procedural requirements and past problems, all of these serving as reminders to the employees. Some workplace regulations were also based on the Japanese parent company models and were supported by locally devised rules and sanctions. (This point will be discussed in more detail in the appraisal section.)

The factory's HR practices differed significantly from those of the Japanese parent plant in many ways. First and foremost, there were fundamental differences in employee relations. The Japanese managers tended to assume that an effective management system was the best way to support production, an assumption which did not seem to be accepted by local management.

The [Japanese] manager always asks us to provide suggestions to improve rules at the workshop. But our problem is not that we do not have enough rules, but how we put them into effect...Rules mean nothing if people keep ignoring them, right? (Line Supervisor, Chinese, 37, male)

Japanese managers also expressed frustration about the difficulty they faced in maintaining workplace discipline. But they seemed to believe this was caused by the lack of employee involvement in setting up the workplace regulation.

It is sometimes difficult to know whether the workers agree or not before any rules are put into effect. We had implemented a rule that workers in the shop floor have to wear a cap. However, when we are in the workshop, we constantly see people [who were not wearing their caps] put them on in a hurry. We asked why and they said it was too hot to wear a cap. Why did they not say so before the rule was implemented? (Head, Division of Production, Japanese, 53, male)

Instead of seeing communication difficulties as the major cause of problems at the workshop, the local managers were more inclined to blame the ineffectiveness of the rewards/penalty system. Many expressed the idea that the Chinese workforce displayed low quality when compared to the Japanese workplace. By "quality", the managers meant compliance with company regulations.

We are not willing to admit this but quality [suzhi] of the workers is far worse here than that of Japan. We always have employees behave the way that is obviously not acceptable at work. I am not saying that all our employees are like this. And of course there are problematic employees in Japan as well. But it is that there are more such employees here in China than in Japan. This is why management has much more to do here...The only way to prevent such behaviour is to link the workers' behaviour to their pay, but we are not authorized to do so. (Deputy Head, Department of Quality Control, Chinese, 42, male)

In other words, the local managers saw the local workforce's lack of compliance and sought to motivate them with tangible and material incentives. This drove them to suggest the need for close supervision and a scheme of rewards and penalties. Japanese managers, by contrast, tended to evaluate the "quality" of the workforce in terms of workers' learning abilities. Although they agreed that workplace discipline was a problem, they were not sure if imposing penalties would be a long-lasting solution. Seeing that workers experienced stress due to fear of penalties, Japanese managers were rather concerned that penalties resulted in unwanted outcomes such as restricted employee creativity, reduced loyalty and lower overall performance.

Local HR practice remained under re-evaluation and adjustment. At the time of this research, the factory had implemented some elements of the Japanese parent company's HR practice and some elements from the old SOE's (WG-A Co.'s Chinese parent company) HR practice, and some elements borrowed from other local practice. WG-A Co.'s HR practice differed from the Japanese parent plants in several significant ways.

Workforce composition

The composition of the workforce was much more diverse than on the Japanese side. The factory recruited three types of employee: collectively recruited employees [*tongbian zhigong*] (47%), contracted employees [*hetong gong*] (18%) and temporary employees [*linshi gong*] (35%). The collectively recruited employees were all from the Chinese parent company, which used to be an SOE. The management recruited about 400 employees from the Chinese parent company when WG-A Co. was established. Over the previous twelve years, some of the employees in this group retired, resigned, were promoted or transferred to the Chinese parent company. But these employees still represented the largest proportion of the workforce. The factory did not offer life-long employment for the new employees as used to be the case with employees of the SOE Chinese parent company. However, it seemed this group enjoyed job security and a larger percentage of them were promoted to managerial positions than either of the other groups. The HR manager explained that this group would be reclassified as contracted employees in the near future in line with the enactment of the reformed national labour law.

There was also a group of employees on short-term contracts, who worked in the company from one to three years. When asked about the reasons for signing short-term contracts instead of long-term ones, HR managers explained that "it was a local labour market norm". Employees felt that a short-term contract would give them some flexibility when "the right job comes along", and this contributed to the instability of the local labour market. A less explicit reason seemed to be a shared understanding of job security at WG-A Co. It was very likely that the contract would be renewed and the company seldom chose to terminate contracts.

One of the problems [with our company] is that we lack effective policies for firing people, and we have been trying to review them for the past several years. But the fact is that we seldom fire people unless they commit serious legal violation. (HR Manager, Chinese, 36, male)

Very few employees chose to leave the company, and this distinguished WG-A Co. from many other Japanese joint ventures. The annual labour turnover of WG-A Co. had been about 3 to 5 per cent over the past few years, while many companies nearby struggled with labour shortages and recruiting difficulties. The average length of service among the contracted employees was seven years, higher than the national average of four-and-a-half to five years. One of the possible explanations for WG-A Co.'s low turnover is its employee selection and retention policies, and these will be discussed in the following section. It is necessary to emphasize here that WG-A Co. intentionally recruited a large group of temporary shop-floor workers and the company adopted separate policies to deal with different segments of the local workforce. Such clear division between the "core" and "periphery" employee groups characterizes WG-A Co.

The company had not established policies for dismissing employees, but they had a supplementary strategy, and thus only a small number of shop-floor workers were contracted employees. These workers were supposed to make up the "core" members of the workforce. At the same time, the company used a large number of temporary workers – mostly migrants from other provinces. Temporary workers were obtained through local recruitment agents, who signed direct contracts with the workers. WG-A Co. only contracted with the agent instead of with individual temporary workers. The number of temporary workers recruited depended on the production season, and they were in the majority on the shop floor, comprising about 80 per cent of the workforce during the peak season. Most of the temporary workers were dismissed at the end of the peak season, and most of them returned to the local agent, who would find new jobs for them.

The factory explained that using a large number of temporary workers was an effective way of reducing costs in a labour-intensive industry. The management pointed out that even though the number of contracted employees was small, their individual salary was higher than the temporary workers. Temporary workers were paid on the basis of the quantity and quality of the products they produced. These indirect salary savings were quite significant for WG-A Co. and contributed to their bottom line in the long run.

Due to the seasonal nature of the sales of WG-A Co.'s products, using temporary workers greatly reduced labour costs during the non-peak season. The other major saving the company made was on the employees' social insurance. For the temporary workers at the factory, the company was only responsible for accident insurance but did not have to contribute to their social insurance package, which, according to the current labour law, comprises 37 per cent of the salary paid to the contracted workers. This seems to be a most important measure that allowed WG-A Co. to keep down labour costs. The management also admitted that they had difficulty in securing a stable skilled workforce and this was also an important reason for the choice of core–peripheral workforce division strategy at the factory.

The Japanese companies are teased for being "training engines" here in China. Unfortunately it is true. We lost many of our employees to our competitors. Then we thought, why not use a real training body. So 5 years ago, we started cooperation with CCC job agent, who are experienced in dispatching workers to many companies, including many of our competitors. (Clerk, Human Resource Department, Chinese, 32, female)

While using temporary workers helped reduce labour costs, it also brought some serious problems. The most critical ones were the lack of commitment among the temporary workers, repeat training costs, and difficulty in securing the desired number of workers at the peak season. Recognizing expanding production and the increasing need for temporary workers, the factory launched a temporary worker recruitment plan to motivate the temporary workers. Those with the best performance were given a chance to join the factory as a contracted worker. As this plan was launched in 2006, the effect is still not very clear.

Recruitment and selection

Unlike the parent plant which in general prefers to recruit fresh graduates and promotes managers internally, WG-A Co. has so far relied heavily on experienced workers and mid-career managers. Apart from the temporary workers, more than 70 per cent of the new recruits are in mid career.

We understand that it is faster for the fresh graduates to learn and adapt to our company. And we do have some wonderful young graduates working here. But they soon leave for better personal development. I think the average length that young graduates worked for our company is about 2 or 2.5 years. This is not good enough for the company. We need our employees to be more responsible and be willing to connect their personal development with that of the company, people who believe in the company and its prosperity and its setbacks. I think my Japanese colleagues agree with me on this point. (Deputy General Manager, Chinese, 49, male)

The above thoughts indicate that there is a shared understanding within the management team about employee commitment. Although the understanding and evaluation of employee commitment at the factory may have varied between the Japanese and Chinese managers, they seem to have agreed to a pro-mature employee approach in the selection of workshop leaders, salesmen and managers. Fresh graduates were more likely to start with clerical jobs, which were described as "repetitive" yet "stressful". WG-A Co.'s external recruitment preference had the effect of encouraging these fresh graduates to seek external promotion, which explains their shorter length of service at WG-A Co. As far as their parent company was concerned, the management preferred to recruit fresh graduates. This was reflected in the selection of employees to attend managerial training programmes in Japan. As part of the localization policy, the Japanese parent company recruited two local fresh graduates in 1998 and 2003 to join the headquarters as management trainees; they were repatriated after three years of on-the-job training to WG-A Co. and one other Chinese subsidiary.

Compared to the parent plant, selection was conducted in a much less formal manner, and the procedure of selection was purely interview-based.

Many of us have worked in the factory since it was established. We know what kind of people the factory is looking for and who might stay longer. We are fully aware of the kind of questionnaires some other companies use to select employees. But that takes a lot of paperwork. And after the interviewing process, we may well end up with the same group of people. (Head, HR Department, Chinese, 36, male)

In contrast, selection in Japan followed very different procedures.

The selection process in Japan is quite standard. We had two rounds of written exams and two rounds of interviews... Here, it is mainly interviews. (Clerk, Accounting Department, Japanese, 29, male)

There were not many written criteria available to investigate what type of people WG-A Co. was targeting. A recruitment advertisement normally included preference for age range, gender, educational background, working experience and residential status. Maintaining ambiguity in selection criteria enabled the factory to conduct selection case by case and gave them some leeway to recruit people for different reasons.

Some people here are really competent and good at their jobs. Some are recruited from the Chinese parent company. Some are hired because they had some connection. We once hired a young graduate because she is the daughter of a former employee, who used to be a security officer in the accounting department and was forced to ask many employees to retire early. (Clerk, Accounting Department, Chinese, 35, female)

Employee selection was carried out by the HR department and the relevant recruiting department. What was observed was that WG-A Co.'s recruitment and selection was more locally oriented and was characterized by a strong preference for experienced workers. An interview-based selection process was common. While the former was a result of navigation through some unsuccessful recruitment experiences, the latter had been delegated to the local managers since WG-A Co.'s establishment. As a consequence, policies and practices that conformed to local practice have also been followed. The Japanese parent company only retained power to influence maintenance of consistent policies and practices when local employees were recruited to work in Japan and continued working as a member of the parent company.

Reward and benefits

The employees' salary structure was largely based on that of the Chinese parent company. Pay was linked to individual performance and some departmental bonuses were given as supplementary rewards. Salary structure contained some elements borrowed from the old SOE wage structure, including basic salary, seniority allowance, position allowance, performance allowance and welfare allowance. There was not much difference between the salary of shop-floor workers and office clerks. The workers' pay was calculated on the basis of the quantity and quality of their production. Office clerks were generally paid a fixed salary with an annual bonus. Salaries in the sales division were mainly based on individual sales records. Monthly salaries and bonuses were put forward by the head of the sales division and approved by both the deputy general manager and the general manager. Salaries for managers on the same job grade could vary by up to 100 per cent. One expatriate expressed the idea that the salary system in the Japanese parent plants is much more "socialistic" than at WG-A Co.:

Salary structure includes many elements: age, seniority, position, performance, family responsibilities. The last one makes a big difference in Japan. I am not married so my pay is half that of my peer, who is married and has got two kids. (Chief Accounting Officer, Japanese, 52, male)

In WG-A Co., the performance-related salary system was cited as the most important element in improving efficiency in the workplace and promoting employee commitment.

A benefits component that distinguishes WG-A Co. from other Japanese subsidiaries was the company accommodation provided to managers. When WG-A Co. was set up, the location was difficult to access and the company built accommodation for the expatriates, the technical support team and some local managers. Later, more local managers were allocated apartments. The managers admitted that allocation of these apartments often caused conflicts among the managers, but having managers living close to the factory allowed them to work overtime and to be called to the office in an emergency. Providing a company apartment was also helpful in retaining some competent managers.

Appraisal and promotion

As we can see from the reward and benefits scheme, WG-A Co. employees were categorized into several groups and managers were evaluated by Management by Objectives (MBO). It should be noted that the MBO in WG-A Co. was designed using a five-point scale, ranging from "no effort made to achieve the goal" to "performance is beyond original target". Appraisal was done in a top-down manner, which was similar to that of the Japanese parent company. However, the difference was that not many levels of management were involved in appraisal. The authority was centralized at the general manager's office and the Chinese deputy general manager took full responsibility for the final results. Decision-making on appraisal and promotion of managers was described as a "black box", which mainly involved the deputy general manager's judgement, though the general manager was consulted for the final result.

Nobody can read the criteria in our deputy general manager's mind. We know that chances are there and we trust our deputy general manager is a wise leader. (Head, Sales Department, Chinese, 43, male)

We all trust he [the Deputy General Manager] will perform justice. (Clerk, Sales Department, Chinese, 28, male)

He works hard but was paid less than many other managers, a pretty honest leader. (Assembly line worker, Chinese, 30, male)

He really believes in equity. In other [Japanese] joint venture factories, you might see the Japanese eating in a different canteen or at least having different meals. Here, the meal is the same for everyone, everyone including the top managers. You see the kind of stage in the canteen? It used to be built for the Japanese to eat there. But after he joined our factory, he persuaded the Japanese not to use it as it is an apparent message of separation. (Clerk, Administrative Department, Chinese, 25, female)

Although some of the appraisal results would be made public to the employees, such as the salesman of the year, an employee's bonus was typically treated as a strictly confidential matter. WG-A Co. implemented a face-to-face discussion (*Mendan*) in order to inform the appraisal result. Face-to-face discussion was conducted between managers and their direct subordinates and this facilitated gathering of feedback from the employees. According to the HR managers, this was actually a way of avoiding jealousy among employees and was not used only to protect their privacy. As it was possible that the subordinates might not express some negative opinions in front of their seniors, WG-A Co. planned to conduct a survey of employee satisfaction in 2007.

Appraisal in WG-A Co. combined practices from different management paradigms. With an SOE background, WG-A Co. did not jettison all the practices, deciding instead to retain some of the practices as a structure. The company also retained some HR practices learned from the Japanese parent company and some other local companies, as well as some practices adopted by Western MNCs built upon the structure.

Training and development

WG-A Co. preferred experienced employees, and tended to recognize external as well as internal expertise. Initial training was given to employees who had recently joined the company. The initial training programme was described by the employees as "more like an orientation". As the majority of the workforce was composed of temporary workers, they were marginalized in any kind of internal training except for orientation. The long-term employees were encouraged to pursue external education or training. They were given incentives in the form of special bonuses for some targeted skills. On-the-job training was said to be given but the employees had different opinions about this issue.

We are not sure if this should be called "on-the-job training" or we are just "on-the-job". Everybody is busy and you just have to figure out how to do the job by yourself. Of course you can ask, but you are not guaranteed an answer. It is pretty much learning while doing it yourself. (Printing Line Worker, Chinese, 29, male)

An element missing here was the practice of job rotation, which is commonly adopted in their Japanese parent plants. This is not a surprising finding considering that a large proportion of the shop-floor workers were employed on a temporary basis. The HR managers had definite plans for the rest of the employees, and suggested not rotating them to different positions simply to suit the Chinese employees' preference for developing depth rather than breadth of skills.

One important training feature that distinguishes WG-A Co. from other companies was their unique management trainee programmes initiated in 1998. As mentioned above, the trainees were not selected from the existing managers but chosen from a batch of fresh graduates. They were recruited as employees in the Japanese parent company and asked to work in the headquarters to gain internal knowledge. Once properly trained, they were repatriated to the subsidiaries. One of the trainees was expatriated to WG-A Co. in 2002 and appointed as junior manager, responsible for supporting the Chief Accounting Officer (expatriated from Japan). She described her work as mainly office paperwork:

I think the major job for me is to establish a so-called management system that could help discipline the employees and prevent adverse behaviours, which seem to be a serious problem here. I am supposed to compare the local management practices with our parent company and design relevant working process, management procedures and employment regulations. (Deputy Head, Accounting Department, Chinese, 33, female)

Employing freshly graduated locals trained at the headquarters clearly showed the parent company's intention to reorganize the subsidiaries by using the existing practice in Japan. However, the newly established written processes and procedures have not proved to be as effective in WG-A Co. as in the parent plant. The same manager expressed her frustration about the difficulty of implementing the management practices which had been developed based on those in the parent company.

I worked so hard when I first arrived in this factory. I went to talk to people in different departments. I worked overtime to figure out the problems with the current measures they used and compared that with what I learned in Japan. Then I worked out some process, procedures, and regulations that will supplement the current management measures and try to make it a system. You see the piles under my desk and in the cupboard? These are all drafts and final editions of my work. But later on, I learnt that most of them won't work. They ended up in just piles of paper as we don't have measures to say what we are going to do if these process, procedures and regulations are not followed. That is the only thing missing in the Japanese management system – punishment. Of course, many of the managers here seem to believe that making the punishment unpredictable could be more effective and the work I am doing will only make things worse. Maybe they are right. (Deputy Head, Accounting Department, Chinese, 33, female)

Again, the junior manager's experience reflects the difference in assumptions between Chinese and Japanese management thinking.

Apart from the programme described above, WG-A Co. seems to have limited resources invested in employee training. Instead, they tend to encourage employees to seek external training and reward employees who obtain certificates from external educational or professional bodies. This was in sharp contrast to the parent company's preference for internal training as reflected in the training of new repatriated managers.

Retention and exit

As explained by the HR managers, WG-A Co. had not so far launched any explicit retention scheme. The individual appraisal and bonus system was cited by employees as one of the most important reasons for their staying with the company. The second important factor was apparently the welfare provided. This could also be an important characteristic that distinguished the company from other companies. Unlike some Japanese-invested companies, which have separate canteens for the expatriates, this company runs a single canteen. All these were seen as WG-A Co.'s endeavour to avoid any negative feelings of discrimination inside the company.

WG-A Co.'s accommodation was also unique among many Japanese-invested companies, most of whom provided accommodation for their workers. WG-A Co. provided apartments for managers. This was something like the company housing which used to be a practice in SOEs. Accommodation was allocated according to the employee's position in the company, years of service, performance and marital status. Family members were also considered while allocating accommodation. The allocation process was similar to that used in SOEs except that employees had to move out when they had purchased their own apartment. As housing was the major expense for households in China, having a chance to obtain free housing early in their career seemed to have a significant impact on young managers' choices when deciding to remain in the company.

5.2.3 The local management team: choices and actions

In WG-A Co., Japanese managers were often at the periphery of decision-making while negotiating for HR system development. The Japanese parent companies sought to increase their influence by employing some repatriation in order to regain power. Research indicates that the number of expatriates in the company followed a 'U' curve. At establishment, there were about twenty Japanese expatriates working in the company, and this number went down gradually to fifteen people within three years. The company encountered serious problems, and most of the expatriates were recalled as a cost-reduction measure. The number remained at about four to five by the end of 2003. When the company started marking a profit, the number of expatriates went up again. The Japanese parent company sent some young managers who were supposed to be expatriated for on-the-job training. Among the eight expatriates in the company, three people were trainees.

The Chinese managers have gained much power in WG-A Co. decision-making since 1998, and this was partly related to the company's history of financial difficulties and low employee morale that was caused in part by corruption on the part of an individual Chinese manager. WG-A Co. was established in 1995 and it ended up in serious deficit by the end of its third year. Besides conflict and inefficiency caused by different management ideologies and poor understanding of the company's market orientation, corruption among some Chinese managers was a major factor that resulted in losses for the company.

The Japanese parent company expatriated a new management team to restructure the company. The new general manager was experienced in doing business with SOEs in China. Detailed background research was conducted and the management sought to clarify connections between certain Chinese managers in the company and the management team in the Chinese parent company. The Japanese side later decided to utilize connections in the Chinese parent company as a weapon to fight and replace those corrupted managers. The information about corrupt practices among managers was released to the Deputy Chair of the Communist Party Committee in the Chinese parent company. An anti-corruption initiative led by this Deputy Chair with the approval of both the Japanese and Chinese parent companies successfully removed the corrupt managers and boosted the morale of employees. The new expatriate team and the Chinese management team gradually rebuilt morale and the company began to move in the right direction, making a profit in subsequent years.

The increased power of the Chinese management team therefore owed something to historical reasons. Unlike some joint ventures with rival ownership, which recruit managers from both the Japanese and Chinese branches for similar managerial positions, the company's

Chinese management team had played a dominant role in sales/marketing and HR management. The Japanese side's influence was more significant in production and quality control. However, with WG-A Co. expanding its business in China, both sides intended to take control of the overall management. The Japanese side found it difficult to incorporate the existing managers and chose to adopt the repatriation programme to enhance parent influence.

5.2.4 Case summary

This is a case where the subsidiary HRM showed some elements of SOE methods, Japanese management style and other locally oriented practices that were developed by companies from other countries. WG-A Co.'s formal organizational structure was similar to many other manufacturing plants set up by the Japanese parent company elsewhere – in Japan or overseas. At first glance, WG-A Co. was not so different from many Japanese manufacturing plants in China. The company provided uniforms to all employees, both long-term and temporary. Free meals were provided to all employees, and expatriates and locals in the factory canteen were served with the same menu. Social activities such as a New Year party (*Bounenkai*) and group tours were arranged. The uniform, factory canteen, employee accommodation and group activities were not new to Japanese-invested companies, which used them to build a sense of egalitarian community among employees. But the company's measures also seemed to have gained some level of commitment among the employees.

HRM at WG-A Co. was characterized by mixed HR practices, the origin of which could be traced to the Japanese parent plants, the Chinese SOEs and some successful local enterprises. While most Japanese thought the management system design and its effective implementation was important for AIRCON's survival, the Chinese seemed to believe it was the *leadership* of the management team that counted. The Chinese and Japanese management teams' efforts to eliminate corruption within the management team seem to have promoted mutual respect and built trust between the Chinese and Japanese managers as well as among the employees. Both sides intended to win employees' recognition and support for the management team's decisions, and the Chinese team proved to be more successful in this race. This was also cited as an important contributory factor in the company's recovery from financial difficulty. Efficiency and productivity were achieved by implementing motivation and disciplinary measures. In general, HR practices in WG-A Co. shared some key features with reformed Chinese SOEs. The Japanese parent company's management practices only affect a limited number of local managers.

The Japanese side's influence cannot be overlooked. They had an established production system and could depend on a relatively stable core workforce, so they sought to increase their influence on management. On the one hand, hard negotiation was going on between the investment partners, as the Japanese side intended to increase their share. R&D was still controlled at the Japanese parent company level and so far, negotiations had not produced any positive results. On the other hand, the Japanese parent company tended to fill the management team with more managers with a local background and who were systematically trained in the parent company. This showed their intention to gradually move WG-A Co. towards a bureaucratic structure and to restrain the power of the local managers at top management level, a policy that had encountered strong resistance among the local managers and employees.

5.3 AIRSYS Co: a ship with a Japanese engine

Organization and management of WG-B Co. provide a sharp contrast to WG-A Co. WG-B Co. shows greater similarity to the Japanese parent company in terms of production and management. WG-B Co. is one of six production bases overseen by the regional Chinese headquarters of the Japanese parent company. It sells 80 per cent of its products to the local market; the other 20 per cent is exported to the USA. While WG-B Co. is mainly in the local market, it differs from WG-A Co. in terms of product composition, sales and marketing channels and major local clients. As far as its financial performance is concerned, the company's sales turnover reached US$377 million with a net profit of US$76 million in 2005. This places it at the top of the eight foreign-invested household white goods manufacturers in China.

A variety of factors contribute to WG-B Co.'s financial success in China. For the managers, the most important factors are the company's persistent efforts to supply technologically advanced products to the local Chinese market and its alliance with central and regional government for sales and distribution. Since rival manufacturers occupied a considerable share in the local household white goods market, WG-B chose to focus on commercial customers. It began its initiative by promoting white goods units for commercial use. Later, it expanded the scope of its products to include high value-added household white goods units. Moreover, the company has shortened the time lag between models launched in Japan and those introduced in China. These efforts have paid off and WG-B now occupies the largest market share for both commercial and household white goods.

In addition, the managers agree that WG-B Co.'s efficiency in sourcing parts and distributing the final products is important to its success in the Chinese market. WG-B Co. is the oldest and largest manufacturing plant among the company's Chinese subsidiaries. It is supported by five other subsidiary factories producing electronic parts and other supplies, and overseen by a local Chinese management headquarters. As a group, these factories make up the east China production base. WG-B Co. has always been regarded as an example of successful transfer of production overseas and a model for the sister subsidiaries. Following the incorporation of the Chinese headquarters in the early 2000s, the production network was further restructured to centralize the Chinese headquarters.

5.3.1 Positioning WG-B Co. in the new business structure in China

WG-B Co. began as a Japanese–Chinese joint venture with 51 per cent investment from Japan and 49 per cent from China. It was a successful pilot venture and the company served as the main base of production. The Japanese parent company has aggressively expanded its investment in China since 1998. After difficult negotiations with its Chinese partner, the Japanese side increased investment in WG-B Co. to 70 per cent. They also built two more wholly owned assembly plants, one as an independent production base and the other as a sub-plant of WG-B Co., in order to expand their production base in China. Meanwhile, several parts manufacturers were set up to supply core parts and chemical materials directly to WG-B Co. and to end the practice of purchasing these items from Japan. They also invested in a trading company to handle the sales of the chemicals produced by one of these independent subsidiaries. These additional trading, production and assembly subsidiaries complement WG-B Co. and form a functional consolidated network.

In 2001, the Japanese parent company reviewed its long-term international strategy and decided to establish four regional headquarters. China is one of the four strategic regions including Greater China, Asia & Oceania, Europe & Africa, and North & Latin America. The Chinese headquarters of WG-B Co. is an investment company and part of the Japanese parent company's investment in China was transferred to the Chinese headquarters. After this restructuring was complete, WG-B Co.'s ownership structure changed to: 58.33 per cent by the Japanese parent company; 11.67 per cent by the Chinese headquarters; and 30 per cent by the local Chinese parent company. The Chinese headquarters is a minority shareholder but its role is quite important. This unit is responsible for strategic planning, financing and management coordination for all Japanese parent company subsidiaries in China. The functions of the Chinese headquarters symbolize a strategic shift in the Chinese market.

[The Japanese parent company] is organized by product groups, which decided when, where, and how to invest overseas. Of course, all investment plans were discussed in board of directors meetings, but basically the product groups' decisions will be respected. So, the subsidiaries in China are actually invested by different parent companies in Japan, though they share the same brand name. With fast expansion and development here, the headquarters feel the need to enhance communication and coordination among these subsidiaries, a function that the liaison office cannot fulfil. The Chinese headquarters, named as WG-B Co. Investment Company, is our strategic centre in China. We are responsible for initiating marketing strategies and action plans, coordination of production, sales, customer services among the subsidiaries, and strategic planning for all HR policies. We have two branches set up in the same city as the production bases to keep close contact with the factories and assist us to realize such functions. (Head of HR Division, WG-B Co. Chinese headquarters, Japanese, 47, male)

To facilitate the work of the Chinese headquarters, two branch offices were set up near the main production bases. Two trading companies and three independent customer services entities were set up along with the investment company to help source raw materials and provide technical support to local users. The companies' network in China has been rebuilt as separate units responsible for performing specific functions (production, sales and customer services). All these units are connected to the Chinese headquarters' branch offices, which are in turn directly controlled by the Chinese headquarters. When questioned about what kind of decision-making power had been delegated to the Chinese headquarters, the deputy general manager stated that, except for large-scale investment decisions, they are the central decision-makers in China.

We have the authority to decide investment plans, provide financial support to the subsidiaries, control and coordinate production, source raw materials and coordinate sales among the subsidiaries, and, HR planning for the Chinese subsidiaries... Well, investment plans larger than US$20 million should be decided by the [Japanese] headquarters. But apart from that, the Chinese matters are decided here. The headquarters are consulted with draft reports or they will send someone to join in meetings here. (Deputy General Manager, Chinese, 50, male)

However, the Chinese headquarters did not seem to be fully functioning at the time this research was conducted. All investment plans were decided at the Japanese headquarters and no new investment projects had been initiated by the Chinese headquarters. Under the Chinese government's Foreign Currency Control Regulations, non-financial institutions cannot have either internal or external financing functions, which means that the Chinese headquarters' proposed financing function is not legally feasible. Moreover, the company had expected to be able to import products from Japan to be sold in the local market in the future, but so far this has not been approved by the local government. The functions of control and coordination are very important in the company. The three branch offices of the Chinese headquarters near the production bases play a vital role in assisting the purchase of raw materials and sales of the products both locally and on an international level.

Some of the managers in WG-B Co., seeing the Chinese headquarters as a trading entity, said that the supportive functions of the Chinese headquarters were merely an overlap of the functions the factory already had.

While the local branch [of the Chinese headquarters] is actually now a trading company, which actually handles sales of our products. Our department used to sell the products directly and we still do. But our main job is to contact the correspondents [in the investment companies' local branch] to get orders and report on progress of production. Of course we need more coordination. The company fell apart. (Deputy Head, Sales Division, Chinese, 37, male)

But the same person also acknowledged the advantage for negotiation in the manufacturer–retailer relationship provided by the Chinese headquarters.

Our clients always negotiate contract price using the price at the major electronic superstores, telling us how [it is] difficult to compete. We used to negotiate on the quality of our products. Now we will say, look, it is the series of products at this price level and the company contracted it for this quantity for an annual contract. The retailers are reasonable as long as you have sufficient evidence to support your price indication. (Deputy Head, Sales Division, Chinese, 37, male)

The manager in the technical support department saw the restructuring as related to "service upgrading". He described how their new technical support centres work.

It is a common practice among the household white goods manufacturers to use third parties for customer services. Our customer services centre is a third party within our corporate group. A major improvement is the computer database applied in the customer services centre. Before, we had to ask for the customer's name and address before sending the technical staff when we receive a fault report. With the new database system, our products' barcodes are linked to the customers who purchased it. The customer services centre will receive the fault report and decide which factory is to be contacted. The goal is to provide timely services to the customers. The local consumers might like this way because it is professional. (Deputy Head, Technical Support Division, Chinese, 34, male)

After this round of restructuring, many of the local retailers and downstream service providers were marginalized. This producer-directed distribution is explained as suiting "the general preference to avoid intermediaries in the local market". In the meantime, WG-B Co. restructured its retail network with the aim of bringing products directly to local consumers.

WG-B Co. did not contract with any of the dominant electronic superstores but instead pursued direct transactions through its corporate network. The company chose to contract with large-scale real-estate project organizers for commercial electronics. Only a limited amount of sales is channelled through a handful of electronics engineering trade companies. Products are mainly handled by the trading bodies (wholly owned subsidiaries of the Chinese headquarters) contracted by the real-estate developers, so that the white goods are directly installed in the apartments/houses. Because it is tempting to bring products directly to consumers, WG-B Co. also initiated franchised professional shops in two municipal cities. The shops are similar to "4S" shops that are commonly observed in automobile retail. These kinds of sales are explained by WG-B Co. as a means of "competing with the large-scale electronic superstores and keeping product price under the control of manufacturers". Due to the growing local consumption of luxury electronics and the rise of the new middle class in China, the pilot professional shops seem to be well accepted by local consumers. This strategy has allowed WG-B Co. to realize a producer-centred sales network.

The investment companies, customer services centres and production plants constituted three pillars of support for the purchase–production–supply chain of WG-B Co.'s central production region. Together with the other two production regions, WG-B Co.'s Chinese headquarters mapped out a triangular chart, which stretched out into relatively developed regions in China. The establishment of a Chinese R&D centre reinforced this triangular production network. The R&D centre was a laboratory plant co-hosted by one of the top local universities and was located in the same city as the Chinese headquarters. The aim of having R&D transferred to China was to serve both technological innovation and personnel training and development purposes.

We chose to establish the R&D centre as part of our China strategy. Many Japanese companies withdrew from the Chinese market because they tend to judge the local market with their Japanese experience. For us, it is important to rely on the local capabilities. We want to utilize the university's expertise in engineering innovation and talented people to develop new models for the Chinese market. At the same time, we hope to develop promising people for the future of the company. (Head of HR Division, WG-B Co. Chinese headquarters, Japanese, 47, male)

When I conducted this fieldwork, WG-B Co.'s R&D centre was a place to test product models designed and developed in Japan and make sensible modifications to suit local production and markets. No original product model had been developed for production. This kind of innovation was said to be "the direction the R&D centre is heading". The R&D centre also helped to train and retain locally recruited engineers. When I visited, the R&D centre was operated by expatriate engineers and locally recruited engineering graduates were at the training stage (training was done both locally and in Japan).

Like WG-A Co., a large proportion of WG-B Co.'s product parts used to be imported from Japan and they have gradually shifted to local procurement. Together with the restructuring in the company network, WG-B Co. persuaded major sub-contracting companies to establish operations in its surrounding areas in China. This was aimed at shortening delivery time and reducing product costs, and it replicates the home-country practice: vertical integration of production with long-term business relationships (Gerlach, 1992). However, WG-B Co.'s reliance on such vertical integration cannot be overstated. In searching for a balance between quality and cost, WG-B Co. had also integrated a number of local parts suppliers into the cluster. These parts suppliers included some invested by Taiwan, Hong Kong, or by local producers, although the core parts were purchased from Japanese sub-contractors.

Overall, WG-B Co. had been integrated into an intra-company network, where more interaction with the sister subsidiaries can be observed. This is closely related to WG-B Co.'s intention to promote the image of high-tech, high quality products, which has led to its technological reliance on the Japanese parent company and the coordination provided by its Chinese headquarters. Expatriate managers are assigned critical roles in connecting this network. The majority of Japanese managers are expatriated to the Chinese headquarters and the R&D centres, which control local distribution, sales, remodelling and testing respectively. The Chinese headquarters also plays an important role in connecting and coordinating production networks in China. This has created important differences in the way WG-B Co.'s products are sold and how services are provided. Finally, the Chinese headquarters serves as an HR centre to the subsidiaries, and this will be further discussed in the next section. While such marketing strategies seem to have contributed to the financial success of WG-B Co., they also placed considerable pressure on the cost and quality control side of production – something which increased tension in employment relations at the factory. At the same time, the problem of how to localize management in the subsidiaries became critical over the course of its rapid expansion.

5.3.2 *The power struggle in organizing production*

In addition to the process of replacing expatriate managers with local managers, WG-B Co. put significant efforts into reproducing production and management practices, based on those of the parent plants.

As I observed in the case of WG-A Co., the level of automation was cited as the major difference between the Chinese subsidiaries and the Japanese parent plants. Work in WG-B Co. involves a great deal of manual labour such as welding, assembling and packing, which require limited skills from the workers. Welding is done by automated welding machines operated by semi-skilled workers, whereas assembly and packing are more routinized manual jobs. Many managers at WG-B Co. also commented that the parent company was more organized in terms of the production material planning and storage control.

In Japan [the parent plant], everything is in order and many techniques are used to help maintain that order. Here, as you can see, parts, tools, and sometimes personal belongings are not put in the right place. Even though we use the techniques learned from Japan to help us to know when to place an order for certain parts, we always need to double check. Otherwise, we might end up ordering in new parts only to discover a whole lot that had been stored in the wrong place. (Team leader, Department of Supply, Chinese, 27, female)

Managers have found it very difficult to implement Japanese practices due to the workers' understanding of job responsibilities.

What we are trying to do is to enhance workplace education to expand workers' ideas about their individual jobs. For example, it is normal to clean

the working area after finishing the workday in Japan. But here, our workers seem to think that cleaning is to be done by the cleaners. We can afford
to hire a cleaner but the employees won't learn to be responsible for the
working environment. So, we need to take some time to allow the workers
to get used to keeping the place clean. It works eventually. You may think
this is a mess here, but if you compare this place to when I first arrived three
years ago, it has got much better. (Factory Manager, Japanese, 65, male)

The deputy production manager also commented that self-discipline
had improved since the company set up its pre-work training centre and recruited from the trainees. But this comparison must
be qualified, since there were demographic factors that influence
self-discipline. In particular, most of the workers from the training
centre were migrants from other areas. The factory had sponsored
them to obtain residence permits to be able to work in the city and
thus it was easier to implement disciplinary measures among these
workers in contrast to those from the local technical school and university graduates.

Discipline problems at WG-B Co., however, did not seem to be
resolvable simply by providing further education and training. Causes
of tension and conflict at WG-B Co. included demands for increased
productivity, alliances between local and Japanese managers, and the
wage gap between workers and managers. Tension at WG-B Co. often
manifested itself in workers' misbehaviour and, sometimes, sabotage
and stealing. Preventative measures did not seem to stop this behaviour. For instance, the administrative office kept a detailed inventory
of office equipment and stationery, but nobody noticed that the hard
disks of two used PCs, which had been left unattended for months,
were missing. This was merely one example amongst several similar
stories.

As in most Chinese assembly plants, work on the shop floor at
WG-B Co. was very intense and stressful. Workers were pressured to
adhere to a strict standard production time per unit. And while there
was an increase in market demand, local government regulations limited overtime to 36 hours per month. Many of the shop-floor workers
expressed the feeling that management seemed to be setting increasingly high production standards. Also, rules regarding "standard time"
were applied to many settings outside the production line, such as
the company accommodation, changing rooms and smoking cubes.

Tension rose as team leaders repeatedly asked workers to adhere to standards regarding time, procedures and safety measures. Workers interpreted "standards" negatively as disciplinary measures rather than "management know-how" or other positive formulations. For instance, many employees thought that wearing uniform and protective shoes, which was generally considered an essential safety precaution, was part of the "standardization" through which their individual talents and contributions were ignored.

The only thing they care about is the standard, procedures and rules. They don't really care about our ideas. I tried to make some suggestions, but what I got was the "you think I didn't know this" look. (Team leader, Chinese, 25, male)

We are required to follow the rules and obey what the seniors say. This place is a seniority-based caste [system]. (Office clerk, Chinese 23, male)

I don't want to be bothered with making improvement suggestions. This factory is too bureaucratic to make any change. (Shop-floor worker, Chinese, 28, female)

I can put up with the bad working environment. I don't mind the Japanese culture. But it seems hopeless to change the company, as people who do not seem to be capable of doing the job occupy the managerial positions. Maybe the Japanese feel that it is safe to have more managers who are dependent on them? (Group leader, Chinese, 22, male)

This reflects the atmosphere of the shop floor at WG-B Co., where many Japanese management practices have been implemented. Such practices ranged from technical and procedural manuals to team-building techniques such as morning gatherings and more sophisticated production systems such as quality control cycles. Training was provided at all levels and employees learned about what to do, how and why to do it as they moved up the career ladder. However, shop-floor workers were more likely to be at an early stage of their careers and were trained to follow the routines, with very limited opportunity to be creatively involved in the production process. Training had little effect on their discipline and job satisfaction.

Workplace knowledge was a combination of the simplified tasks, firm-specific applicable production know-how, and "Japanese" team-building activities. The local employees tended to be more enthusiastic about learning "universal" production know-how than engaging in "activities rooted in Japanese practices".[1] Many of the locals seemed to believe that Chinese were more individualist than the Japanese people and were unwilling to conform to some collective activities originated by the company. Although this sounds simplistic and stereotyped, considering that WG-B Co. was likely to have been most local employees' first experience of Japanese management practices, it is not surprising that some rejected those activities and labelled them "Japanese". Many employees, for example, were not pleased with the practice of doing calisthenics together.

Tension was further generated by the differences in knowledge and education among the workers and how this affected their chances of promotion. Many current senior managers received long-term training in Japan and were in their late 30s or early 40s. The training and socialization of a core local managerial team into Japanese cultural and management practices was called successful "localization" in WG-B Co. These local managers accepted that the practice of internal promotion and a slower advancement in their careers was the case in Japan. Their career orientation was internal and comparison was often based on their peers in the parent companies:

I think we [local managers] are some exceptional examples among Japanese companies. Normally it will take more than 8 years to be promoted to manage a department and a further 5 to 8 years to manage a division in the parent company. We had made considerable progress to engage local managers into the management team. For example, the general manager at our sister plant in Guangzhou is one of the competent local managers. (Manager, HR Division, Chinese, 35, male)

Senior expatriate managers also praised and supported local managers.

We want our employees to understand that our products win with high quality. Following the manuals guarantees this high quality. We do respect individual creativity and we always encourage people to use the suggestion system to make improvements. But we also need people to work according

---

[1] One important point to note here is the anti-Japanese emotion among the young Chinese, publicly expressed at its height by the anti-Japanese demonstration in 2005. This may help explain why the parent plant practices interpreted as "culturally rooted in Japan" encountered strong resistance in WG-B Co.

to the production manual until it is officially revised. (Manager, Quality Control Division, Japanese, 53, male)

However, this internal promotion principle seemed to have provoked more complaints among many young university graduates who joined the company as managerial candidates but did not seem to be promoted as fast as their predecessors. Without clarified policies of promotion, many of these graduates felt that the pursuit of senior management positions was hopeless. In reply to the question "How do you see your future career development in the company?" many employees gave rather negative responses:

I don't think the company values us as much as they say they do. (Office clerk, Accounting Department, Chinese, 24, female)

Room for development? Not much. (Line supervisor, Chinese, 27, male)

I think most of the male graduates who entered this company with me have left. It is discouraging to be always in a candidate position. We joined this company since we were told we would be given training and promotions when positions became available. But, the real question is when? (Office clerk, Sales Department, Chinese, 25, male)

In addition to promotion opportunities, wage differences created severe conflict among the employees. Most fresh university graduates admitted that they were satisfied with their pay (university graduates' starting salary was RMB2,800, which was said to be above average compared to the starting salary at other companies in the local area). Wage differences between workers, line supervisors, and sub-department managers and senior managers in the office seemed to have provoked more complaints among the shop-floor workers than among university graduates, who were often assigned a team leader role. The shop-floor workers' salary was based on the quantity of units they produced per month and it ranged from RMB1,000 to RMB1,800 depending on experience. Shop-floor workers' wages increased only gradually each year (5 to 8 per cent) but these workers had little chance for promotion. The provision of welfare packages, employees' cafeteria and accommodation did not seem to have motivated the workers as much as was expected by senior management.

Although their effectiveness was debatable, such parent company promotion policies as annual self-assessment and peer assessment were implemented at the Chinese headquarters of WG-B Co. Local managers who were trained tended to accept these practices, while recent university graduates and shop-floor workers either rejected or were sceptical about them. Conflict in the workforce and local managers became more apparent after the Chinese headquarters started to centralize strategic HR planning. But despite all these negative factors, local managers, especially those who held senior management roles, remained committed to adopting management practices from the parent company.

5.3.3 Job design and HRM routines

The company's localization strategy was manifested in its HR practice of putting local managers into senior positions. WG-B Co.'s Chinese headquarters was also the HR centre of the Chinese subsidiaries. An HR manager in the Chinese headquarters explained that they "provide guidelines" to the subsidiaries so that they could determine their own HR practices. However, the headquarters provided WG-B Co. with more than just guidelines. With an aggressive localization policy and fast expansion during the past five years, the headquarters had initiated measures to "enhance the efficiency of management" that specifically affected HR.

Composition of workforce
WG-B Co. showed a strong preference for new graduates of technical schools and universities. Most employees in WG-B Co. joined the company as young graduates and had to work under fixed-term contracts. As a direct result of this HR policy, WG-B Co. did not recruit as many temporary workers as WG-A Co. did but recruited twice as many contract workers. The two factories, however, share similar investment scale and annual output. WG-B Co. did not inherit many workers from the Chinese parent company and looked towards young students to make up the majority of the workforce.

Technical school students made up the majority of shop-floor workers and performed semi-skilled jobs such as welding and wiring or unskilled routinized work such as packing. These groups were not recruited randomly or by recommendation from existing workers as other factories normally do (Smith, 2003). Instead, WG-B Co. signed an agreement with the local government to establish a "youth training centre" to train vocational and technical school students and awarded technical certificates upon their completion of the training programme. While there was no written agreement between the trainees and the companies, it was commonly understood that joining the training centre was a gateway to recruitment to WG-B Co.

New university graduates were the second leading source of employees. WG-B Co. recruited them with the intention of promoting them to shop-floor leader or junior managers after two to three years' training in the factory. However, this group was mobile and only a limited number of employees had stayed long enough to be promoted. Mid-career job-seekers had been targeted for shop-floor leader and junior manager positions with the departure of younger candidates.

Although they demonstrated a preference for new graduates, recruiting mid-career employees was not new to the company. With HR reform under way, WG-B Co.'s parent plants launched a mid-career recruitment scheme, which was applied in their overseas subsidiaries as well. The HR managers of WG-B Co. presented themselves as flexible in terms of their recruitment policies and willing to recruit both new graduates and mid-career employees. However, mid-career employees were in a disadvantageous position under WG-B Co.'s pay scheme. Just as in the Japanese parent companies, wages for mid-career employees were normally 3 to 5 per cent less than the wages for employees who joined the company as new graduates. Also, as will be illustrated in the following section, recruitment of mid-career employees was far less systematic than recruitment of new graduates. Recruitment of new graduates outnumbered recruitment of mid-career employees. (The only exception was the technical engineers, who were mainly in mid career.)

Recruitment and selection

WG-B Co., like its Japanese parent company, preferred to recruit new graduates for clerical and technical positions, who might later be promoted to managerial roles. WG-B Co.'s selection procedure was very similar to that of the parent company. In accordance with the principle of "selecting potential employees to promote localization", WG-B Co. conducted careful screening of applicants. While no written test was included in the selection process, three rounds of interviews were conducted to select the most appropriate personnel to work for the company. Each round had a different focus. In the first round, interviews focused on the applicant's background and personality; in the second, on the applicant's knowledge relevant to the position; and in the final round, on the applicant's adaptability. Throughout the selection process, WG-B Co. focused on identifying the applicants' adaptability to a new environment, which was again consistent with the parent company's practice.

Previous knowledge can be a very useful resource. But we don't select people only based on previous experience. It is more important to be able to face new tasks and challenges in this company. (Deputy HR Manager, WG-B Co. Chinese headquarters, Chinese, 37, male)

These principles, again, were very similar to those of the Japanese parent company. For the recruitment of workers, WG-B Co. partnered with the local government in the provision of internship programmes. Many workers were selected from the students attending these internship programmes. The HR manager explained the rationale of using self-trained workers as compared to recruiting through employment agents.

Job agents cannot guarantee the quality of workers we need. It is difficult to describe what kind of people are right for us and even if we do so, we are not sure if the workers meet our requirements. So, training centres are a good place to observe the worker while they are working. It is a good resource for us. And, the workers learned a skill at the training centre. This is good for us and we make a contribution to society. (Deputy HR Manager, WG-B Co. Chinese headquarters, Chinese, 37, male)

WG-B Co. seldom used agencies to recruit mid-career employees. Vacancies were advertised on the company website and the factory accepted both internal and external applicants. Selection was based on the applicants' qualifications and performance at the interview. However, it was more likely that internal applicants would be offered the position given their familiarity with the company and inclination for leaving their current post for promotion. Overall, the selection practice in WG-B Co. gave priority to internal employees and a majority of the employees joined the company directly after graduation.

Training and development

As in many other Japanese subsidiaries, repetitive elementary training was the major task of team leaders and group leaders. The local managers tried to resolve the problem by shortening the initial training given to the starters and incorporating more on-the-job training, which put more pressure on the line managers and supervisors.

Many of the new employees did not get adequate training. This might be the reason why our company cannot guarantee the quality we expected. Our engineers are very busy, not with work in the factory, but running around to the customers to resolve various problems. (Supervisor of Assembly Line III, Chinese, 30, male)

Tension on the shop floor forced managers to find some long-term solutions to the quest for a better-trained workforce. In addition to the technical redesign of work, WG-B Co. began to develop a long-term programme to incorporate training in the selection process. The critical step, in partnership with local government, was to set up a youth training centre to provide pre-work training to vocational school and technical school students. Training was thus prolonged and WG-B Co. managed to secure an enlarged pool of candidates from which to select employees.

Besides technical training, WG-B Co. provided two other types of training: hierarchical and occupational training. This practice was similar to the parent company. As the names indicate, hierarchical training was associated with the needs of employees gradually moving up the career ladder, whereas occupational training programmes aimed to provide specific job-related knowledge and skills. Although WG-B Co. differed from its parent company in the sense that it recruited more applicants with a refrigeration and heat engineering background, all employees were still expected to have "general knowledge", meaning knowledge about the factory and production:

Whatever the employees' background and position in the factory, we want them to know the basics about design, manufacturing, management, control, and sales. We want them to understand that the company is a unit and jobs are done by division into steps and cooperation among these steps. It is very important that our employees understand the whole process. That's the only way to realize coordination in the process. (Deputy HR Manager, WG-B Co. Chinese headquarters, Chinese, 37, male)

Training in "general knowledge" (or company knowledge) was designed by the Chinese headquarters and each subsidiary was encouraged to

develop relevant content, timetables and facilities to conduct training. For technical and managerial training, WG-B Co. relied heavily
on expatriate engineers, managers and HR experts. Designing and
conducting technical and managerial training programmes was seen
as a function that would be inherited by the Chinese headquarters,
"when it is ready", although at that time, managerial training was
still largely controlled by the Japanese parent company. Centralized
training programmes were provided to potential managers and were
generally performed at the headquarters, with the HR department at
the factory responsible for selecting competent and loyal employees
to attend these training programmes. The HR manager in WG-B Co.'s
Chinese headquarters described the Chinese subsidiaries as entities not
yet in a position to provide training at an advanced level.

Appraisal and promotion

Like the young graduate-centred recruitment policy and internal
training programmes, WG-B Co.'s appraisal scheme also seemed to be
identical to that of the parent plants. The pay and promotion scheme
in WG-B Co. used to reflect seniority and signs of a seniority-based
appraisal system remained even after major HR reforms. Most of the
managers were promoted internally and their tenure in the factory
ranged from seven to eleven years. Those in higher managerial positions were generally older than their subordinates. While in WG-A Co.
the young managers were supported by a group of more experienced
ones, this did not seem to be happening at WG-B Co. At the same
hierarchical level, pay to the seniors was generally higher than the less
experienced workers. Seniority, at least in the past, seemed to have
helped to maintain order.

A major review of the company's HR strategy in China started in
2003 and HR reform was initiated by the Japanese headquarters and
modified at the Chinese headquarters to suit conditions in China. The
reform aimed at a performance appraisal system of promotion on
merit rather than on seniority:

The achievement is results-oriented. We focus on our employees' achievements based on their potential. The aim is to help our employees to develop
with support from the company, their seniors, peers and subordinates so
that they can achieve their maximum potential, which they may not be con-
sciously aware of sometimes. (HR Manager, Chinese, 35, male)

Shop-floor workers were assessed by total output. For the rest of the employees, performance was assessed by reviewing their annual targets and action plans, which were settled at the beginning of each year. The employee would be awarded an annual bonus, based on self-assessment, senior managers' re-assessment and peer evaluations. This appraisal process replaced the twice-yearly fixed bonus. Appraisal had thus become more individual than it used to be under the seniority-based system.

Retention and dismissal

WG-B Co.'s published annual staff turnover was about 10 per cent, which was below the average level in the local area. It appeared that the junior managers were more likely to resign than remain, which was largely due to the fact that there were not many opportunities within the company through which they could further their careers, but it was also due to the lack of retention policy. It seemed many of the senior managers assumed that, as a leading electronics manufacturer, the company was attractive enough to stop employees from leaving.

> We don't really have any special programme designed for retention. We provide our employees with opportunities for self-development and help them map out feasible career plans. Such opportunities are the attraction to the employees. (Deputy HR Manager of WG-B Co. Chinese headquarters, Chinese, 37, male)

> We examined people who quit and I would say the majority of them quit because they cannot adapt to the fast development of our company. For the competent ones, we don't think the company should stop them from seeking better opportunities. (HR Manager, Chinese, 35, male)

It is not surprising that WG-B Co. displayed this confidence given the large pool of younger graduates leaving university each year and Shanghai being a popular city for graduate job-hunters from the nearby provinces. Many of the employees seemed to agree that opportunities to learn were the most important reason for their decision to join the company. However, the reason for leaving the company was ironically similar: pursuing further learning opportunities, which might be furthering studies, a higher position in a different company, or simply a change of job.

> I don't think the company really cares about retaining people. People leave but more people join. The problem is the repetitive training. We put a lot

of effort there but it did not seem to improve the skill of the employees. (Manager of training and development, HR department, Chinese, 35, female)

WG-B Co.'s company-centred "self-development" did not seem to match the employees' desired "self-development". Training opportunities alone did not seem to be enough to retain them. Some of the employees explained that WG-B Co.'s welfare package served as a "reasonable" compensation for a relatively "stressful and underpaid job". This family-friendly welfare package was only good for those employees that stayed long enough to become eligible to claim it. Again, such practice was commonly adopted in the Japanese parent plants, where long-term employment was still pursued.

5.3.4 Case summary

HR system development in WG-B Co. was largely influenced by the parent companies' restructuring of their Chinese business. Compared to WG-A Co., expatriate managers in WG-B Co. were found to be playing more dominant roles in subsidiary management. Reliance on importing product models was a key source of parent control. While the business network was largely locally constructed, business relations with the sister subsidiaries had somehow reinforced the influence of the parent company. As WG-B Co. strengthened its business strategy to develop long-term relationships with real-estate developers, the power of the parent company and a systemic support network were used to enhance the leverage of WG-B Co. in winning tenders and contracts. At the same time, direct parent company support was indispensable for winning these tenders, which, again, reinforced the Japanese parent company's influence in subsidiary management.

Another important aspect was that the internally trained managers played critical roles in adapting to reform and reshaping employment practices in the subsidiaries. Conflicts were observed, but such conflicts and confrontations did not just occur between expatriates and locals, or managers and workers. Most of the time, discussions with, and negotiations through, the expatriates seemed to have been institutionalized in WG-B Co. For the senior managers who had worked in the company since its incorporation, alliance with different groups of expatriates was often observed when the subsidiaries intended to initiate change. Chinese managers, however, lacked decision-making power in WG-B Co. even though some of them had been promoted to senior positions.

5.4 Key learning points

All household white goods manufacturers face the challenge of balancing the requirements of quality and cost control. Both the sample companies had faced growing competition in the local market, especially during the past five years with technical upgrading of local manufacturers. By adopting the strategy of providing products with high technological value to domestic and commercial users, the companies established their brand profile and became known for their high-priced and high quality products in China. However, rising production costs were a major concern for subsidiary management. Both companies had reviewed their HR strategy in China, aiming to improve HR efficiency and bring down HR costs.

Despite a similar product range and production arrangements, the factories ended up targeting different segments of the local labour market. In view of the high mobility level of the local labour market, the companies developed different recruitment policies to maintain a relatively stable workforce at the factory. In accordance with the seasonal characteristics of production, WG-A Co. chose to use temporary workers, who were generally easily available. This led to simplification in terms of the job design to ensure that workers could start working with limited training. This practice was partly consistent with Morris and his colleagues' (2009) observation that in MNCs with a labour-intensive production strategy, limited selection, low-skilled tasks, short-term training and orientation, centralized control and close monitoring of the production process tend to be found. However, WG-A Co. was able to retain a relatively stable core workforce made up of some technical workers and experienced managers originally from their Chinese parent company. This group of employees operated as an effective force against the Japanese parent company's influence. The Japanese parent company still intended to transfer some, if not all, aspects of parent HR practices to WG-A Co., partly with a view to balancing the power of local managers in subsidiary management. Given that WG-A Co.'s existing HR practices virtually discouraged fresh graduates from staying for promotion opportunities, the parent company had implemented an "inpatriation-repatriation" plan to bring potential young managers to the parent company for training purposes. In short, HR practices performed in WG-A Co. were far from developing a hybrid HR model because the various HR practices applied to different employee groups seem to be isolated and it was very difficult for employees to move from one particular group to the other.

In sharp contrast, WG-B Co. showed significant difference in terms of HR practices adopted. The workforce was much younger compared to WG-A Co. In the face of a high level of labour market mobility, WG-B Co. turned to the fresh graduates, vocational and technical school students, who were less favoured in the local labour market and therefore were easier to source. Setting up a youth training centre assisted WG-B Co.'s aim of combining selection and initial training. Fresh graduates were carefully selected and trained during or before the start of their service in the company. The well-trained ones were in a position to train later recruits, which indicates WG-B Co.'s preference for an internally rather than externally trained workforce. Selection and training were not the only HR aspect which showed strong influence from the Japanese parent. Dominance of the parent company in HR development did not seem to have encountered such strong resistance as I observed in WG-A Co. In fact, WG-B Co.'s HR practices concerning performance appraisal, the promotion process, employee welfare and dismissal showed some important parent company characteristics. This result is not surprising given the fact that many local managers were mainly trained internally and had limited external work experience. More importantly, many local managers tended to seek the parent companies' influence in support of the development of local business networks. Struggles for power were observed, but such struggles often took the form of passive actions rather than direct confrontation.

The above discussion highlights one of the key factors that mark the difference between WG-A Co. and WG-B Co. – local networks. Critical differences in terms of the subsidiaries' position in the inter- and intra-corporate networks were observed. Both subsidiaries developed a local-market centred business strategy and pursued some level of localization. WG-A Co. was found to be a more self-sufficient entity that centralized most functions except for R&D, which was under negotiation. Most decisions were made in the subsidiaries and parent companies were seldom directly involved in the decision-making process. Making use of management expertise and experience of dealing with the local workers, the local managers in WG-A Co. successfully integrated a number of local practices into organization and management of the subsidiary, disregarding the origin of these local practices. WG-B Co. was less independent yet supported by parent-related parts manufacturers, R&D institutions, sales and customer services networks, financial bodies, and administrative and HR functions. The parent company initiated the independent sales networks in China, which left WG-B Co. the manufacturing function. Also, the local managers were internally trained and promoted and had exposure to very limited external training. The vested interests of seeking internal promotion opportunities seemed to have encouraged them to form stronger alliances with the expatriates. These points will be further discussed in Chapter 7, where I compare WG-A Co. and WG-B Co. with the synthetic fibre manufacturers – SF-A Co. and SF-B Co.

6 | *Synthetic fibre manufacturing plants: developing a regional production base*

This chapter focuses on two synthetic fibre manufacturers: SF-A Co. and SF-B Co. Unlike WG-A Co. and WG-B Co., which had a local-market-oriented production base, SF-A Co. and SF-B Co. were set up with export-centred production bases, supplementing their sister plants in ASEAN countries. The products were mainly exported to the international market, predominantly Japan. I assumed that there would be stronger evidence of the transfer of parent plant HR practices in these two subsidiaries because of the capital-intensive nature of the synthetic fibre industry, the role of the subsidiary as an export-oriented production base, and whole ownership by the Japanese parent company. This assumption is partly supported by the empirical findings. However, closer comparison indicates that HR functions, policies and practices differ significantly between SF-A Co. and SF-B Co., despite the fact that these two subsidiaries share some important features in terms of product range and production scale, as well as manufacturing process and procedures. Major differences lay in the way local employees were trained, motivated and integrated into the management team, which again suggests that the companies have developed substantially different interpretations of "localization". SF-A Co. is, according to my observations, dominated by the parent company and managers here are more pressured to develop subsidiary HR practices with important parent characteristics. It is, in fact, a production base that is tightly controlled through the hierarchy of management and rigorous top-down supervision. SF-B Co., by contrast, delegates more autonomy to the Chinese headquarters, which assumes the role of developing short- and mid-term HR plans, prescribing general guidelines and facilitating the implementation of HR strategy in the subsidiaries. Local managers in SF-B Co. take more initiatives in local HR policy formulation and implementation and, as a consequence, HR practices applied to the workers show more variation from those employed in the parent plants and other sister plants. Apparently, SF-B Co. applies unified HR policies to govern the local senior managers and expatriate managers.

In this chapter, I compare SF-A Co. and SF-B Co. in terms of the HR function, policies and practices. The first section provides a brief overview of the locality – Nantong, an industrial cluster of Japanese FDI concentrated in the textile industry. While the cluster effect, to some extent, attenuates locality as a constraint on parent management transfer (Beechler and Yang, 1994; Sharpe, 2001, 2006), mobility of labour undermines the efficiency of the internal labour market-based HR policies and practices. Labour market conditions in the area were characterized by a large supply of unskilled rural labour and high mobility among the skilled workers, technical personnel and managers. A key HR issue for both subsidiaries therefore was to source and retain trained and skilled personnel. Following this theme, the second and third sections offer detailed discussion of the two sample companies. Localizing subsidiary management is found to mirror the comparative position of the subsidiaries in their corporate networks as well as those in competitive networks in this industrial cluster. Although neither subsidiary seems to have achieved the goal of "localization" as specified in its HR strategy, and turnover among the mid-level managers remained high, both the companies had engaged in developing effective HR practices to maintain a relatively stable top management team. The very last section summarizes the cases with a discussion of the implications of the differences observed.

6.1 Nantong: a textile industry cluster

As shown in Chapter 4, Japanese-invested manufacturing plants are geographically concentrated in two regions in China: the traditional industrial centres and newer industrial clusters. Nantong is the latter – an industrial new town to the north of the Yangtze River. Compared to Shanghai, where our cases of household white goods manufacturers were located, Nantong is a new manufacturing base transformed from a traditional agricultural area as a result of government-led industrialization. Structural transition has created a large surplus of young unskilled rural labour, which is reflected in wage levels. The average wage in the Nantong area was about 30 to 40 per cent lower than nearby areas to the south of the Yangtze River (though this difference has decreased in recent years). Meanwhile, land and property prices

were much lower in Nantong, which attracted manufacturers targeting economies of scale in production. Japanese companies in Nantong
are mainly engaged in the textile industry, especially synthetic fibre
plants, spinning mills, weaving and dying yarn and garment factories.

State and local government have played an important role in attracting foreign investment to facilitate the intended structural transfer.
As discussed in the previous chapter, the Chinese government has
announced policies to promote export-led economic growth, including import tariffs and export tax rebates. At the same time, machinery for local production purposes was exempted from import duty,
which serves as a supplementary measure to facilitate export-oriented
FDI. In addition to national policies, the regional government had
also launched a number of preferential policies to compete for FDI.
In the case of Nantong, the local government set a target to attract
large-scale manufacturing plants. The government was keen to build
infrastructure and offered foreign-invested companies customs exemp-
tion for production machinery, tax reductions and local income tax
rebate. The majority of the foreign-invested companies in Nantong
are Japanese paper mills, chemical and synthetic manufacturers. The
arrival of leading companies such as SF-A Co. and SF-B Co. has been
followed by several group companies engaged in the service sector,
such as quality inspection, logistics and trade houses.

This locality has many implications for the HR issues that concern
SF-A Co. and SF-B Co. First of all, the companies faced a relatively
homogeneous employee group – unskilled workers who had previously been employed in agriculture in the neighbouring area. Although
the turnover among migrants is high, industrialization forces a large
number of job-seekers to move into the area each year. This means that
the companies do not need to put much effort into finding unskilled
replacements. Secondly, given Nantong's lower salary levels and prox-
imity to more developed areas, experienced employees often chose to
migrate to areas such as Shanghai and Suzhou in search of better-paid
work. To the Japanese subsidiaries, a critical issue therefore was to
retain the technical and managerial personnel. And last but not least,
employees working for different companies formed the majority of the
local population. Since most employees lived in company accommodation, news of new employment opportunities, working conditions and
pay rates could spread quickly among employees. For the subsidiaries,

this added to the difficulty of controlling employee behaviour such as "hopping" between different jobs in the same area.

6.2 SF-A Co.: a miniature of the parent plants

6.2.1 Production upgrading: changing subsidiary role in the corporate business networks

SF-A Co.'s decision to invest in China reflects the mobility of capital-intensive industry. Compared with the household white goods manu-facturers who upgraded to full automation at the home plants, the synthetic fibre companies witnessed the decline and closure of factories in Japan. Relocation was characterized by restructuring of the product range and reinforcement of innovative capacities in the home coun-try. While headquarters have generally centralized the R&D function, standardized production has largely been moved overseas. There are multiple reasons for the relocation of production. Difficulty in sour-cing recruits was cited as a key reason by many people. The laborious and repetitive nature of work in textile mills makes it "unpopular" with the younger generation and the situation of recruitment was described as "very dreadful":

I am extremely happy to see so many young people working here. In the factory where I used to work, it has been years that we cannot secure new recruitment. No young people are interested in working in factories, espe-cially those like ours. The so-called 3K[1] industry has completely lost attract-iveness. (Factory Manager, Japanese, 62, male)

I went to one of the manufacturing plants 10 years ago when I attended my first training programme in Japan. That's where I learned most knowledge of how production is managed. I visited them again last year. That factory was a complete mess. Everything looks old and moves slowly. It just lacked the kind of vigorousness that a factory needs to survive. (Division Manager, Chinese, 35, male)

In contrast to the situation in Japan, popularity of the job did not seem to be an issue for young job-seekers in Nantong. Many employees working in the factories had left their rural home because the land allocated was not enough to accommodate the whole family. For these

[1] 3K means *kitanai* (dirty), *keken* (dangerous) and *kitsui* (demeaning).

workers, moving back home did not seem to be an option. These workers believed they would be better off if they could gain skills and experience by moving around factories.

Another important reason for SF-A Co.'s relocation was related to the new global division of labour. Establishing overseas manufacturing plants reflected the financial pressures facing the textile industry and the consequent "hollowing out" effect in Japan. The major synthetic fibre manufacturers initiated restructuring to facilitate the headquarters R&D function. The home plants are used to produce a small amount of innovative materials. Bulk production of the low value-added fabric has largely been moved overseas. Unlike companies in the household white goods sector, these companies seem to be less enthusiastic about upgrading production machinery.

From the factory's perspective, we prefer producing standardized fabric, which is more cost-effective. But the trend in the textile industry is that people do not want standardized clothes. Believe me, no company in this industry will invest in full automation as long as there is a place, somewhere in the world, that provides low-cost labour. People are much more flexible than machines, and cheaper as well. (Division Manager, SF-A Co., Japanese, 40, male)

The parent company also tended to emphasize its role in coordinating the marketing and sales function, and transfer of knowledge across subsidiaries in Asia. SF-A Co. was not the earliest overseas subsidiary of its parent company. Rather, it was founded as part of the ongoing process of development; a "second round" relocation of production followed as late-developing countries showed some advantages in comparison with those which had developed earlier. Internationalization among synthetic fibre manufactures occurred in the 1980s, when appreciation of the yen made overseas relocation more cost effective. After the 1990s, China became an alternative location for mass production as political risk reduced and economic development continued to rise. SF-A Co. was initially a supplementary manufacturing base of its sister plant in Indonesia. More clothing and furnishing manufacturers moved labour-intensive production away from Japan and most of these companies were SMEs. These companies seemed to prefer China, the neighbouring country, as a closer location allowed constant inspection of the manufacturing process and faster delivery turnaround. The textile industry also requires close coordination between suppliers and users so as to promote incremental changes in products and provide timely delivery to minimize storage costs. The importance of accommodating the customers can be seen in many aspects of subsidiary management, including recently setting up an R&D division in order to tailor existing products according to customers' colour, texture and quality requests.

Finally, the local market was characterized by increasing competition between the traditional actors in the textile industry – the Japanese brand makers – and the rapidly rising new actors – Chinese start-ups. As discussed in Chapter 4, China has become the major producer of synthetic fibre around the world. The company's general manager said the reason for its internationalization was "very simple":

Synthetic fibre manufacturing develops at an incredible speed in China. We [the parent company] felt that it would be too late if we didn't set up factories here. The market potential is huge. We can see this just by comparing the wardrobes of Chinese and Japanese women. Japanese women normally have two or three wardrobes, full of clothes. But Chinese women normally have one and it is often half empty. (General Manager, SF-A Co., Japanese, 58, male)

The general manager's explanation seems to indicate a local-market-driven orientation at SF-A Co. Due to lower production costs, the fast-growing textile industry in China has put significant pressure on the Japanese textile fibre manufacturers. While Chinese companies have mainly concentrated on producing fabric with lower added value, their R&D resources have lagged far behind. Lower property prices and labour costs have facilitated the Chinese manufacturers' pursuit of cost leadership. At the macro-level, China has become the largest producer and consumer of textile fibre. While Japanese synthetic fibre manufacturers remain competitive in terms of production technology and new product development, reliance on economies of scale for profit has forced most Japanese synthetic fibre manufacturers to relocate to low-cost production bases, such as China.

6.2.2 The power struggle at subsidiary level

Internationalization has led to some important characteristics in production and management of the textile fibre industry. One key issue was subsidiaries' overall reliance on the headquarters to source raw material and handle the sales of end products. When SF-A Co. was first set up, all raw materials were imported from Japan and all finished goods were exported. SF-A Co. merely assumed the role of production. By the time I visited SF-A Co., the parent company's influence remained apparent in its trade relations. More than 70 per cent of SF-A Co.'s production material and around 60 per cent of the products were handled by the parent company or parent-company-owned trade houses, whereas SF-A Co. itself only controlled a small proportion of domestic sales. The managers explained that expansion of SF-A Co.'s domestic sales was critical for them to gain further autonomy.

In fact, the major accomplishment for SF-A Co. during the past decade was the upgrading of production technology and capacity rather than exploring the local market. The managers said that replacing the Indonesian sister plant as the predominant production base was crucial as the headquarters was considering restructuring the overseas subsidiaries. At the same time, gaining local business was also of critical importance to their survival. In the early 2000s, SF-A Co. started to set up self-directed sales branches and a technical support division (which was, however, called R&D). The company aimed to serve local clients better by incorporating more functions.

Our company's target for the next 10 years is to increase our domestic sales. To do so, we set up our own sales offices in Shanghai and then three other cities: Shenyang, Wenzhou, and Guangzhou, which covers north, central and south China. We also discussed setting up a new branch in Qingdao to explore the east China market. While the sales record has not reached our expectation so far, we believe we will achieve the goal in the near future. (General Manager, SF-A Co., Japanese, 58, male)

R&D [technical support] is a critical function of this company. We believe we have the full ability to develop new material with assistance from the parent companies. But so far, what we are doing here is to make adjustments to the product design according to customers' requirements. [We] think this division's future lies in being able to develop products to suit the Chinese market. (Manager of the R&D division, SF-A Co., Chinese, 39, male)

However, as I will discuss in the following section, subsidiary-directed functions created many conflicts within SF-A Co. as well as between SF-A Co. and some key partners in its business network.

Subsidiary-developed business and parent-controlled business

While there was seemingly a consensus on the company's past achievements, the managers found it hard to agree on what SF-A Co. should
do in the future. Most local managers believed that setting up the sales
and R&D functions would bring about a steady increase in domestic
sales and more subsidiary autonomy. However, this did not seem to
be recognized by headquarters. As far as local sales were concerned,
the general manager explained that their aim was to achieve a balance
in the three major markets: one-third to Japan, one-third to Europe
and one-third to local manufacturers. By the end of 2006, sales in
the Chinese market accounted for 25 per cent of the company's sales
turnover, whereas exports to Japan shrank to 45 per cent. As exports
were handled by the parent company, it is very unlikely that SF-A Co.
would go far towards autonomy. Furthermore, among the 25 per cent
of SF-A Co.'s sales to local customers in 2006, a proportion included
the Japanese market-oriented suit makers. SF-A Co. still relied heavily on the parent company to coordinate different clients. The sister
trading company in Shanghai often got involved in the process of
trade negotiation as well as quality inspections. In this sense, the parent company's influence on production and quality control remained
strong.

We used to get orders from our trade house and they provide us with a large
quantity, which may be from different customers. What we have been doing
is that we are trying to build direct connection with some large sportswear
and smart suit makers and leave the smaller companies to be channelled
by the trade house instead. This is more sensible for the factory and we
don't need to worry too much about the problem of the small clients' creditworthiness. (Deputy General Manager, SF-A Co., Japanese, 49, male)

To accommodate the self-directed business and trade through sister
companies, SF-A Co. had divided the sales division into two functional
sections: a business division in the company and a few sales offices in
some major cities. Separation of the sales division was expected to
"be sensitive to the market and keep close contact with production".
However, separation posed a critical issue of coordination as the sales
function was semi-externalized and different sales agents had been
integrated. The business division was thus expected to channel business between the companies and various clients.

The business division is the window to all sales functions including our sales office, our group trade house, and the parent company's representative office. We receive orders from them and pass on to the production planning division. We can put together orders from different clients so that the production division can make plans accordingly. (Deputy divisional head, Business Division, SF-A Co., Chinese, 36, male)

However, coordination was sometimes bypassed due to the business division's lack of authority to gain accurate information from both production and sales divisions, and this business division was actually responsible for performing more administrative functions.

It is difficult and awkward when there is a disagreement on production and delivery time. Sales will tell us all orders are urgent and production always say they do not have capacity. If the production division say they cannot deliver as sales division require, what we can do is to pass this message on. Sales normally will speak to the managers in the production division directly rather than negotiate with us. Much of the time, they just get the same as we informed them. I sometimes wonder if we are just record keepers. (Clerk, Business Division, SF-A Co., Chinese, 25, male)

What we do every day is act as information passers. We get order information from the sales company in Shanghai, and inform the production planning division. We then record the order and track the progress of the order through production. We are not supposed to develop new business, which is the role of the sales department and we are never assessed by our performance based on our business record. (Clerk, Business Division, SF-A Co., Chinese, 24, female)

Many of the salesmen in this office, like myself, used to work in the factory's business division. I felt that I've learned most product and production related knowledge there. We also gain some basic business knowledge. The business division is like our training centre. (Sales associate, Shanghai sales office, SF-A Co., Chinese, 36, male)

Separation of the sales division, however, had reinforced the parent-directed business network since the sister trade house had taken up the business development role that SF-A Co.'s business division might have played. Both the business division and the sales offices were incapacitated by the more experienced and resourceful sister trade house. It was a fact that SF-A Co.'s profitability generally came from economies of scale and this gave priority to bulk orders, which generally came from the sister trade house. As a result, the development of a factory-centred local business network became more important than maintaining relationships with the parent-controlled sales for SF-A Co. Self-directed clients were restricted to a limited number of OEM factories, which manufactured foreign-brand sportswear, medical and surgery wear, and casual and smart wear. The general manager's judgement of the three-stream business pattern was that it seemed to be more practical than a fully subsidiary-directed business network.

Product development and R&D

SF-A Co.'s pursuit of a "compete by best quality" business strategy necessitated close contact with the parent company. The managers explained that their local market strategy had to be consistent with its global market strategy.

We are a high-profile brand and our products are made to meet the requirements of the brand. The products must meet the quality standards set by the parent company. I don't think there is "too much quality" as you described. Our material is much more durable. It provides better protection. And, the colour won't fade easily. Will you call these qualities "too much"? You are right that it does cost a bit more, but it lasts for longer use. So, our product is cheaper. (Sales Associate, Shanghai sales office, SF-A Co., Chinese, 34, male)

In Japan, our brand sells itself. We need to put much more effort here than in Japan to promote our products, which is understandable as we are well-established in Japan for years but we're just a new-comer here. Our price is higher. But what we could do is to provide products and services that the major competitors cannot, for example, timely delivery, stable quality and smaller minimum lot requirements etc. (Assistant Manager, Shanghai sales office, SF-A Co., Japanese, 26, male)

When associated with such a marketing strategy, the sales offices required more resources from the parent company including technical, marketing and personnel support. Although the company had set up an R&D function, it continued to provide technical support and an after-service role. The department generally engaged in making minor adjustments to the materials developed in Japan to cater for some clients' requirements. The department did not assume any new product development function. For the expatriate managers, having this R&D division was more about gathering information and making necessary product suggestions to the headquarters, which was a reflection of the company's global restructuring. SF-A Co.'s strategic importance remained as a major overseas production base for the parent company. However, textile fibre was no longer the core business that contributed to the company's growth. The headquarters had shifted its attention to developing high-tech industrial fibres, and the textile fibre division had become peripheral.

SF-A Co.'s stance in its corporate networks translated into some controversial policies concerning future directions of this business unit. The headquarters function was planned to be centralized in the R&D centre in Japan but the resources allocated to developing high-tech industrial fibres and R&D investment in textile fibre were rather limited. Local managers tried to persuade the expatriates that SF-A Co. needed to engage in developing their own new products. But this view was unfortunately not supported.

I think the headquarters does not have a focus. We are not sure about the future direction of this company. All efforts we make at this point to invest in developing new products and new markets may well be in vain next month or next year, because the headquarters may change the policies. Producing and delivering the best quality fabric is more feasible than developing a kind of novel material. (Divisional Manager, Shanghai sales office, SF-A Co., Japanese, 45, male)

In this sense, global restructuring had weakened SF-A Co.'s competitive position both within the corporate networks and in the local market. In fact, the local managers took a rather cautious stance concerning subsidiary autonomy.

There is not this general understanding of what the company will be like in the future. We have to figure it out by ourselves, which requires close contact with the headquarters. One thing is clear. Textile fibre is no longer the money-maker for our headquarters. I know they have been discussing closing down the factories in Indonesia. So, why not us? (Manager of the R&D division, SF-A Co., Chinese, 39, male)

The most important reason that I would stay in this company is to lead the Chinese employees. Japanese, they are just here for the "short term" and their decisions are thus on a short-term basis. But we have to think for the long term. If the Japanese withdraw their investment, we have to make sure that the factory can still operate properly. (Deputy Manager of woven factory 1, SF-A Co., Chinese, 35, male)

The reaction in response to the question of whether they foresaw the closure of SF-A Co. in the near future seemed to be rather optimistic. One deputy factory manager put it this way:

Well, there is always this kind of discussion about what to do when the road gets rocky. The headquarters aims to make money here and if this company doesn't, they might choose to give it up. But the local government cannot afford not having such a leading company. There is the possibility that the ownership will change and our factory may be sold to local investors. I think it is important that we will be prepared for one day, when the Japanese are all gone, we have to at least be able to keep the factory going. (Deputy Manager of weaving factory 2, SF-A Co., Chinese, 36, male)

In this sense, the local managers showed they had some incentive to seek autonomy. As the managers indicated, SF-A Co. intended to be "a self-sufficient manufacturing plant under parent guidance". However, restructuring in the textile fibre section within the corporation had raised significant uncertainty about the future of SF-A Co. The managers thus showed more inclination towards maintaining the current situation than acting more aggressively to seek subsidiary autonomy.

Local business development and credit control
A final issue related to the difficulty of developing more subsidiary-directed business was the nature of the local market. The concern of local creditworthiness rose as clients requested delayed payment after delivery. The headquarters had enforced its control over SF-A Co.'s local transactions by setting up rigid creditworthiness criteria to determine the reliability of local clients.

We have to be cautious about local transactions. It was years ago, that we were circulated a report about how a local salesman took advantage of payment after delivery and collaborated with some dummy company. Cargo was delivered and disappeared but payment never came to the company account. Having rigid criteria will prevent our company from making such types of loss. (Deputy General Manager, SF-A Co., Japanese, 47, male)

The enforcement of the creditworthiness criteria meant less flexibility for the sales division, who were not able independently to decide on

possible clients, than for the accounting division. Some possible contracts might have to be "suspended" or "terminated" as the targeted
clients could not meet the criteria. SF-A Co.'s target of developing a
self-directed sales network was constrained by the barriers set by the
parent company.

In this section, I have highlighted SF-A Co.'s changing role in
the corporate networks. After rapid expansion in the late 1990s,
SF-A Co. encountered the shrinking of the international textile fibre
market and had faced growing competition from local textile fibre
producers since 2000. Late development as a fully functioning company, particularly the lack of R&D capacity, had created substantial
subsidiary dependence on the headquarters. While the subsidiary
managers believed that developing local business was critical for
SF-A Co., there were several obstacles to the transformation of a
parent-company-controlled production plant to a strategic business
unit. Some key factors included SF-A Co. remaining heavily dependent on headquarters for R&D and technical support; a large proportion of business being handled by headquarters-owned trade houses;
and credit control restraining the number of potential business partners. Also, SF-A Co.'s attempt to strengthen its responsiveness to
the local market had largely been constrained by the decline of the
textile industry in Japan and the headquarters' partial reduction in
textile fibre-related R&D investment. Headquarters' restructuring
of international business and closing down of some overseas operations increased the uncertainty SF-A Co. was facing. This in turn
deterred the more vigorous pursuit of subsidiary autonomy.

6.2.3 Management learning in the construction of subsidiary management practices

Parent company influence permeates both the HR design and implementation. The headquarters dispatched a short-term mission to help
design the local HR policies and practices. The China representative
office also provided "advice" to guide the implementation of HR policies. Besides direct parent control, expatriates and local managers in
SF-A Co. closely supervised control of production and management
procedures. In fact, many of the expatriate managers expressed the
idea that they were expecting the local managers and employees to

learn "everything" from Japan so that they could be promoted to higher managerial positions to run the company.

> I think that the local managers need to polish their managerial skills. I mean, they need to learn quickly. I am expecting the local managers to learn everything from Japan, knowing how to operate and manage this factory. Then, we don't want any expatriates in this factory. (General Manager, SF-A Co., Japanese, 58, male)

> I don't think the Japanese managers trust us well. We had a meeting with a group of senior managers from Japan. The Japanese managers described us as "sibasiba yushu [outstanding]". But if they do think so, what's the point of having such tight monitoring of our work. (Deputy Factory Manager, weaving factory 2, SF-A Co., Chinese, 35, male)

Management control in SF-A Co. was largely realized through formalized control mechanisms and direct personnel supervision, which was not consistent with Harzing's (1999) observation that Japanese subsidiaries employ a high level of expatriate control. This theme is discussed in more detail in the following chapter.

Visualization of rules and regulations

SF-A Co. comprises four factories that produce a full range of synthetic fabric. Export-oriented production plants normally adopt parent production and management practices and SF-A Co. was no exception. The factories performed particularly rigorous quality control, which included implementation of standardized production processes, quality inspection procedures, and safety and protection measures. To highlight some key procedures, bilingual posters and whiteboards were displayed in areas which could be seen easily. The only exception was the key quality inspection procedures, which were all written in Japanese. This, according to the managers, was to "maintain consistency" in the production and inspection process and avoid possible confusion.

The careful following of standardized procedures was considered to be essential to maintain "workplace safety", which was specified as "complete implementation of 5S". These workplace rules and regulations were usually translated into and largely accepted by the locals as "learning the parent way of management". Besides overseer manuals and other translated paperwork, expatriate managers acted as role models for local managers, who were expected to learn from them the art of implementing the process and procedures. Following the guidance of expatriates, local managers could easily perform supervisory roles on a daily basis.

I don't think there is much space for individual ideas here. The guidelines and principles are clear. Based on these principles, we can compose our proposals and report to the top managers and they will normally give us some advice. We constantly report our progress to the top managers and gain feedback for improvement. Similarly, we encourage our subordinates to report to us frequently and offer some advice to them. (Deputy Factory Manager, SF-A Co., Chinese, 38, male)

You know Japanese managers. They care about details. Our factory manager is an advocator of "genba shugi [work on site]". He walks around and gives us improvement suggestions. As site managers, I feel we are expected to be able to detect these problems before he points them out. (Departmental Manager, SF-A Co., Chinese, 37, male)

All managers in senior positions were given a specific monitoring role to detect and correct problematic behaviours on site. They also took turns to be the key "workplace safety" inspectors. The principal duties of the local managers included tours around the factory, meeting with the subordinate group leaders, composing production reports and reporting to the senior managers. Senior managers were involved in monitoring as well. A formal "factory inspection tour" was organized once a month and all the senior managers met with the factory managers, shop-floor managers and junior managers to check whether production was performed according to the procedures and other requirements. Photographs were taken wherever something "odd" was detected and these were presented at the monthly managerial meeting. The person in charge of the workshop was supposed to take responsibility for improvement and photograph the "improved" situation for the following monthly meeting.

Hierarchical supervision and close control

SF-A Co.'s organizational structure was carefully designed and featured a rigid hierarchy. Figure 6.1 shows the hierarchical structure in one of the factories.

Workers at the bottom of this hierarchy were divided into working groups to make up three shifts. Group leaders reported to line leaders and they in turn reported to shift leaders. Group and line managers were treated as junior managers; departmental managers, divisional

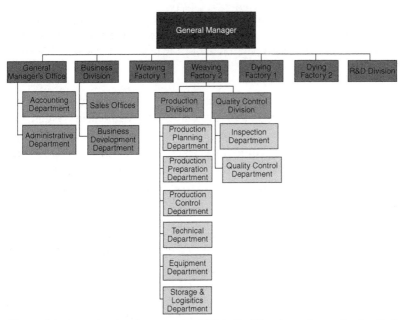

Figure 6.1 Organizational structure of SF-A Co. The chart shows the detailed structure of Weaving Factory 2, but the other factories shared a similar structure.

managers and factory managers comprised the senior managers. The dividing line between senior managers and workers was clear, and this reinforced the symbolic power of the managerial group. Separation between managers and employees was reflected in many aspects of HRM, a point I will come back to again in the next section. Such symbolic power could also be observed as managers wore name tags and workers number tags at work. The managers were offered different food in the canteen. The dormitory rooms allocated to the managers were shared by fewer people.

The managers explained the practical effects of having a rigid hierarchical structure and a clear division between managers and employees and said that it was an important measure to help maintain control of the production process.

Discipline, rules, senior managers' instructions...these are the basics and indispensable to a company's success. The reason these are not available in Japan is because people are following these rules and disciplines. Here, we have to clearly communicate with the employees and make sure that they all follow these basics. Unless employees behave by instinct, we will need some measures, system and people to monitor the behaviour. (General Manager, SF-A Co., Japanese, 58, male)

Formal control measures were seen as provisional and replaceable. The managers explained that the current "management system has not reached the effects expected". Direct supervision was considered necessary because "the company is too young to cultivate a corporate culture to influence the individual's behaviour". Being at an early stage of development was also often cited to explain why the nature of managers' jobs was more routinized and tightly controlled.

I think the relationship between me and my subordinate managers is like father and sons. I am expecting them to grow up and take responsibility as real managers. (Factory manager, SF-A Co., Japanese, 48, male)

I am very on-site oriented [genba shugi]. I believe a lot of things have to be confirmed by my own eyes. Even so, there are always unexpected things, unexpected happenings, or staff put in unexpected places. This is what a factory job is like. (Factory manager, SF-A Co., Japanese, 61, male)

Managers, especially the site managers, are the pillars of the factories. There is no specific job responsibility to describe how to be a site manager. We have to learn by observing the senior managers, by seeking their advice. Basically, we are responsible for planning daily work, resolving problems at site and training the new employees. (Head of Production Preparation Department, SF-A Co., Chinese, 34, female)

A firm managerial hierarchy and tight control were not restricted to the actual work. Managers were expected to control many aspects of working life. Managers were responsible for supervising maintenance of dormitory hygiene. They were also responsible for the dormitory inspections that were scheduled monthly but actually only took place occasionally. Photos were taken where the room hygiene fell below the 5S standard. These photos of "bad examples" were then displayed on a whiteboard close to the dormitory gate. The managers in charge of the rooms were responsible for supervising the improvements as well.

Consensus building and teamwork

The influence of the parent companies was also reflected in some "consensus-building" activities. For example, problem-solving was a group activity. All four factories had "production quality meetings", where managers met once a day to discuss problems found in the factory, either detected during their tour around or reported by the workshop leaders. These meetings served the purpose of communicating problems to factory managers and seeking advice and suggestions from the whole managerial group. The site managers would try to get the consent of the expatriate factory managers, and would then apply their proposed solutions as well as provide feedback at the next meeting. All the local managers seemed to accept and reiterate the concept of "*hou-ren-sou*" – which stands for *houkoku* [report], *renraku* [communication] and *soudan* [consultation] – a common practice in the Japanese parent company.

Group-based problem-solving was explained as a very important measure to promote teamwork. Meetings were commonly observed in SF-A Co.'s daily routines. For example, each factory held a "morning gathering" every day in order to remind the employees of some critical issues in the working procedures. The morning gathering was an opportunity for the group leaders to obtain first-hand information about what was happening in the factory. At the gatherings, the group leader stated any problem that had occurred in the previous shift and asked for suggestions to avoid similar problems. The group members were required to take turns to remind the groups of the possible problems and the rest of the group was supposed to give suggestions/advice so that they could arrive at the most reasonable plan for maintaining the procedures during their shift. This practice was repeated when the next shift took over, and the two group leaders were expected to exchange information about problems on the previous shift. In practice, however, workers were frequently not attentive during the meetings and committed similar mistakes despite the group leaders' constant warnings.

The managers were also expected to get feedback from the employees through the "suggestion scheme", a practice commonly adopted in the Japanese parent plants. Unlike Taylor's (1999) observation that monetary reward was used to motivate workers to participate in providing suggestions, SF-A Co. did not use a direct link between suggestion and bonus. Though some were awarded an "Outstanding Suggestions Prize" at the end of the year, the amount was merely nominal. As the managers explained, the local managers were very keen to cultivate employees' voluntary participation by boosting their sense of belonging to the company.

We believe that our employees should think themselves as members of the large family – the company. At least, I think I am responsible for taking care of my employees and I feel many of my colleagues feel the same way. (Divisional Manager, SF-A Co., Chinese, 35, male)

It takes time for our employees to get used to providing improvement suggestions. However, when they are used to these, they come up with suggestions spontaneously, even after they leave this company. (Manager, Administrative Division, SF-A Co., Chinese, 38, female)

What has to be highlighted is that the managers were well aware of the difficulty of cultivating this sense of belonging. The first problem was that many workers were short-term. The average tenure of employees was two-and-a-half years. Another difficulty encountered was the employees' unwillingness to contribute to continuous improvement, as many workers expressed the idea of being "pressurized" to take part rather than "motivated" to do so.

We are responsible for many off-work activities. It is said to be voluntary, like attending the Japanese courses. But if we don't attend, the managers will take it that we are not interested in working in this company for long, then we won't be fairly assessed. (Worker, Chinese, 29, female)

Our assessment is not just about quantity and quality but also the managers' impression of our work attitude. We have to show a positive attitude, like giving suggestions to avoid production accidents or cleaning of the machines. (Worker, SF-A Co., Chinese, 20, male)

Here again, direct control by the managers seemed to be important. To monitor employee behaviour closely, monthly assessments were conducted and those who did not meet the performance criteria, which included quantity, product quality and following workplace discipline, would have an amount deducted from their monthly bonus or salary.

6.2.4 *Job design and HRM routines*

Managers' work, to a large extent, was to control and monitor the operation of the factories. SF-A Co. showed a strong tendency to transfer policies and practices developed in Japan and this was reflected in the HR function. HR practices that showed important parent company characteristics included a long-term recruitment strategy, comparative appraisal policy, internal promotion, combined on-the-job and off-the-job training, as well as a non-specified dismissal policy. There was no local HR strategy in place until 2005, when the headquarters conducted a major review of the HR function to enhance HRM efficiency. Expatriates from the headquarters' HR division were dispatched to SF-A Co. to help restructure the local HR system. SF-A Co. served as a key overseas production base. To the managers of SF-A Co., their HR policies and practices were an extension of the HR reform at headquarters. As the current HR manager put it, the review of HR policy made SF-A Co. "a miniature of the parent company".

Recruitment and selection

Recruitment in SF-A Co. was overwhelmingly focused on young graduates, as in many other Japanese subsidiaries located in Nantong. Given the lack of skilled workers in the local area, the young graduate-centred recruitment policy was more a reflection of local labour market conditions than a strategically planned transfer of parent practices. SF-A Co. did not have specific selection criteria apart from health requirements. The largest number of shop-floor workers were recruited from local technical schools. The majority of the locals currently in managerial positions were recruited two years before SF-A Co. was officially set up. They joined the company straight after graduation from technical school and were trained in Japan before working as junior managers at SF-A Co. Only two of the local managers had previous experience, but their current job bore very little resemblance to what they used to do. They had gone through a similar training process to the group of technical school graduates and worked in SF-A Co. for several years before being promoted to a higher managerial position. SF-A Co. thus had a core group of managers who shared some homogeneous internal experience, whereas very little had been done to develop HR strategy concerning the future generation of managers until 2005.

The rationale for SF-A Co.'s preference of recruiting young graduates seemed to be similar for both the Japanese and Chinese managers. The Japanese managers tended to believe that young graduates were more flexible about accepting the "company way" of working, which is consistent with the intention to transfer production and management know-how. The local managers also acknowledged young graduates' ability to learn the company way. However, they pointed out that targeting young graduates was more practical when facing the high level of employee turnover in the local area. As one manager stated:

Let's face it. Our employees won't stay long. They are fresh, they are young, and they change their gadgets, their girlfriends, and their jobs. But at least, they learn things very fast. If we recruit more experienced workers, they will still move but they are much less flexible in accepting how things are done in our factory. (Production Manager, SF-A Co., Chinese, 38, male)

When deciding the future HR plan for recruiting potential managers, the managers agreed on the young graduate-centred policy. However disagreement arose concerning the key selection criteria. The local managers saw people with a background in chemical engineering, machine engineering or textile manufacturing as most suitable for potential managers since most of these young university graduates were expected to start as workshop group leaders. Those with limited technical knowledge might be looked down upon by the workers and thus lose their authority as managers. The expatriate managers, however, intended to improve communication with workshop managers. Providing long-term intensive language training was financially impractical without a headquarters subsidy. To the expatriates, "communication skills" often translated as being Japanese literate, and this was thus the top selection criterion. The expatriates also suggested that candidates with Japanese proficiency were more likely to be settled in the company and develop technical knowledge internally.

Differences in selection preferences led to conflicts between the HR division and the factories. With recruitment centralized by the HR division, factory managers were involved at the final stage of the selection process. Since the HR division reported to the general manager and to the HR division at the headquarters, priority was generally given to candidates with a Japanese-speaking background. More than 60 per cent of the young graduates recruited since 2005 had majored in Japanese, while the remaining 40 per cent studied Japanese as a second language. Many factory managers expressed resentment that candidates recommended by HR were not suitable for the job. The local HR managers who had assisted in the reform of the local HR system were said to "know nothing about the nature of factory work".

Conflict during the selection process was more than just preference for the particular knowledge or skills that young graduates might be able to offer. Rather, such conflict reflected tension between the current managers and young graduates. Facing a new group of potential managers, existing managers attempted to justify their expertise in managing the factories. They tried to influence the selection process by suggesting technical criteria. They were also found to be less cooperative with the newly recruited university graduates, who did not seem to encounter the particular difficulty in managing the experienced workers that had been predicted by the existing managers. But coordination with other site managers was said to be extremely hard. Many expressed frustration at not being given accurate information on the previous or following production procedure or time for feedback from the senior managers, difficulty in scheduling a co-worker group, and limited chances of using Japanese.

Training and development

In general, SF-A Co. emphasized internal and on-the-job training as well as an off-the-job training system, which was generally consistent with the headquarters' HR policy. As mentioned previously, most local managers in senior positions received intensive training in Japan before being promoted to their current position. The young graduates from technical colleges were recruited and dispatched to the parent plants for one or two years. They were then sent back to SF-A Co. and worked as assistants to the expatriate managers as a follow-up training programme. For the young college graduates recruited in recent years, the entry-level training was done in SF-A Co. Training in the parent plants was only offered to some selected employees and the length of training had been shortened to ten months, and later six months. Since the parent company had withdrawn the training subsidy for subsidiary employees, SF-A Co. had been paying for employees to attend training programmes at the headquarters. However, many managers working in Japan claimed that what they did in Japan had very little to do with the job they were doing in SF-A Co. For example, the sales and marketing staff were also sent to Japan for training, while they were supposed to concentrate on developing the Chinese local market. In this sense, off-the-job training in Japan epitomized SF-A Co.'s intention of rewarding employee loyalty.

Another important characteristic of SF-A Co. was the Japanese language training provided to all employees. To improve overall proficiency in Japanese among the employees, SF-A Co. offered different levels of language training depending on the employees' position in the company. For the workers, the company offered basic Japanese courses. Even though many workers were not interested in learning Japanese, they had to go through some basic training to be able to recognize the Japanese terms used in the quality inspection process. There were also many signs in the companies written in *Kanji* [Chinese characters], the meaning of which had to be learned either through school education, formal training provided by the company or self-learning. The computer system was also in Japanese. Employees working in materials supply, business development and stock control thus had to learn Japanese to be able to use the system. The employees were encouraged to take a Japanese Language Proficiency Test (JLPT) and those who passed the test were awarded a monthly skill allowance. Proficiency in Japanese was essential for those pursuing managerial positions in the company. SF-A Co. recruited Japanese tutors to provide small group courses for the local managers. The Japanese of these tutors was at an advanced level.

Besides language training, local managers received management training mainly through working with expatriates. Consider the divisional managers' on-the-job training, for example: factory managers asked individual divisional managers to work out a proposal prior to the start of a particular project (such as introducing a new type of fabric). Based on the proposal, advice and suggestions would be given and a revised proposal would then be implemented. The divisional managers were expected to follow the progress of the project and gain feedback from their peers and subordinates, consult the factory managers for improvement suggestions, and modify the original proposal where necessary. When the project was completed, the divisional managers were supposed to reflect on the process and produce a final report. Ideally, departmental managers gained similar training by working closely with the divisional managers. However, many local managers showed no incentive to share their experience and saw self-directed learning as the way training was obtained.

Giving suggestions and advice is not easy. Our young managers need some more experience to understand the work. If I tell them what to do, they can get the job done. But they still don't understand why. They have to learn through their own experience. (Divisional Managers' Assistant, R&D division, SF-A Co., Chinese, 34, male)

I don't think the senior managers are willing to teach me anything. When I ask them questions, they normally will say "go read this", or "go ask A". I think some of my colleagues have similar experiences. So, I finally get it. When I have a question, I'd better figure it out myself and then ask the seniors if my idea is acceptable. (Clerk, Business Development Department, SF-A Co., Chinese, 24, female)

The introduction of a reformed HR system increased internal competition for promotion opportunities. It was not surprising that current managers lacked the incentive to share their knowledge and experience. Expatriates were trying to encourage on-the-job training by introducing more team activities such as daily production meetings. The formal appraisal procedure also partly served as training. Junior managers got advice and suggestions through formalized consultation and performance assessment meetings.

Reward and compensation

SF-A Co.'s pay-for-job grade system shared many elements with that of the parent plants. Each job grade indicated a basic salary and position allowance. *Technical skill allowances* were paid to individuals who obtained company-recognized technical certificates. Employees were also paid *Competence Allowance* if they passed JLPT. (The size of the allowance differed according to the level of the JLPT certificate an employee held.) Employees with English proficiency certificates such as TOEIC were also recognized and paid a Competence Allowance. However, as English proficiency was not linked with promotion criteria, those who spoke English were "in a disadvantageous situation" in terms of competing for senior positions.

Those who do not speak Japanese are in an extremely disadvantageous position in competition for promotion opportunities. Not impossible, but extremely disadvantageous. Personally, I don't mind my subordinate speaking English to me or in the company, but for their own future in this company, I encourage them to attend Japanese courses. (Divisional Manager, Shanghai sales office, SF-A Co., Japanese, 45, male)

By linking the reward package with proficiency in Japanese, SF-A Co. aimed to control mobility of the skilled workers and managers. In line with SF-A Co.'s internal promotion policy, the company needed

to have a pool of candidate managers. The benefits package prioritized company-specific knowledge and skills. Proficiency in Japanese
was considered the foundation for building technical and managerial
skills internally. Also, given that Japanese was less widely spoken than
English, employees with only Japanese proficiency had fewer opportunities to seek external career advancement. In particular, SF-A Co.
and SF-B Co. were the largest employers in the area before smaller
Japanese-invested companies arrived. There was no consensus between
SF-A Co. and SF-B Co. to employ each other's leavers, even though
they offered similar salary levels and welfare packages. Local managers expressed the idea of moving next door but this was considered
as "neither worthwhile nor practical". However, linking proficiency in
Japanese with the reward (as well as appraisal) policy did not guarantee low turnover among the skilled workers and managers. One reason
for this was similar to Elger and Smith's (2005) observation that the
cluster of Japanese-invested companies could have weakened the company's control over labour mobility. As explained at the beginning of
this chapter, the Nantong government's policy of attracting FDI also
increased the demand for skilled workers and experienced managers.
For example, SF-A Co. lost a group of managers to another Japanese
fibre manufacturer, which set up a production plant in the same area
in 2002. An equally important reason for high turnover among the
skilled workers and experienced managers related to Nantong's location. Fast economic development in nearby cities such as Shanghai
and Suzhou encouraged many experienced employees to seek career
advancement outside Nantong. Labour turnover was not merely a
cluster effect but also related to the increased regional differences that
characterize China's emerging economy.

    Another important element consistent with the headquarters' com-
pensation policies was the relative compensation policy, which was
particularly relevant to deciding managers' end-of-year bonuses.
Managers were graded according to four performance ranks: A (performed outstandingly), B (over-performed), C (performance goal
achieved) and D (under-performed). The rank reflected how well they
were able to achieve their performance target compared with other
managers. This meant that a manager might well achieve his or her
own performance target but still be ranked as "D" if they were not
as good as the other managers. According to the general managers of
SF-A Co., the purpose of introducing the relative compensation policy

was to instigate internal competition and encourage the managers to achieve their full potential.

Appraisal and promotion

SF-A Co. lacked clear promotion criteria, apart from length of service. As mentioned earlier, SF-A Co. had only one generation of local managers. Seniority therefore did not have the same meaning as in the parent plants. On average, the divisional managers worked two or three years longer than the departmental managers, who served the companies slightly longer compared to most shop-floor supervisors, line and shift managers. The age range among group leaders varied because some of them were promoted after working for the factories for several years and some were newly recruited young graduates. A large proportion of the local managers had worked for five to six years before they were promoted. They commented that new managers were expected to work much longer before being given the chance of promotion. The HR manager explained that promotional opportunities were "open to all eligible candidates" but "subject to availability of a position". While technically the length of service requirement for the university graduates was designed to be shorter than for the workers, in reality SF-A Co. might not have vacant positions for this group of trainees by the time they had fulfilled the requirement. Since most local managers in senior managerial position were in their mid/late 30s, promotion opportunities for the newly recruited university graduates were rather limited unless existing managers chose to leave the company or the headquarters recalled more expatriates. There were local managers who suggested that the number of expatriates could be reduced in the near future.

Two of the factory managers are expatriates here on contract basis, not directly from the parent company. When their contract ends, I suppose local managers should be promoted to these positions. (Assistant Manager, SF-A Co., Chinese, 32, male)

However, more locals seemed to believe that factory managers would still be expatriated, given SF-A Co.'s past unsuccessful experience in localizing one particular management position. This trial localization will be discussed later in this section. More importantly, local managers were aware of the problem of redundancy in the parent plants. The message to subsidiaries, according to the local managers, might be an increased number of expatriate managers to share the personnel costs with the parent company. As there was no clear promotion route, recruitment of young university graduates was suspended in 2007.

Retention and dismissal

SF-A Co. encouraged a long-term employment relationship. While there seemed to be very limited chances for promotion, those who had served a long time in the company were compensated by an incremental salary rise. Dismissal policy was ambiguous, especially with regard to managers. According to the HR manager, the company had "never fired a single manager" and "wanted the employees to feel cared for and useful" at work.

The HR reform reinforced an "internal transfer" policy as a retention measure. While the HR manager interpreted this internal transfer as part of job rotation within SF-A Co., people generally saw the transfer as a demotion and proof of not being competent in a particular job. The HR manager also admitted that the most difficult job was to persuade people to accept the company's transfer decisions as employees generally interpreted them rather negatively. The internal transfer policy had a rather negative effect in terms of securing the long-term employment relationship. Rather, resignations had increased since its introduction. In practice, this kind of internal transfer was judged a form of indirect dismissal.

Using internal transfer instead of direct dismissal did not seem to have resolved the problem of turnover among the junior managers. Instead, it had made more junior managers and senior employees re-evaluate their position in the company. Many local managers saw SF-A Co.'s HR policy of retaining employees as "not suitable to local conditions".

Most of the employees in the companies are young and are not afraid of taking up challenges. At the same time, they care more about how much they gain for the efforts they have put into their job. They may not plan for the long term. And, they will not hesitate to leave a job if it is proved to be hopeless. This is the condition of the workforce in China. (Assistant manager, SF-A Co., Chinese, 26, male)

In dealing with employees who turned out to be less competent, SF-A Co. tended to arrange internal moves instead of dismissing them.

Many reasons were given for SF-A Co.'s lack of a dismissal policy and parent influence could not be discounted. Like many large-scale Japanese companies, the Japanese parent company used to offer a long-term employment relationship, especially for those expatriate managers who used to be managed by a "lifetime employment" practice, who tended to prioritize long-term employment relations and an internally promoted management team. The local managers in SF-A Co. did not seem to have an incentive to develop more sophisticated dismissal policies given the 30–40 per cent turnover among local employees. Having a more effective retention policy was more critical to future HR development in SF-A Co. As explained by the managers, the loss of core mid-level managers had seriously affected the plant's productivity.

6.2.5 Case summary: the process of integrating local managers

SF-A Co.'s dependence on the parent company was central to the subsidiary–headquarters relationship. To meet the quality standard for exports, standardization of the production process and formalization of production procedures have characterized production arrangements. Expatriates have dominated production process design, supervision and review in the subsidiary. As a result, standardized procedures and formal regulations were generally drawn from parent company policies or interpreted from common practices experienced by expatriates. Expatriate dominance was justified by their experience and familiarity with production and quality management. Close supervision was applied to ensure standard processes and procedures were followed and implemented, and supplementary rules could be enforced wherever necessary. When exports dropped due to the shrinking international synthetic fibre market, SF-A Co.'s local business strategy to compete by product quality in the local market tended to reinforce standardization of production and formalization of management.

In terms of localization, a pilot policy was once introduced and one divisional manager was promoted to be factory manager. However, this trial only lasted for half a year. The factory encountered more quality problems than ever and the Chinese manager was not able to resolve these problems properly. He described the time as the "most difficult period in my life".

All of a sudden I was told to be the manager of this factory but without information of how to manage it. I worked as hard as I could ever imagine but things just didn't work out right. Old problems piled up and new problems kept emerging. I just don't think I have got sufficient managerial training to do the job. (Divisional Manager, SF-A Co., Chinese, 36, male)

The local manager's claim of lack of experience reflected the limitations of SF-A Co.'s HR policy, which discouraged professional education and overemphasized language training and on-the-job managerial training. More importantly, tension and conflicts among the local managers as a reaction to the promotion decisions is salient.

He [Department manager] is in his fifth year and he should be called back to the parent company by the end of next year. We are not sure what is going to happen after that. I guess I might be promoted to this position, but most of the departmental managers will not be happy because they are all older than me and have waited for promotion for years. If any of these local managers is promoted, I am sure there would be more problems. I guess the best choice may be that the parent company dispatches another expatriate, more experienced than us. That will soothe the tension and avoid further conflicts. (Assistant Manager, Sales Office, Japanese, 30, male)

Given that most local managers shared very similar experiences and formal performance appraisal was only introduced after 2005, senior managers found it difficult to distinguish between different subordinates' performance when making promotion decisions. In addition, limited promotion opportunities and the top-down nomination system always generated complaints and disagreements among local managers, and this often led to managers choosing to leave the company. In fact, turnover of the experienced workers and junior managers was much higher than that of the senior managers. Losing more competent junior managers was also an important cause of many workplace problems. As the general manager has admitted, many existing managers were "familiar with the production site but not good at coordinating and managing across functions". Recruiting Japanese-speaking young university graduates might, in the short run, fill in some vacancies and improve communication between expatriates and shop-floor managers. However, turnover among this group could remain high if their career expectations were not met in SF-A Co.

In summary, development of HR policies and practices in SF-A Co. was more reactive than strategic. The problems that SF-A Co. was facing, particularly turnover among experienced workers and junior managers, were not only a reflection of structural and locality mismatch, as pointed out by studies of the transfer of Japanese management systems (Beechler and Yang, 1994; Graham, 1995; Elger and Smith, 2005). SF-A Co.'s HR policies and practices also failed to match the HR goals they intended to achieve. For example, tight control and supervision of managers' daily work conflicted with the attempt to encourage initiative amongst local managers. A rigid distinction between junior and senior managers ran counter to the intention of building teamwork and promoting learning among the managers. The homogeneous local manager group also challenged the effectiveness and perceived fairness of "relativity-based appraisal". Clarification of local HR policy by HR reorientation might have helped SF-A Co. successfully attract some university graduates to fill vacancies. But the mismatch in HR policies appeared to constrain significantly the retention and development of a local management team.

6.3 SF-B Co.: a subsidiary adopting "global best practices"?

SF-B Co. was set up in 1996. Although the subsidiary was incorporated two years later than SF-A Co., it soon overtook SF-A Co. to become the largest Japanese company in Nantong. Like SF-A Co., SF-B Co. also integrated weaving and dying of a full range of synthetic fabrics. The development track of SF-B Co. was also similar to that of SF-A Co. More than 90 per cent of its products used to be exported to Japan and Southeast Asian countries in the late 1990s. Sales in the Chinese market went up steadily from 2000 and domestic sales eventually exceeded exports to reach 60 per cent of the total sales turnover by 2005. Changing corporate structure indicates SF-B Co.'s transition from a supplementary production base to a fully functioning strategic business unit. The marketing, sales, R&D and HR planning functions have been separated from it. Within SF-B Co., a well-structured hierarchy is in place to control the manufacturing process and procedures. Nevertheless, some major differences between SF-A Co. and SF-B Co. can be observed, mainly as a result of SF-B Co.'s strategic orientation and latest review of corporate structure in China.

6.3.1 A regional headquarters-centred network

The operation of SF-B Co. reflects a multi-regional business structure, in which China is one of the strategic regions. Nantong is intended to become a production and R&D cluster. The general manager of SF-B Co. explained that the current task for the company was to "develop the core competence of individual subsidiaries and link up the production chain effectively". For SF-B Co., they intend to lead competition in the Chinese market by continually introducing new products.

> We understand the market potential of China and we have been developing local business since our establishment. We have a very clear local strategy, that is, to always offer products that our competitors do not have, or better products than what the competitors already have. (General Manager, SF-B Co., Japanese, 52, male)

> The scale of the Chinese market is the largest in the world. But we have to know in which segment we can compete. One of our junior members once proposed to channel the products in a mass market. I have been there myself and it was just not the right place for our products to be sold. Our products are never cheap, but all our fabric is unique. (Sales Manager, SF-B Co., Chinese, 40, male)

Compared with its major competitors such as SF-A Co., SF-B Co.'s product range was more specialized filament fibre for sportswear and healthcare use. The structure of SF-B Co.'s network in China and the HR system were designed to consolidate this "compete by specialization" strategy. In terms of business networks, the Chinese holding company functioned as an administrative centre covering the trade houses, manufacturing plants (including SF-B Co.) and several local R&D centres.

The group network of SF-B Co. in China used to be similar to that of SF-A Co. The manufacturing plants were supported by the Beijing and Shanghai representative offices, which coordinated trade between various subsidiaries in China and the headquarters. In view of the fast growth of the Chinese domestic market and intensified competition, the company reviewed its Asian strategy in the early 2000s and started restructuring the Chinese network. The Chinese holding company replaced the Shanghai representative office as the regional headquarters, centralizing the strategic planning, investment and trade coordination functions. The Beijing representative office's function, in contrast, was weakened. However, as noted in the previous chapter, the holding company was not able to fulfil the role of mediating local trade due to the Chinese government's policy constraints (Guan and Fan, 2003). A trade agent, co-invested by the parent company and the Chinese holding company, was thus formed to facilitate domestic trade. In the following years, three R&D centres were also set up, two within the manufacturing cluster in Nantong and one in Shanghai. The managers explained that the ultimate function of the R&D centres was to develop new products with local resources. At the time of writing, the R&D centres focused on tailoring existing products to meet local clients' requirements. By restructuring the Chinese network, SF-B Co. strengthened its position as a production centre.

Unlike SF-A Co., which was struggling to become a self-directed subsidiary by integrating more strategic functions, SF-B Co. concentrated on improving the production capacity and its product variety. In terms of the key functions of marketing and R&D, the company had constructed a collaborative network, mainly with sister subsidiaries.

I think we have a well-balanced trade structure. We have our own sales division in each of the factories. International trade is handled by the Chinese holding company. Local business is channelled by several agents. I don't have accurate data on how much local business is handled by our sister trade house and how much we trade through local agents. But I would say half and half. The group trade house was set up in 2004 and they are very specialized. (Board member, SF-B Co., Japanese, 60, male)

To be honest, I think it is good not to keep the R&D function and production in the same company. Production departments do not like trials. By separating R&D and the factories, the R&D centre is treated as a lab. They pay the factory for all the trial costs, which the factories can decide depending on their capacity. Another reason to separate the factory and the R&D centres is that our engineers in the R&D centre earn much more than the engineers at the factory. If they all work in the same company, the factory engineers will definitely be furious. Now that they work for different companies, we don't have these kinds of problems. (Board member, SF-B Co., Chinese, 46, male)

The parent company's strategic reorientation in China aimed to build a network consisting of a number of specialized subsidiaries and two coordination centres: the Chinese holding company and the representative office. SF-B Co. was one of the production bases, specialized in making textile fibres. Within the cluster, two sister plants were engaged in producing industrial fibres and industrial films. R&D facilities in Nantong were on the same scale as those in Japan and specialized in the three product lines. This allowed close cooperation with the respective production plants. With various subsidiaries specializing in either production or development of a particular line of products, the Chinese holding company coordinated across various subsidiaries. While the Chinese holding company was a minor shareholder of these Chinese subsidiaries, headquarters delegated considerable decision-making power to it. It has thus centralized the roles of financing, marketing and administration.

> The Chinese headquarters makes investment, business and management related decisions. Meetings are held here and our headquarters will dispatch staff to attend the meetings. (Board Member, SF-B Co., Chinese, 45, male)

> We have the authority to make most decisions related to the subsidiaries. To name a few, we make decisions on investment expansion, change of local business strategy, restructuring of the subsidiaries, etc. (HR Manager, Chinese holding company, Japanese, 52, male)

The Chinese holding company's regional headquarters function was further strengthened by filling the HR planning role and centralizing some key HR functions such as training, development and expatriating subsidiary managers.

6.3.2 Production upgrading: the role of the local management team

Like SF-A Co., SF-B Co.'s production machinery was semi-automated and the factories recruited a large number of unskilled and semi-skilled workers. As Nantong has become a cluster of the synthetic fibre industry and has seen the rise of several other garment manufacturing clusters nearby, the factories have experienced difficulty in sourcing skilled workers and managers from the local labour market. Continuous expansion of production capacity necessitated the use of more migrant workers. By the time SF-B Co. was visited in 2007, migrant workers formed the majority of the workforce. Managers explained that it was almost impossible to control the migrant workers by written contract, and retaining bonuses became a more practical alternative.

The workers are unpredictable. Our factory has an average annual labour turnover of 34 per cent. Turnover fluctuates over the year and the situation is particularly bad during the Lunar New Year. When the workers go back home, we never know if they are coming back. (HR Manager, SF-B Co., Chinese, 37, male)

In addition to labour turnover, managers were under pressure to supervise the production and quality control processes. Compared to SF-A Co., SF-B Co. seemed to be less active in developing employee commitment. The company was also not able to cultivate a cooperative working atmosphere among the workers. The bonding between the company and the workers was, therefore, largely based on direct control, monetary and personal control. As the HR manager explained, basic salary was calculated by reference to the worker's short-term performance and a bonus was paid in relation to long-term performance. Incremental rises were also paid as the employee's tenure at the company increased. While the expatriate HR manager in the Chinese headquarters tended to suggest that increasing the proportion of "seniority-based wage" was a good way to motivate workers to stay with the companies, the local HR managers in the subsidiaries seemed to be very cautious about the use of seniority. The local managers were worried that increasing the element of seniority in employees' pay structure could seriously demotivate the large number of young workers and affect overall productivity. In SF-B Co., again, manipulation of power by local managers (Taylor, 2001) was not observed. The rationale of using monetary control was based on the idea of workers' "short-term" orientation towards work in SF-B Co.

The local managers were responsible for monitoring the production process and employees' behaviour on a day-to-day basis. In terms of product prototype, production, quality control and inspection procedures, SF-B Co. introduced key features of production management from their parent plant. Some of the management techniques, such as the notice board in the workshop and employees' suggestion scheme, were also adopted. However, work-related decisions were made in a "top-down" manner and very limited "bottom-up" communication could be observed, as promoted by the parent company. Some expatriate managers expressed disappointment over the way workers were treated in SF-B Co.

It is not normal that even when all the instructions are followed and quality control measures are applied, the quality of the products still falls to B level or even C level [A is the top level]. I admit there are many factors that impact on the quality of product, but the most important one is that the workers are not happy being under surveillance all the time. (Factory manager, SF-B Co., Japanese, 57, male)

The local managers played a critical role in maintaining the progress of production and they seemed to be more results-oriented:

The procedures and instruction can never be overemphasized. If we say this job has to be done 100 per cent according to the manual, the workers will just do 80 or 70 per cent. If we need a result of 100 per cent, we have to make to requirement at 125 per cent or maybe more. After all, we are not in Japan. (Line manager, SF-B Co., Chinese, 34, male)

In the absence of alternative measures to motivate the workers, economic and personnel control seemed to be a makeshift arrangement for keeping daily production on track, based on detailed instructions of manufacturing procedures.

The problem with using economic and personnel controls to support production management largely borrowed from the parent plants was that the workload for the local managers was much more than that of the parent plants. Much attention was given to following the procedures and there were occasions when site managers lost sight of the bigger picture. One example was the distribution of a new set of daily quality checking forms. The work record was used to check the progress of production. To keep more details of work progress, a new form of work record was designed and the shop-floor managers were in charge of making sure that all workstations started to use the new work record on the same day. At the daily quality meeting, production department managers reported that all the workers understood the differences between the new form and the old one. However, the factory manager asked where the old forms had gone and none of the workshop managers seemed to have an exact answer. The factory manager then advised that the old forms had to be collected and destroyed to avoid workers confusing the two forms.

We are very keen to encourage the employees, especially the managers, to develop job "depth" and job "breadth". However, our managers sometimes treat jobs as separated. This is why many of the managers here cannot foresee problems. (Chairman, SF-B Co., Japanese, 46, male)

Again, we see that the transfer of parent company management practices was restricted to some artefacts, such as the parent company's production documents, physical facilities and articulated management techniques. The company dormitory and canteen had a limited effect on developing an egalitarian working atmosphere or building commitment among the local employees. Rather, these features helped exert some control over the employees in a highly mobile labour market and drove the need for frequent overtime. These results are quite similar to research findings obtained from other foreign-invested companies in China (Pun and Smith, 2007). Since many of the "artefacts" aspects of the parent company practices were enforced rather than emerging from the company, the notion of shared values embodied in these practices seemed to have gone missing in SF-B Co. These "artefacts" were either indoctrinated among the employees as canons to enhance production efficiency and reduce cost or applied as convenient measures to exert control over employees.

6.3.3 Formalized integration: local managers in the global HR strategy

What distinguished SF-B Co. from other Japanese subsidiaries was that their "pay-for-job grade" system was linked to that of the parent company. For employees at lower levels, the scale was merely a wage scale and had little to do with job security or career development. This was because the employment contracts were on a short-term basis and job rotation rarely occurred in the organization. Senior managers were integrated into the "core employee" group, the assessment of whom was then separated from the local HR system. This policy seemed to be an extension of the parent company's core–periphery division, except that in SF-B Co.'s case, this division was not based on gender, form of employment or nationality as in Japan (Koike, 2000), but was more based on the employee's position in the career hierarchy. This policy was aimed at integrating more locally recruited managers into the corporation's international management cadre. It had been made clear to the employees where they were placed within the corporate hierarchy. By expanding promotion opportunities beyond the realm of SF-B Co., the new policy extended the scope of senior managers' career prospects. In fact, SF-B Co.'s sister plant recruited managers from Malaysia and Thailand, which served as an example of international promotion. The parent influence on HR management practice was restricted to the senior management level. SF-B Co. seemed to rely on these local managers' expertise and their familiarity with both countries' institutions. This facilitated the development of specialized and diversified products to suit the Chinese market.

We have a wide range of products and the R&D centres follow the product lines. The location choice is aimed at exerting local advantages. For example, our Shanghai (R&D) centre is small, but it has close cooperation with the local universities, which extends our innovative capacity. The ones at the factory site are more efficient in turning new products to large-scale production. (Head of Shanghai R&D centre, SF-B Co., Chinese, 41, male)

As such, the HR practices employed showed more signs of strategic planning and had long-term implications for building a local management team.

Recruitment and selection

Fresh graduates remained an important source of new recruits. Every year, the Chinese holding company centralized advertising in universities and selection of the candidates. SF-B Co. looked for more experienced individuals when recruiting engineers and managers, who were sourced from various channels, including local employment agencies and job centres as well as some personal recommendations. This differed from the parent company's practice, which generally encouraged recruitment of "generalists" who would gain production and management knowledge in-house. In SF-B Co., line managers, supervisors and departmental managers had more diverse backgrounds. Some were promoted internally and some were directly recruited to their current position, such as the head of the administrative department. Senior managers, however, were generally recruited from internal sources. The Chinese holding company coordinated expatriation of subsidiary managers and the Chinese managers at board of directors' level were all expatriates from the Chinese holding companies at the time of the research. Japanese managers were expatriated from the Japanese headquarters.

The HR division of SF-B Co. only retained partial control over employee selection. Given the high turnover of the local workforce, SF-B Co. did not conduct systematic screening in the selection process. For university graduates, screening was generally done at the Chinese holding company and SF-B Co. retained responsibility for hosting formal interviews. Most production managers, quality control and inventory control managers were internally promoted because of the need for more company-specific knowledge and skills. Some had experience of working in the parent plants and all had visited the parent plants for observation and to learn factory operations. More mid-career managers were recruited for positions in the administration, sales and accounting departments. There relevant local knowledge was considered the most important selection criterion. This made a sharp contrast to the parent company, where more technical managers were sourced externally.

Training and development

On-the-job training was cited as the most important way employees gained and developed work knowledge. However, the scope and depth of job development an employee could gain through job rotation was related to the level of their position. Workers were normally put to work after elementary orientation at the factories and gained most training "on-the-job". A senior member would be assigned to train the newly recruited workers in basic skills. Job rotation was cited as an important training practice in the parent company but this was only selectively applied in SF-B Co. due to the high level of labour turnover. Workers, in general, would have the chance to work on different tasks. Nevertheless, most tasks were standardized and routinized, and therefore required limited skills. Employees who had stayed with the company for about ten years would not be able to develop broad and specialized skills, unless they struggled to move up the career ladder. Managers explained that high turnover was what made deepening work knowledge "impractical" and tasks had to be foolproof so that production would progress as scheduled. Managers at the junior level would have a chance to work in different functions but it was very unlikely that these junior managers would be transferred across factories, each of which was treated as a basic manufacturing unit. Senior managers would have the chance to be transferred within the corporate network for training purposes, depending on their willingness, their adaptability and their seniors' recommendation. In theory, senior managers at SF-B Co. could be expatriated to other subsidiaries for training, but none of the local managers of SF-B Co. had been selected for this type of training at the time of the research.

Management training also took the form of on-the-job training. The head of each department led a team of managers who worked as understudies for their seniors before being assigned to a managerial position. Internship at the parent company was another important form of on-the-job training adopted by SF-B Co. Unlike SF-A Co., which used training at the parent plants as a reward for loyalty, training programmes in SF-B Co. seemed to be linked to retention policies more directly. The employees selected to attend long-term training programmes in the parent plants were generally in the early stages of their career and they were supposed to sign a long-term contract of five to seven years instead of the one-year contract typical of most of the employees. Economic control was also exerted. An accumulative deposit served as a guarantee of return. Salary was not paid in full while the employees attended internship in the parent company. The unpaid salary was saved in the employee's account and served as a deposit, which would be refunded incrementally until the contract ended. On-the-job training combined with economic control became a management practice to control employees, a practice commonly observed in the local context. As explained by the HR manager, the possibility of resignation was negatively related to the tenure of the employees. The practice thus helped create an internal pool of candidates, which allowed SF-B Co. to enforce an internally based promotion policy at the senior management level.

SF-B Co. also offered a financial subsidy to senior local managers in order to encourage them to gain professional training through professional training bodies. While the parent company had a policy of recommending potential employees to attend MBA courses, SF-B Co. did not make the reward policy clear concerning those employees seeking an MBA degree by themselves. Employees' basic salary contained an "occupational stipend", which was linked to the technical and professional certificates commonly recognized by the local Labour Bureau. Employees got a rise when they gained a master's degree but the company seldom refunded the tuition fees. In terms of internal training, the Chinese holding company started to organize centralized training for local managers. Courses were generally short-term (ranging from a day to a week), in which parent company staff or external training bodies were invited to give seminars.

Reward and appraisal

Most similarities between SF-B Co. and the parent companies were found in the appraisal procedure. For employees, the pay-for-job grade system was a device that adopted the parent plant's system as a template.

This pay-for-job grade system was used to decide the wage level of the employee and provided an important basis for the understanding of the appraisal system in SF-B Co. Local employees were placed in different job ranks and separate appraisal procedures were adopted. SF-B Co. had two parallel career advancement routes: a technical route and a business route. The "accumulative point scale" was used to assess employee performance. Points were given to a range of skills required for a particular job stage and job rank. When the employees achieved satisfactory points for the skills, they were ready to move up a stage/rank. To be a member of the company's global management team, the local manager had to be promoted to positions at "Rank C", and this meant the manager had to be promoted to a position equivalent to deputy general manager (Table 6.1).

Applying a "pay-for-job grade" similar to the parent company created some sense of unity. However, this pay scheme did not necessarily entail seniority-based career advancement, which used to be a dominant factor in the parent company appraisal system. In fact, serious disagreement arose concerning the leverage of seniority in assessment criteria. As noted earlier, local managers seemed to be very critical about seniority as it "causes inefficiency as in the old SOEs" and tended to support a "merit/competence-oriented" assessment. The expatriate managers did not seem to agree with the local managers' judgement of the role that seniority could play. They tended to suggest that giving more priority to seniority would help reduce conflicts generated by wage differences.

Table 6.1 *Pay-for-job grade in SF-B Co.*

Rank C	Stage 7	Board of Directors	
	Stage 6	General Manager	
		Deputy General Managers and equivalents	
Rank D	Stage 5	Divisional Managers and equivalents	
	Stage 4	Deputy Divisional Managers and equivalents	
		Departmental Managers and equivalents	
		Deputy Departmental Managers and equivalents	
Rank E	Stage 3	General Skill 6	Specialized Skill 6
		General Skill 5	Specialized Skill 5
	Stage 2	General Skill 4	Specialized Skill 4
		General Skill 3	Specialized Skill 3
	Stage 1	General Skill 2	Specialized Skill 2
		General Skill 1	Specialized Skill 1

Source: Abstracted from FIBRE Co. company documents, 2007.

No appraisal criteria could be completely objective and merit based. The company requires the employees to be categorized into four scales. But how can you justify that people who performed well but were slightly below the top category and the ones who performed a bit better than the worst ones should be in one category. Let alone that the jobs themselves are different. (HR Manager, SF-B Co. Chinese headquarters, Japanese, 48, male)

The expatriates' perception of local employees also made them persistent about showing the value of "seniority". The head of the HR department in the Chinese holding company explained it as: "Chinese people say they want to be assessed by ability but believe in seniority at heart." As a result, seniority remained a key assessment criterion while the gap between merit and seniority had slightly increased.

The performance assessment procedure was standardized and adopted by all Chinese subsidiaries. Appraisal meetings were held three times a year (beginning, middle, end of year) and all managers were supposed to present their performance reports to the senior management team that provided improvement suggestions and advice on the managers' action plans. By the end of the year, individual department managers' self-assessment was reviewed by the senior managers and the final assessment was reported to the general manager for approval.

A face-to-face consultation meeting was then held, in which individual managers would have a chance to discuss their performance with their direct senior managers. The HR division in SF-B Co. generally stepped aside from this process, which again reflected the company's reorientation to centralize more strategic HR functions in the Chinese holding company.

Retention and exit

SF-B Co. had an annual labour turnover of 34 per cent, and thus I assumed that having a retention policy would be a critical issue for the company. However, apart from some of the economic and personnel control measures mentioned earlier, the company did not seem to have employed measures specifically aimed at retaining employees. SF-B Co. had never conducted an exit interview to understand the reasons for leaving. The recruitment policy, extended career development opportunities, incremental wage rises and benefits were claimed to be "good enough" to attract local employees. The senior managers' assumption that employees only left because of better pay was not always the case. Among the mid-level managers, the most important factor that seemed to encourage them to leave the company was difficulty in expressing ideas and lack of support from the seniors to coordinate across different functions. In other words, an absence of voice. While the managers explained that having retention measures was aimed at screening out individuals who were "not suitable" for the job or the company, they also admitted that the company had lost several "very talented" managers in the process. We need to note here that since the Chinese holding company had centralized some HR functions, SF-B Co. had very few resources to develop subsidiary-specific HR policies and practices. The HR function in SF-B Co. was partially paralysed due to budget cuts and lack of HR specialists. The headquarters HR strategy of retaining senior managers might not have much effect on reducing the turnover among subsidiary managers. This was because only the very top layer of local managers was integrated into the headquarters HR system. This group of managers tended to be less mobile. In fact, senior managers often explained that it was very difficult for them to seek external promotion opportunities because their work knowledge was mainly gained internally. At the same time, centralizing HR planning in the Chinese holding company further limited SF-B Co.'s ability to resolve the most critical HR issue encountered – high turnover among the mid-level managers and shop-floor supervisors.

6.3.4 Case summary

The restructuring of the corporate business strategy and HR strategy in China reflected the financial pressures the company was facing. Localizing the subsidiary management team therefore is better understood in the context of cost-reduction management. On one hand, the headquarters recalled a number of expatriates in SF-B Co. The board of directors had seven members, including four Japanese expatriates and three Chinese managers. At the managerial level, many expatriates were called back to the headquarters. However, this did not necessarily mean that local managers were promoted to all senior managerial positions to fill the vacancies. Several local managers were promoted but a number of positions remained vacant, which the HR manager explained was because "no capable personnel were available". Almost all senior managers were appointed to multiple positions, supported by several assistant managers, who were expected to be promoted in the near future. These measures helped to reduce some direct personnel costs as well as motivating the local managers by clarifying their career advancement route. On the other hand, SF-B Co. also sought to lower the HR costs by outsourcing some HR functions such as using local job centres and employment agents to recruit workers. The HR practices towards local workers thus showed more similarities to local practices.

The subsidiary had gained bounded autonomy, which meant management control of the local workforce was largely delegated to the local managers and strategic HR planning remained centralized in the Chinese holding company. Compared to SF-A Co., expatriates in SF-B Co. were much less involved in subsidiary HR policy formation. The HR function within SF-B Co., however, had not become more strategic. Due to rising production costs and appreciation of the renminbi, the corporate strategy of rapidly expanding the Chinese production base to serve the international market did not achieve its sales and profit goals. Having reviewed the global business structure, the headquarters shifted its focus to compete through economies of scale and reinforcing the new production development capacity of the Chinese production base. The corporate HR strategy was redirected towards facilitating the coordination and integration required by the business strategy. For SF-B Co., however, the implication of the corporate strategy was that they had very limited power to change the management style, which was considered to be critical to the turnover problem SF-B Co. had been experiencing.

6.4 Key learning points

This chapter has compared two companies in the capital-intensive sector. Despite the hypothesis that more intensive transfer would be observed in this sector leading to more similarity in subsidiary HR policies and practices, the findings indicated that the two companies showed substantial differences in terms of local business strategy, employment relations, and the way that local managers were integrated into the management team. Some similarities were also observed. For example, the subsidiaries shared some key features of production arrangements, which was a sign of strong parent control. This observation was not surprising given that both subsidiaries carried out standardized and routinized production. After seeing the rapid expansion of the local synthetic fibre market and competition from local fibre manufacturers, both companies conducted major restructuring of their Chinese business networks and aimed to consolidate a regional strategy. The focus on "enhancing product quality and shortening delivery time" had an impact on both the nature of production and quality control, which in turn justified the technical advantage of the parent management practices. This explained why I observed increasing parent control over various subsidiary-level issues, including subsidiary HR practice development.

Tensions between the headquarters and subsidiaries put pressure on management to implement a more regionalized HR strategy. I thus observed both intended and unintended consequences. In terms of intended consequences, HR restructuring in SF-A Co. enlarged the pool of managerial candidates. For SF-B Co., the locals started to see an extended career progression route, which motivated some employees. However, the unintended consequences were equally, if not more, critical to both subsidiaries. In SF-A Co., many experienced managers chose to leave as the new HR policies increased uncertainty and the difficulty of internal career advancement. Conflicts between existing managers and managers recruited under the "managerial trainee programme" also caused serious workshop conflicts, which led to the suspension of this programme in 2007. The "localization strategy" did not achieve the goal of developing a competent, committed and internally trained management team. In SF-B Co.'s case, the company's strategic orientation increased the financial pressures facing the subsidiary. Headquarters shifted to enhance the new production development capacity of the Chinese business group. SF-B Co. went through a major HR revision to enhance the efficiency of the local HR functions. To the individual subsidiary, however, headquarters' localization strategy meant losing some HR control to the Chinese holding company, which further limited the HR division's capacity to develop HR policies and practices to resolve subsidiary-specific HR issues such as high turnover among experienced workers and mid-level managers.

These findings reconfirm the significance of subsidiary moderation of both environmental and corporate-level forces in shaping the HR practices adopted, which I observed in the household white goods sector in Chapter 5. Subsidiaries have cultivated different interpretations of a localization strategy. For SF-A Co., localization meant that local managers should be able to replace the expatriates to realize parent control whereas for SF-B Co., localization meant integrating a limited number of locals who survived in long-term, on-the-job selection. I cannot deny that the overall corporate strategy, the locality and the subsidiary's role in the corporate and local business networks have affected how its localization strategy was interpreted in the respective subsidiaries. But more importantly, the process through which the localization strategy was translated into subsidiary HR practices was contested and subsidiary managers mediated the consequences and effects of such strategy. These points will be further developed in the following chapter.

7 | *Management learning, strategic repositioning and power struggles: dynamics in developing subsidiary HRM*

The previous chapters show that subsidiaries are complex sites of HRM development. HR practices reveal some significant differences in the four companies despite the general HR strategy of "localizing subsidiary management". In this chapter, I will discuss what accounts for such differences by focusing on the dynamics in subsidiary HRM development. As discussed in Chapter 2, pressure of parent company dominance, host-country institutions, influence of best practices, industry sector and production norms all cast constraints on subsidiary managers' choices. However, global and local constraints do not rule out strategic choice at subsidiary level (Geppert et al., 2003; Kristensen and Zeitlin, 2005; Edwards et al., 2010; Ferner et al., 2012). In this chapter, the primary objective is to define the trajectory of subsidiary managers' actions in developing subsidiary HR practices. I focus on the competing pressures facing subsidiary management teams, the actions taken by the managers and consequent HR practices at each of the subsidiaries. I will compare and contrast the four cases and summarize similarities and differences in terms of the power struggles experienced by the management team, the construction of subsidiary strategic choice and the learning cycles of subsidiary HR practice development.

Synthesis across the cases will reveal the patterns of interaction among the subsidiary managers, whose active and bounded choices moderate the institutional, structural and corporate pressures faced by subsidiaries. The focus here is the complex process through which corporate HR strategies were implemented, subsidiary HR policies were formed and HR practices were institutionalized. To gain a comprehensive picture of how different HRM practices emerge, I decided to link institutional, structural and corporate pressures with the management process. Through analysing the actions and choices of subsidiary managers, country context and industrial sectors were connected with workplace realities. I argue that institutional, structural and corporate pressures do not merely set the scene or leave a space. Rather, these pressures are manipulated to endorse managers' fight for power within the MNCs. These pressures give rise to subsidiary initiatives to reposition subsidiary functions in the face of corporate strategic reorientation. Also, these pressures embrace the management resources and knowledge base that managers tap into in order to develop management practices.

My analysis in this chapter will address several debates within the existing research on managing HR in MNCs in China. The first debate lies in how (or whether) management transfer occurs from an advanced economy (Japan) to a less advanced economy (China). Discussion will draw on previous research conducted by Campbell (1994) and Hong et al. (2006) (who suggest a progressive track of management transfer from the parent plants to the subsidiaries), and Taylor (1999, 2001), Gamble et al. (2004) and Morris et al. (2009) (who argue that management transfer is not happening). The results suggest that the subsidiaries are neither in the process of converging to an ideal type of parent practice, nor are they becoming programmatic assemblers characterized by high turnover, job simplification and cost reduction. Instead, continuous differentiation in subsidiary HR practices is the outcome of a dynamic process, in which *transfer* (adopting existing management practices employed by the parent company), *adaptation* (taking on local management practices), *localization* (replacing transferred parent practices with local practices) and *re-Japanization* (replacing local practices with parent practices) operate in parallel. Differentiation will persist and new forms of management practices emerge during this process, although the sample cases are "reproductive" subsidiaries rather than "learning" subsidiaries in Fruin's sense (1992). The political struggle among the subsidiary management team often shapes how HR practices are institutionalized in the individual subsidiary context.

Second, the research findings extend the mainstream strategic IHRM approach grounded in contingency theory. I assessed the strategic IHRM approach by focusing on the "localization" strategy adopted by many MNCs in China. While some authors argue that an expatriate-centred staffing strategy has a negative impact on the morale of the local managers (Legewie, 2002; Yoshihara, 2004), critical factors, such as the lack of well-trained local managers, are also found to be practical obstacles for subsidiaries in integrating more locals into the senior management team, particularly in China (Gamble, 2000). However, these arguments speak from the headquarters' perspective. This study offers a critique of the headquarters-centred research design by showing subsidiary HRM outcomes when the headquarters takes action to localize subsidiary management. The findings suggest that headquarters' localization strategy developed on the basis of the "best fit" rationale has varied effects on subsidiary management. Subsidiary managers often see strategic reorientation at the headquarters as an opportunity to reposition the subsidiary in the corporate networks. The strategic "best fit" in the parent companies' sense does not always reconcile with the "best fit" from the subsidiary managers' point of view. Consequently, subsidiary managers often moderate the impact of corporate HRM strategies in order to advance subsidiary interests in corporate strategic redirection and restructuring.

Finally, the research results question the prevailing assumption that a larger number of expatriates inevitably indicates stronger parent influence in developing subsidiary HRM. The subsidiaries in my study were not very different in terms of the number of expatriates. More importantly, the subsidiaries selected for this study shared important structural features such as their size, age, international experience, internationalization strategies, home country and subsidiary locations. Even so, significant differentiation in subsidiaries' HRM was observed. The research results revealed a variety of expatriate assignment purposes, ranging from strategic planning of management development to management training for junior expatriates. Diversity in the roles played by local managers was also found to be relevant to different HR policies and practices developed at the subsidiaries. I therefore argue that researchers need to bring in context-based analysis to reflect the different expatriate assignment purposes, background and experiences of subsidiary managers as well as the social dynamics involved in developing subsidiary HRM.

The chapter is organized in the following way. The following section discusses how management learning, strategy enactment and the power struggle among the managers shape HR policy and practice development at subsidiary level. Unlike some previous studies suggesting that companies may adopt a "close hybrid" or "open hybrid" pattern of adaptation (Beechler et al., 1998), I found that development of local HR policies followed different tracks, and differentiation of subsidiary management practices persists. I then move on to consider how the subsidiary management team moderates institutional, structural and corporate-level forces in order to shape subsidiary HRM. The chapter concludes by considering the significance of the research findings for addressing the debates within the existing literature on managing MNCs in China from an HRM perspective.

7.1 Management learning

7.1.1 Cognitive learning: constitution of subsidiary knowledge through members of the subsidiary management team

The constitution of management knowledge is largely affected by the composition of the subsidiary management team. Previous empirical studies on the composition of subsidiary management teams mainly focused on the number and proportion of expatriate managers. Given the role of expatriate managers in linking parent companies and subsidiaries, the number of expatriates is argued to be positively related to parent control and transfer of parent practices. While the variables of number and proportion of expatriate managers are easy to access, this study found that they do not provide sufficient support or explanation of differentiation of the subsidiary HRM. Table 7.1 shows the key configuration of expatriate managers in the four sample subsidiaries.

All four subsidiaries had greatly reduced their expatriate numbers during the first five years after incorporation. They had also expanded the scale of the subsidiaries. More local managers were recruited to replace the vacancies left by departed expatriates. As a result, the proportion of expatriates went down significantly and at the time of research all four subsidiaries had a proportion no higher than 1 per cent, which was below the average level of Japanese-invested companies in China (1.12%, calculated by the author based on Toyo Keizai Data Bank, 2007). This result reflects the general "localization" policy as promoted by these companies. In terms of the ratio of expatriates to local managers, three of the subsidiaries maintained about one-third expatriate managers in the management team. The only exception was SF-B Co., which had reduced the expatriate managers to occupying one-sixth of the managerial positions. However, the presence of expatriate managers did not seem to guarantee that

Table 7.1 *Expatriate managers in the subsidiaries*

Company name	WG-A Co.	WG-B Co.	SF-A Co.	SF-B Co.
Number	8	10	8	6
Expatriates/local employees	1.0%	0.8%	0.7%	0.4%
Expatriates/local managers	33%	31%	32%	17%
Distribution (number of departments led by expatriates)	4	12	10	6
Average cumulative tenure (years)	3.35	4.5	4.15	3.25

subsidiary HR policies and practices would be consistent with those of the parent companies. What was observed was that a higher proportion of expatriate managers made WG-A Co. highly localized in terms of deviation from the Japanese parent company's HR model, whereas SF-A Co. shared significant similarities with their Japanese parent company. To further understand the constitution of management knowledge, I considered the *accumulative tenure* of expatriates (i.e. the length of expatriate assignments at subsidiaries), the *frequency of flexpatriates* (i.e. the number and form of short-term expatriate missions dispatched by the parent companies) and *management embeddedness* (i.e. the knowledge and experiences of the members of subsidiary management teams).

Accumulative tenure of expatriates

Expatriates' length of service is critical to the flow of knowledge between parent companies and the subsidiaries (Tsai and Ghoshal, 1998). Here, I use the accumulative tenure of expatriates, which is an important indicator of whether there exists a dedicated core managerial cadre at the subsidiaries. I found that the Japanese parent companies had differentiated policies in terms of dispatching expatriates to the same subsidiaries. In WG-A Co., Japanese expatriate managers generally worked for three years. It was very unlikely for one expatriate to be assigned to the same country more than once. As discussed in Chapter 5, WG-A Co.'s Japanese parent company intended to increase

its influence by integrating Chinese managers into training in Japan and
repatriating them to the subsidiaries on a long-term basis to gain the
advantage of managers with knowledge of both countries. However,
this also increased the HR cost and the company had to take the risk
of repatriates "going native". This Chinese expatriate explained that
learning and implementation of the parent company practice was not
an easy task due to the contextual differences of the workforce in the
home and host countries:

The thing is Chinese and Japanese think in very different ways. The Japanese
managers are more engaged in their workgroup. I have asked why they follow all the procedures so rigidly. Their responses were like "It will bring
trouble to people around if I don't do so". But when the Chinese are asked
why the procedures are not followed, they are more likely to say that "I will
be all right". It is very hard to generate voluntary participation in a country
with such different group orientations. (Department of Management, WG-A
Co., Chinese, 33, female)

The repatriates may "go native" due to their background and being
away from the parent companies for long periods. This explains why
repatriation has not been promulgated widely among WG-A Co.'s sister plants and expatriation remains the mainstream HR policy.

Accumulative tenure of expatriates in WG-B Co. is slightly longer.
Expatriates in WG-B Co. generally stay for two to four years.
However, as at WG-A Co., the chances of an expatriate manager
being assigned to the same country or the same subsidiary were very
low, though some of the expatriate managers were mainly assigned
to international missions during their career. In SF-B Co., most of
the expatriate managers were assigned to their post on a three-
year basis, though in some exceptional cases, expatriate managers
had worked in the subsidiary for more than ten years and moved
to the Chinese headquarters. The cumulative tenure of expatriate
managers in SF-A Co. was longer. The company had settled the tenure of expatriates at five years for the general managers and three
years for the other expatriates. Many of the expatriates had been
repeatedly expatriated to China, and some even to the same subsidiary. Some younger expatriates had progressed their career mainly
in China, which meant they moved between the parent companies
and the Chinese subsidiaries every two to three years. At the same

time, there were also expatriate managers who were expatriated just before retirement and they were normally assigned production management related roles. Accumulative tenure reflected the company's global HR strategy. In companies with a parent-company-centred HR strategy, expatriate managers were more likely to be dispatched on a regular basis and the parent influence was realized through repeated expatriation. Companies implementing a global HR policy, like SF-B Co., intend to develop a management team with diverse experience. Expatriate managers in one subsidiary were from different backgrounds and with different experience and assignments at the subsidiary.

Frequency of flexpatriates

The knowledge flow between the parent companies and subsidiaries was also facilitated by missions of flexpatriation. Frequency of flexpatriates therefore reflects the subsidiaries' reliance on the parent company for technological and managerial routines. This study found that all four subsidiaries followed a pattern of reliance on the parent company in terms of importing product models developed in the parent companies. However, the parent company seldom chose to increase the number of expatriates in production upgrading. Generally, parent company personnel would be dispatched to provide short-term support when the subsidiaries faced major production and product upgrades or encountered technical problems. In these missions, flexpatriates were also involved in providing training to the local managers, which facilitated the management transfer process on a short-term, continuous basis. Of the two electronics manufacturers, WG-A Co. had far less frequency of flexpatriates than WG-B Co. This mirrored the subsidiaries' doubts about the contribution of these short-term missions and resistance to the Japanese companies' involvement in subsidiary management.

The local managers are very unhappy with the parent company sending short-term expatriates here. Actually, our chief manager is strongly against accepting people from the parent company on short-term [assignments]. They cannot really help. They come here and pick on things. We've made it very clear to the parent company that our department will not accept any short-term expatriates from this year. (General Manager's Office clerk, WG-A Co., Chinese, 36, female)

WG-B Co. accepted flexpatriates on a regular basis. Not only were they dispatched when the subsidiary set up new production lines or introduced a new series of products, they also made regular visits to WG-B Co. to provide on-site advice. During their missions, flexpatriates facilitated learning of tacit knowledge for the local managers who learned while working as a team with the parent company personnel.

The synthetic fibre manufacturers generally maintained a lower level of flexpatriation. This was largely due to the longer life-cycle of their products and because the companies' production was based on mature technology that used to be adopted by the parent plants. Also, many of the textile companies' parent plants in Japan had been closed as a result of the downturn in the synthetic fibre industry there, and major production bases had been moved overseas. Expatriation had occurred on a long-term basis rather than through any short-term missions. In SF-A Co., inviting flexpatriates was considered an indispensable step when the subsidiaries were facing strategic change. For instance, SF-A Co.'s major HR reorientation was led by a group of flexpatriates running the project in several Chinese subsidiaries. SF-B Co. took a different approach. Expatriation was mainly on a long-term basis and the flexpatriates were occasionally dispatched to provide technical support. However, expatriates in the Chinese headquarters played similar roles to flexpatriates. They paid regular visits, attended management meetings and provided training to the local managers.

The make-up of expatriates helps to map out several important aspects of the parent–subsidiary relationship in the process of developing subsidiary HRM practices. In particular, cumulative tenure informs the longitudinal knowledge transfer between the parent companies and the subsidiaries. Frequency of flexpatriate usage is also an indicator of knowledge input from the parent company. The parent's influence was often realized by constantly checking on the management processes with different groups of managers dispatched to the subsidiaries on a short-term basis. However, the Chinese managers and the context in which they gain skills and knowledge are critical to management learning as well.

Management embeddedness

Subsidiary managers' knowledge, skills and past experiences shape their thinking and behaviour. Here, I use the term management embeddedness to refer to managerial knowledge, skill and experiences accumulated through internal and external sources. Two major types of embeddedness are assessed in this study: *internal embeddedness* and *external embeddedness*. Internal embeddedness stands for the corporate knowledge base which managers gain as they work with the company and through internal on-the-job and off-the-job training. External embeddedness, on the other hand, shows the extent to which managers develop their knowledge base from sources such as school and professional education or work experience in different companies. The extent of internal embeddedness and external embeddedness is an important precursor to the relative absorptive capacity (Lane and Lubatkin, 1998; Lane, 2001) of the subsidiaries, which helps to explain the trajectory differentiation observed in HR strategy implementation.

Management embeddedness constrains managers' efforts to translate certain HR policies into subsidiary HR practices. Companies with a more internally embedded management team show the ability and motivation to assimilate and apply parent company practices in the local context. Managers seem to perceive that the "internal fit" (Huselid, 1995) of the parent company HR repertoire contributes to a higher level of productivity and subsidiary managers endeavour to build subsidiary HR practices that fit with the existing HR practices. Subsidiary managers do not see parent HR practices as replicable in the subsidiary given the significant differences between China and Japan in terms of labour market conditions and composition of workforce. However, they try to articulate some abstract norms that they presume contribute to the parent plants' higher productivity, and attempt to develop HR practices that formalize these norms. Differentiation of subsidiary HR practices emerges as managers interpret existing HR practices.

SF-A Co. was a case where managers' internal embeddedness largely outweighed external embeddedness. The local managers were significantly younger than the expatriates. They developed their work knowledge in the parent company and within the subsidiary. Flexpatriates with professional HR knowledge were integrated on a project basis. As the local managers were not considered to have developed sufficient knowledge for top managerial positions, they were generally in supporting roles. The policy of "localization" here was interpreted as "learn and do the same". The managers also identified organizational factors that do not transfer, such as "employee loyalty" [*chushin*], "pride of craftsman" [*shokunin kishiki*] and "egalitarian community" [*shakai shugi*]. These were often verbalized as "notes of behaviour", which were displayed in appropriate places to remind the employees of the company's expectations. On the doors in the toilet, for instance, the note reads, "Be considerate to others. To avoid confusion and unnecessary waiting time, keep this door open when it is not occupied". Some of the expectations were visualized. They were reflected in the practice of managers getting used to taking photographs when "non-expected behaviours" were detected, showing the pictures in management meetings and displaying them in the places where it happened. A comparative photo would be hung next to it to remind employees of the expected behaviours. While many local managers understood that these measures were learned from the parent company, the expatriate managers commented that these were "not necessary" because "people are doing [things] in the expected ways by instinct". In addition, policy implementation was associated with close supervision over the process, scrutinizing the short-term effect and adjustment of policies to achieve the intended "prototype" of local HR practices.

Furthermore, internal embeddedness imposed restrictions on managers' motivation to utilize knowledge gained from external sources. Corporate-based knowledge was the key assessment criterion for promotion and, consequently, managers with overarching knowledge dominated the subsidiary management team. One of the local managers commented on the learning experience:

It is not that we don't know how other companies are managed. We attended several seminars and companies talk proudly about the effectiveness of an organic structure. The structure looks perfect for information sharing. But in practice, it will end up creating a big mess as the functions are overlapping with each other. (Senior Manager, HR Department, SF-A Co., Chinese, 35, male)

Local managers were observed to be more cooperative when the policy reflected existing management practice employed by the parent company or sister plants. Local management practices were integrated when they were perceived to be supportive of the intended HR practice.

In companies where there is a dyadic embeddedness (which means internal embeddedness and external embeddedness are parallel in the management team), subsidiary HR practice development does not start by prototyping what were considered as effective HR practices at the parent plants. Managers tend to take a more pragmatic approach, in which the internal HR repertoire and external HR portfolio are viewed as a repository for managers to refer to when developing subsidiary HR practices. Paralleled internal and external embeddedness stimulate managers to search for the "external fit" (Huselid, 1995) between certain HR practices and the goals they intend to achieve. Subsidiary HR practice differentiation emerges as the managers assess the relevance of existing HR practices.

SF-B Co. is an example of this type of dyadic embeddedness. The HR manager in SF-B Co.'s Chinese headquarters explained that the aim of the localization policy was to "put the capable person in the appropriate position". For managers at junior level, relevant knowledge and experience was considered most essential. The company provided training in the individual subsidiaries, and also encouraged managers to seek professional training through external institutions. Unlike SF-A Co., who chose to invite external training bodies to provide in-house training to the local managers, SF-B Co. took the approach of giving reimbursement to managers who gained professional certificates. As managers moved up the managerial ladder, the impact of corporate knowledge increased while professional knowledge remained part of the management knowledge base. The consequence of this pattern of HR practice development was that the subsidiary represented various practices that might fit in organizational and host-country contexts. This helped to explain the differentiation in HR practices applied to the local employees and local managers. Management of senior managers was centralized in the Chinese holding company to realize global coordination. By contrast, less control was observed in the local HR management as reflected in the practice of leaving local HRM to the local personnel managers who had the relevant knowledge and experience in managing the local workforce.

In addition, management embeddedness had the effect of reinforcing the current knowledge base, which drove continuous differentiation in management practices across companies. Different approaches were observed in HR policy redirection in the companies' retention schemes as part of the "localization" policy to promote local managers into the management team to replace expatriate managers. Both SF-A Co. and SF-B Co. decided to enlarge the pool of candidates by expanding the management team. The major difference lay in the measures adopted. SF-A Co. took the socialization approach by introducing a management trainee programme to speed up promotion; this was considered as the major "incompatibility" between the HR management adopted by the company and the more mobile labour market of China. Socialization allowed internal embeddedness within the management team to be reinforced so that the company could become a "miniature of the parent plant". SF-B Co., by contrast, expanded the local management team by conflating the job responsibilities of the managerial positions. The functions of the divisions and departments were further divided and new jobs were created. With more managers joining SF-B Co., HR practices concerning the local workforce became more diverse. SF-B Co. therefore developed more hybrid forms of HR practices than SF-A Co.

Findings in the household white goods sector confirmed those from the synthetic fibre industry. Embeddedness of managers' knowledge drove a trajectory of differentiation in subsidiary HR practice development. WG-A Co. and WG-B Co. both faced problems in enhancing the performance of the company in the early stages of operation in China. WG-A Co. displayed the characteristic of dyadic embeddedness. WG-A Co.'s local managers were more experienced, had long tenure, and many of them shared some experience working in the Chinese parent company, which had formed strong solidarity among them. More importantly, local managers earned management legitimacy by resolving subsidiary-specific issues in the local context. Faced with the problem of corruption among the local management team, the parent companies of WG-A Co. reached an agreement that the senior managers should be more experienced and respectful in order to be able to lead the team. New general managers and deputy general managers were expatriated from the Japanese and Chinese parent companies, respectively, and had defined responsibilities on the basis of the expertise of the managers from different sides. This endorsed the distribution of the managerial roles as they currently were. It also created the basis of competing management repertoires rooted in the Japanese parent company and Chinese parent company, which characterized both the HR practices and the policy implementation process in WG-A Co. In contrast, WG-B Co. was a more internally embedded subsidiary. A large proportion of local managers joined the company after graduation and developed their knowledge mainly through internal training and work experience at WG-B Co. To improve subsidiary financial performance, the managers sought resolutions from the Japanese parent company and the expatriate managers took the leading role in setting up an "efficient management system", which was largely on the basis of parent company HR practices. With the establishment of the Chinese headquarters, the Chinese parent company was gradually shunted to the periphery in subsidiary management. Managers from the Chinese parent company were either replaced by the graduates trained in WG-B Co. or the Japanese parent company or socialized by joining project committees or internal training programmes. The leverage of internal embeddedness hence rose over time.

There is no fixed and systemic "Chinese management model" given the transitional nature of the Chinese economy and the consequent transformation in the way the indigenous companies manage people. Rather, management with "Chinese characteristics" entailed the co-existence of contrasting management practices, and companies continuously learned practices from companies with different countries of origin operating in the locality (Warner, 2008). The findings of this study mirror these observations. Not only did the companies incorporate HR practices from different management systems, but subsidiaries constantly reviewed their HR management practices by referring to other companies' experiences, successful or disastrous. Learning was also achieved by competition between these companies. Most of the local managers interviewed showed good knowledge of major competitors' market orientation, general financial performance and HR practices. However, they were also very critical about adopting similar practices, either due to the distinctions between companies or confidence about their own management repertoire. These findings reflect the selective side of managers in developing subsidiary HR practices.

Management embeddedness reflects the learning cycle of policy implementation. Managers in the subsidiaries had different sources from which to learn, and corporate boundaries marked the main sources of learning. The management team used their experience and knowledge to interpret policies to be implemented and took different approaches when conducting implementation. The existing knowledge base of the management team was important in deciding what approach to take, which in turn affected the HR practices adopted by the subsidiaries. In general, more parent–subsidiary differentiation was observed in companies with higher levels of external embeddedness. The subsidiaries integrated a wide range of managers, and learning occurred as the managers experienced new things in their environment. Subsidiaries showed further differentiation in relation to the overall embeddedness of the managers in the knowledge base of parent companies and the host country.

7.1.2 Routine-based learning: partial transfer of parent company management practices

Production arrangements and transfer of manufacturing techniques
A major similarity shared by all four subsidiaries was having job design to support a standard production process, which was not surprising given the subsidiaries' role as regional production centres. The parent company practices were observed in all aspects of production, which was tightly controlled to meet the quality requirements and inspection procedures settled by the parent company. Table 7.2 summarizes the comparison between the parent companies and their subsidiaries in terms of job design.

Similarity in job design across subsidiaries reflects the dominance of Japanese production practice in less developed economies (Abo, 1994; Campbell, 1994). Parent companies' influence can be seen through subsidiaries' reliance on parent company production resources such as financial, technical, knowledge and sometimes personnel support. Since the Chinese subsidiaries employed less advanced production technology, managers seldom compared productivity to that of the parent plants. The rationale for adopting parent production processes, procedures and techniques was often related to the quality standards of products. However, what cannot be ignored is that cross-sector similarity is also a consequence of the internationally recognized ISO90001 standard, which all subsidiaries have to meet, irrespective of their business strategy in China. Some deviations from the parent production arrangements were also observed. For instance, stock control was much less rigorously implemented because the location choice not only gave the subsidiaries some leverage in securing relatively low-cost storage spaces but also allowed subsidiaries to rely on

Table 7.2 *Job design in the case subsidiaries*

Company name	WG-A Co.	WG-B Co.	SF-A Co.	SF-B Co.
Production prototype	Product blueprint Product modification procedures	Product blueprint Product profiles Design approval and modification procedures	Product qualification forms Product modification and notifications procedures	Product qualification forms Product modification and notification procedures
Production procedure	Standard unit time Standard daily production quota Semi-automated assembly lines Factory layout to allow product flow Spare parts and product stock records	Standard unit time Standard daily production quota Semi-automated assembly line Factory layout to allow product flow Spare parts and product stock records Long-term relationship with contracted suppliers	Carefully calculated production turnaround Semi-automated production lines Factory layout Stock records	Carefully calculated production turnaround Semi-automated production lines Sequence of production and factory layout Stock records
Production process	Production planning forms Operation manual Quality control booklet Technical instructions Machinery maintenance records	Production planning forms Operation manuals Quality control booklet Technical instructions Machinery maintenance records	Quality control manual Traceable production record Production manual Machinery maintenance records	Quality control manual Traceable production record Production manual Machinery maintenance records
Production techniques	Whiteboard Individual movement record Co-worker teams Regular management group meetings	Whiteboard Co-worker teams Morning gatherings and midday gatherings Production meetings Monthly management group meetings	Daily inspection tour Morning gatherings Whiteboard Daily quality meetings Monthly factory inspection tour Monthly managerial group meeting	Standard unit time Daily inspection tour Whiteboard Weekly quality control meetings

Source: Based on company documents and fieldwork notes.

production material and enabled them to outsource some spare parts internationally.

Besides production processes, procedures and techniques, some routines and ritual activities, which are generally interpreted as symbols of corporate identity to boost teamwork, were also observed in all four subsidiaries. For instance, all subsidiaries required employees to wear a company uniform and identity tags (name tags and number tags) at work. All subsidiaries offered a company canteen, in-house health centre and employee accommodation, although these facilities served different employee groups in different subsidiaries. The companies also arranged some social activities, such as *Bounenkai* (New Year party) and an annual company trip to encourage interaction among the employees outside work, similar to the parent companies. Most companies used routine meetings to encourage group communication and gather on-site suggestions from the employees, although the frequency of such meetings varied across subsidiaries.

Some scholars argue that transfer of such practices' "physical architecture" is an important measure to socialize the local employees and such transfer thus serves the purpose of replicating the corporate context in subsidiaries (Guan and Fan, 2003; Hong et al., 2006: 1043–5). However, from my observation, transfer of the symbolic rites, routines and management techniques did not necessarily indicate transfer of the meaning that these practices possessed in the parent company context. Rather, as some expatriates commented, parent practices often lost their original meanings and were given different interpretations in subsidiaries. One example is the so-called *kanpan* system, which is used to facilitate the production process and enhance productivity in the parent company. In the subsidiaries, however, the whiteboards were used to display some general guidelines, production plans, reminders of workshop accidents and, sometimes, movement of employees. It is unlikely that *kanpan* was being used as a sign of employee involvement in continuous improvement; it was more likely being used as a means of top-down control and indirect communication. As I will show below, changing the function of parent practice was commonly observed in the HR field in the subsidiaries.

HRM routines adopted at the subsidiaries

Subsidiaries incorporated some of the parent companies' HR practices to support production. While all of the subsidiaries employed a combination of home-country practices and local practices, as the previous literature on hybridization has described (see Elger and Smith, 2005: 71–80 for a review), the path by which each subsidiary reached its current HR practices varied. Some of the subsidiaries moved ahead of the parent companies in terms of taking on "new" management practices, whereas others adopted a more conservative position by following the parent company management repertoire. Table 7.3 lists the technical HR practices employed at each subsidiary.

If I put the subsidiaries on a spectrum in terms of Japanese parent dominance in the development of subsidiary HR practices, SF-A Co. would stand at one end, representing a subsidiary that shows strong similarity to the parent plants. Managers of SF-A Co. described current subsidiary management practices as a "miniature" of the parent plants and the parent-directed HR restructuring and "localization" had encountered less resistance from the local management team, who received professional training in the corporate headquarters and the parent plants. At the other end, WG-A Co. stands out as a subsidiary in which local managers take control of the HR management, and subsidiary HR practices show more local characteristics. HR policy concerning the local managers was largely based on a "reformed SOE" model and the Japanese parent company's influence was rather limited. The Japanese parent company's intention to transfer parent company management practice had encountered strong resistance from the local management team, including some instances of rejecting expatriates. The Japanese parent company took an eclectic approach to repatriating the local managers trained in the parent company to enhance parent company influence over subsidiary HR issues. SF-B Co. and WG-B Co. stand in between these two. The Chinese offices have centralized the HR planning functions, and subsidiary managers have less control over many HR issues such as the recruitment and training of potential managers. Still, HR practices differed between WG-B Co. and SF-B Co.: the former lagged behind HR reform back at the parent company and the latter had adopted some pilot HR practices that had not been exercised elsewhere in the corporate group. In WG-B Co., the expatriates controlled HR management and local managers played more supportive roles. In contrast, HRM of local employees had been largely delegated to the local managers in SF-B Co.

The subsidiaries show some similarities in their use of complicated pay-for-job grade systems and lacked sophisticated retention and

Table 7.3 *Technical HR practices employed by subsidiaries*

	WG-A Co.	WG-B Co.	SF-A Co.	SF-B Co.
Recruitment	Mainly mid-career managers and experienced workers University graduates for the "inpatriation-repatriation" programme	Mainly technical school, college and university graduates Experienced engineers	Almost all technical school and university graduates A limited number of workers and managers with experience	No clear preference for young graduates
Selection method	Mid-career managers: Agents' recommendation Interviews Experienced workers: Agents' recommendation University graduates for the "inpatriation-repatriation" programme: Bio-data screening Written test Interviews	Both young graduates and experienced employees: School recommendation Bio-data screening Written test Interviews Training centres	Technical school graduates: School recommendation University graduates: Bio-data screening Interviews	Experienced and non-experienced workers: Local job centres and agents' recommendations Young graduates and mid-career managers: Bio-data screening Written test Interviews

Key selection criteria	University graduates for the "inpatriation-repatriation" programme: Japanese proficiency General knowledge Mid-career managers: Relevant experience Flexibility to fit into the corporate culture	For both young graduates and experienced employees: Personality Adaptability to different working environment Relevant knowledge and skills Mid-career engineers: Knowledge and experience	Technical school and college graduates: No clear selection criteria are specified University graduates: Japanese proficiency Adaptability	University graduates: General knowledge Japanese or English proficiency Mid-career employees: Japanese or English proficiency Experience
Training and development	Not much training given to mid-career managers Young graduates joining the "inpatriation-repatriation" programme receive long-term on-the-job training in Japan	Training centres offering technical qualification training Basic training Mainly in-house on-the-job training Company funds selected managers to attend professional training programme	Japanese language training Progressive technical training Job rotation Japan consultant companies are invited to offer managerial training in the company (quasi-off-the-job training) Mid-term and long-term on-the-job training in parent plants Compensation to employee with professional certificates	Mainly on-the-job training The Chinese headquarters organize some short-term training Off-the-job training for the senior local managers Selected managers attend centralized training at the headquarters

Table 7.3 (*cont.*)

	WG-A Co.	WG-B Co.	SF-A Co.	SF-B Co.
Performance assessment and appraisal	Pay-for-job grade system tailored on basis of the Chinese state-owned parent company Merit-based assessment Paternalist, top-down assessment procedure with deputy general manager making all the decisions on regular employees' performance results	Pay-for-job grade system tailored on basis of the Japanese parent company Semi-annual performance assessment Assessment criteria are based on tenure, merits and performance Top-down assessment procedure with senior managers deciding subordinates' performance results	Pay-for-job grade system tailored on basis of the Japanese parent company Annual performance assessment Achieving performance targets are the main assessment criteria Top-down assessment procedure with senior managers deciding subordinates' performance results	Pay-for-job grade system linked to the Japanese parent company's system Semi-annual performance assessment Assessment based on tenure, merit and performance, though the leverage of tenure has been weakening Top-down assessment procedure with senior managers deciding subordinates' performance results
Retention	Monetary and other material rewards	Job security Internal promotion opportunities	Job security Training opportunities in the parent company Corporate-based knowledge structure	Global promotion opportunities
Dismissal	No specific dismissal policies	In-house transfer or demotion Tenure-based compensation	In-house transfer or demotion	In-house transfer or demotion

Source: Summarized from fieldwork notes.

dismissal policies. While these HR practices resembled those of the parent companies, we cannot simply take the practices as having been transferred. The institutionalization of the pay-for-job grade system in each subsidiary involved managers' interpretation of the local labour market conditions in the wider corporate context, negotiation for job-grade templates and reviews of the existing system. The subsidiary job grade reflected this kind of active construction. SF-A Co. cut down the numbers of job grades to shorten the career progression route for local employees and to reinforce management authority. SF-B Co. further expanded the job grades to allow more managerial positions as a means of retention and management development. WG-A Co. retained a modified Chinese state-owned job-grade system as a symbol of local management power. WG-B Co.'s job grades, in contrast, showed much similarity to their parent plants. Likewise, the lack of a retention and dismissal policy can be interpreted differently in each subsidiary. Given the high mobility of skilled workers, engineers and managers in the local labour market, the companies collectively experienced some difficulty in retaining these groups of employees. However, all subsidiaries seemed to lack the incentives to develop particular retention and dismissal policies. Only WG-B Co. adopted the parent scheme of offering tenure-based compensation for redundancy. The rationale for not having retention and dismissal policies was mixed. One problem was that the subsidiaries lacked development resources to adopt similar retention and dismissal policies to the Japanese parent company. They also lacked readily available legitimized or institutionalized local dismissal practices, which might have been referred to whenever the need arose. But more importantly, as some managers suggested, current retention and dismissal practices permitted flexibility in negotiation with the employees. Ambiguous dismissal policies gave the companies more leverage in controlling the local workforce.

As stated earlier, assessment of management transfer cannot be based solely on the comparison of similarities in parent and subsidiary HR policies and practices. Parent company practices often served different purposes in the subsidiary context (which will be referred to as *parent HR practice differentiation*). Subsidiaries also developed HR practices that conformed to the expectations of the local institutions as well as those subsidiary-specific practices that reflected the situational and long-term development track of the subsidiaries (which will be referred to as *subsidiary HR practice differentiation*). These types of differentiation characterize the development of subsidiary HR practices, which I will further elaborate in the following sections.

7.1.3 The social process of management learning: differentiation of HR practices

In addition to cross-subsidiary differences in HRM practices, I also found that subsidiary HR practices continuously changed their functions in the face of various organizational and environmental pressures. The first point needs to be highlighted as it represents the distinction between the personnel (or white-collar) management [*jinji*] and the labour (or blue-collar) management [*roudou*] in these subsidiaries. This reflects the level of subsidiary integration into the parent company's HR system. The distinctiveness of HR practices indicates that subsidiaries had varied definitions of the "management group" and implemented varied "localization" strategies. Figure 7.1 shows the distribution of employees in the four subsidiaries:

WG-A Co. distinguished between four groups to whom different HR policies were applied in the organization: the expatriate managers (including managers under the "inpatriation-repatriation" programme), the local managers, the long-term employees and the temporary employees. The management team referred to expatriated managers and local managers who were promoted to positions higher than departmental manager. WG-B Co. had three different sets of HR policies covering the expatriates (centralized to the Japanese parent company), local managers (centralized to the Chinese headquarters) and local employees (controlled by the subsidiary). WG-B Co. had a larger managerial base. Leaders of working groups, shifts, production lines and supervisors were all members of the managerial group. Employees of SF-A Co. were divided into four employment groups: the expatriates, the local managers, the local employees and the management trainees. SF-A Co.'s local management group included all employees in positions higher than departmental manager and the trainees on the managerial track. In SF-B Co., a line was drawn between senior managers (including expatriates and local managers) and local employees. The former were managed under parent HR policies and the latter were further divided into the managerial group and working group and they were managed by different HR policies and practices. Only board members and factory managers were considered part of the

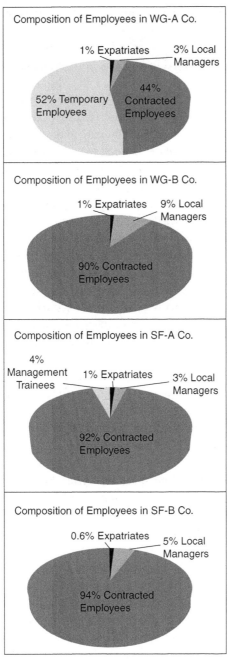

Figure 7.1 Distribution of employees with different HR policies applied

management team and many management decisions were made at the Chinese headquarters.

Applying different HR policies and practices among different employee groups is well documented in Japanese companies, particularly those in the electronics industry (Kenney et al., 1998). For the subsidiaries in this study, different HR practices created a distinction between the core and peripheral groups. While gender and social background were found to be important in the division between core and peripheral groups in the parent companies, subsidiaries divided the employees according to their position on the career ladder. In most of the subsidiaries, the workers formed a large majority, whereas junior and mid-level managers were at the periphery. Only 1 per cent of the employees were considered core. This core was carefully selected, offered better pay and welfare benefits and continuous training and job security as compensation for relatively limited promotion opportunities. The core group was much smaller compared with the Japanese parent plants, where employees under temporary contracts were considered periphery. For the rest of the employees, the subsidiaries normally offered a better starting salary than major competitors in the same sector. But salary increased slowly and salaries for middle-level managers were generally lower than the major competitors offered. Basic work orientation and training were provided to everybody but only selected employees were given intensive training opportunities. Job rotation was also limited for the majority of employees, though the skills range of the employees differed in the two sectors. The household white goods manufacturers performed more simplified and routinized production procedures compared with the synthetic fibre manufacturers.

From a strategic HRM perspective, a firm's HRM policies and practices are expected to develop its employees' knowledge, abilities and skills, to encourage employee involvement and teamwork, and to retain competent employees. In the end, all these will contribute towards the performance of the firm (Huselid et al., 1997). For the subsidiaries, the desirable outcomes of "localization" were to enhance employee morale and commitment, to encourage continuous quality improvement, and to develop and retain employees with desirable skills, abilities and the propensity to stay with the company for the long term. I summarize the parent HR practice differentiation and subsidiary HR practice differentiation in Table 7.4 to link the HR practices and their function in the subsidiaries.

Table 7.4 *Differentiation of the subsidiary HRM practices*

		WG-A Co.	WG-B Co.	SF-A Co.	SF-B Co.
Recruitment and selection	Subsidiary-specific				
	Local characteristics	Outsourced selection; unstructured interview; newly recruited managers are mainly from external sources	The youth training centre: selection method Japanese language proficiency as key selection criterion	Japanese language proficiency as key selection criterion	Recruitment of mid-career managers, experience in Japanese companies preferred; priority given to people with Japanese language proficiency
	Parent differentiation				
	Convergence with parent practices	Selection criteria for the repatriation candidates	Preference for young graduates; rigorous recruitment procedure; adaptability and general knowledge in recruitment selection criteria	Simplified selection procedure Preference for young graduates; general knowledge and adaptability as selection criteria	Selection procedure and key selection criteria

Table 7.4 (*cont.*)

		WG-A Co.	WG-B Co.	SF-A Co.	SF-B Co.
Training and development	Subsidiary-specific	Repatriated local managers	Internship		
	Local characteristics	Managerial training is seldom provided	Management trainee programme	Extensive language training; management trainee programme	Uses external consultant body for managerial training
	Parent differentiation			Off-the-job training at headquarters or parent plants	
	Convergence with parent practices			Job rotation	
Rewards and compensation	Subsidiary-specific	Company accommodation; pay-for-job grade			
	Local characteristics	Individual performance outcome-based bonus; 5+1 social insurance package	5+1 social insurance package	5+1 social insurance package	5+1 social insurance package
	Parent differentiation				
	Convergence with parent practices	Pay-for-job grade	Pay-for-job grade	Pay-for-job grade
Relative assessment criteria	Pay-for-job grade

Appraisal and promotion	Subsidiary-specific	Deputy general managers make HRM-related decisions		Extended responsibilities; current managers are in the same age range	Local expatriation
	Local characteristics	Appraisal largely based on individual performance	Individual presentation is adopted for performance assessment and promotion decisions	Shortened tenure requirements for promotion	
	Parent differentiation	MBO appraisal	Seniority-based appraisal	Performance appraisal at the end of March	Performance appraisal at the end of March
	Convergence with parent practices	Internal promotion	Mainly internal promotion; MBO appraisal	Distinctive labour and personnel systems; internal promotion; MBO appraisal	Internal promotion; increased leverage of merits; MBO appraisal
Retention and dismissal	Subsidiary-specific	Managers sign long-term contract with the company	Contract length 1–2 years; trainees in Japan need to sign long-term contract and local wages are retained by the company	Contract length 1–2 years	Contract length 1–2 years
	Local characteristics		Job rotation as dismissal measure	Job rotation as dismissal measure	Job rotation as dismissal measure
	Parent differentiation		Tenure-based compensation		
	Convergence with parent practices	Dismissal policy not specified		Dismissal policy not specified	Dismissal policy not specified

Source: Abstracted from fieldwork notes.

Cross-subsidiary and subsidiary–parent plants comparison results indicate that a "localization" strategy entailed different HR policies at each subsidiary. For the local managers in WG-A Co., the priority of localization was to gain further control over the R&D function. Tension arose as the Japanese parent company prioritized the enforcement of new management procedures, which technically weakened local managers' power over many HR issues. The Japanese parent company held onto several key positions and some junior managerial positions, which were assumed by managers under the "inpatriation-repatriation" programme. To WG-B Co. and SF-B Co., the Japanese parent companies' localization meant centralizing strategic HR at the Chinese headquarters. This led to constant negotiation and conflict between subsidiary managers and managers from the Chinese headquarters. For SF-A Co., however, localization was ideally expressed as "subsidiary adopts a full range of parent management practices", the feasibility of which was highly doubtful to most local managers.

Parent practice differentiation is particularly relevant to the long-term employment relationships which had been exercised in the parent companies over several decades. While some of these HR practices may have functioned as retention measures, they also served the purpose of exerting direct control over the local employees. For example, WG-A Co. was the only subsidiary that provided apartments to managers before they purchased their own property. This differed from the old SOE company accommodation in the sense that company housing was supposed to be a short-term, contract-based lease and the company was under no obligation to provide accommodation to all employees. Neither was this practice consistent with the parent company practice, where company accommodation was considered a form of compensation for young employees on low wages. Instead, dormitories not only helped retain local managers but also extended their working hours as they were generally expected to work voluntary (unpaid) overtime. The workers would leave the premises when the eight-hour work shift was over. The managers, by contrast, would normally stay longer and might be called back if something required urgent attention. In fact, WG-A Co. did not enforce any policy to persuade staff who had purchased their own apartment to move out of the company accommodation. This showed that company accommodation served the purpose of providing convenience to managers with additional after-work duties rather than compensation to the young low-paid employees. The managers' comments confirmed such differences between the parent company and the subsidiary practices.

We might be the only [Japanese] company in China having a company housing system like an old state-owned company... Our company dorms in Japan are for single employees and they are very small and they are 1 hour away by train. The employees will normally move out of the dorm after 2–3 years. But here, I don't think anyone would move unless they are forced to do so. (Manager in Accounting and General Management Department, WG-A Co., Chinese, 33, female)

Besides accommodation, some parent company management practices were also applied to control mobility and absenteeism. WG-A Co. used company mobile phones to keep a record of the movement of local managers.

The company will retain the list of calls of all the company mobile numbers. We sometimes detect that someone applied for sick leave and he/she used the mobile in other regions. The "sick leave" then won't be verified and the person will get a deduction. (Clerk in Administrative Department, WG-B Co., Chinese, female, 36)

SF-A Co. offered healthcare benefits with its in-house health centre, which centralized approval of sick leave.

We cannot get sick leave based on a doctor's diagnosis from the local hospitals or health centres. The diagnosis and days of leave have to be approved by the company healthcare centre. And normally, the days of leave will be half of what you normally get from the hospitals. (Management trainee, SF-A Co., Chinese, 27, female)

Again, these HR practices took the same form as those of the parent companies but involved different interpretation by management. In view of the difficulty in cultivating commitment in a local labour market with much higher mobility, direct control was presumed to be a viable alternative to the indirect control through forming a social relationship between employees and the company which was once celebrated in Japan.

7.2 Repositioning subsidiaries in the corporate networks

The dynamics in subsidiary HR development was also reflected in the enactment of corporate strategies. Subsidiary managers' capacity for influencing strategic planning at headquarters level has been documented in existing literature (Kristensen and Zeitlin, 2005; Edwards, Colling and Ferner, 2007). My focus here is the subsidiary level. Strategic reorientation of the parent companies often affects subsidiaries' relation to the parent company, sister subsidiaries, and the major suppliers and clients (see Figure 7.2).

The organizations-as-networks approach proposed that the functional position of a specific subsidiary reflects its resource reliance in the network, which will affect the way people are managed in the whole entity. While it is useful to take subsidiary role in consideration when assessing the development of subsidiary HR practices, I found this approach too passive for capturing the construction of subsidiary functions. Drawing upon global commodity-chain analysis (Gereffi, 1999), I considered how subsidiary HRM was shaped by the subsidiary's projected position in the stratification of production functions within the corporate networks. While parent companies influence subsidiaries' construction of internal and external networks, my findings suggest that subsidiary managers often seek to reposition the subsidiaries in the *technical networks*, *transactional networks* and *managerial networks* during the process of strategic reorientation. China's shift from a production base to a major consumer market has given rise to initiatives by subsidiary managers to upgrade the subsidiary's function, which often affected HR policy formation and differentiation of HR practices.

Technical networks refers to the structure of product development. I found that the position of the subsidiaries in their technical networks differed significantly. In the electronics sector, WG-A Co. was set up as an independent manufacturing plant and thus relied on the Japanese parent company mainly for product model upgrading. The subsidiary intended to increase its importance in the technical networks by gaining an R&D function, whereas the parent company endeavoured to exert more influence in subsidiary management. Both of these approaches have encountered strong resistance from the other side. WG-B Co., by contrast, internationalized on a group basis with some home-country suppliers following the plant to the local market.

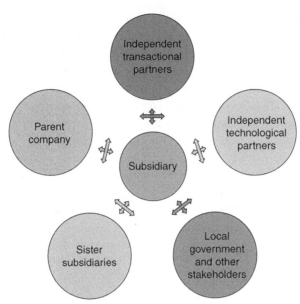

Figure 7.2 The embedded subsidiaries

Technical improvement was realized with a loose structure, and more coordination from a higher-level technological centre became necessary. The Chinese R&D centre was set up partly to play this role. Most of the local engineers in the technical networks were in a subordinate position and assisted the flexpatriate missions with technical projects. The synthetic fibre manufacturers showed similar patterns. SF-A Co.'s engineers and managers in the R&D department played a rather supportive role to expatriates in day-to-day management and to the technical experts dispatched to provide product development advice. SF-B Co.'s technical networks were more decentralized, with separate R&D centres associated with manufacturing plants. Coordination was mainly realized at the subsidiary level and local managers had gained more power. Also, more functions had been moved to the subsidiaries. The local managers and technical team led the local R&D centres and were responsible for day-to-day production management.

Transactional networks concern the competitive strategies of the subsidiaries. The difference between the household white goods manufacturing sector's local market-centred strategy and the synthetic fibre manufacturers' international market-oriented strategy does not adequately explain the subsidiary–parent company differentiation across subsidiaries. This further increased strategic differentiation between the companies. Both WG-A Co. and WG-B Co. had developed locally oriented transactional networks. WG-A Co. showed the least reliance on the parent company for business development in the local market. The transactional networks were mainly locally developed. Though the Japanese parent company intended to somehow centralize local sales by running a wholly owned trading house, business partners and transaction routes were generally diversified and mainly controlled by the local managers. The local managers were mainly from the Chinese parent companies, and thus the HR practices showed more significant similarities to the reformed SOEs than the Japanese parent company. WG-B Co., on the other hand, showed a strong reliance on the local network for business development and only a small proportion of sales (exports) were controlled by the parent company. The company aimed to compete with major rivals in the local market and decided to develop the Chinese market through the local government-related networks. The Japanese parent company launched the theme of "concentrate on government projects" instead of connecting business relations with the local distribution agents, such as large-scale superstores. The parent company had decided that their local strategy was to focus on developing close relations with the local government administrative bodies in order to extend their influence with property developers. They had also developed a cooperative relationship with the local government by providing training to young graduates in the corporate training centre. They responded to the call for "localization" by recruiting, developing and promoting local managers with in-depth local knowledge and networks to senior positions. Cooperative relations with local government helped WG-B Co. to secure a supply of new employees as well as to be selective about new recruitment, which was critical to replicating the parent company practice. At the same time, the government nominated WG-B Co. as a successful model of "advanced technological and managerial transfer" to the host country, which also helped the subsidiaries to integrate more managerial practices from the parent company. These findings show that engagement in the local networks can be used by managers to encourage the transfer of parent management practices.

Among the synthetic fibre manufacturers, the parent companies were more involved in subsidiaries' business transactions due to the nature of their export-centred business structure. This helped to explain why more parent–subsidiaries similarities were observed in this sector, but not a lot of differentiation was visible across subsidiaries. In SF-A Co., not only did the parent company control the supply of the production material, it also handled a major proportion of sales as well. The parent companies were heavily involved in transactions with their suppliers, clients and sister plants. One manager explained this type of parent company involvement when the subsidiary company was in a crisis condition.

One of our sister plants' storage warehouse caught fire years ago and all the materials were burned out. They had nowhere to source the material in time. They sought help from the parent company and we were requested to spare the material we had to them. (HR Manager, SF-A Co., Chinese, 35, male)

From this manager's point of view, the parent company exerted considerable control over the business process in SF-A Co. By so doing, the parent company extended its involvement in the quality cycle, supporting the control of production through documentation, standardization of equipment and personnel controls. The local managers had developed a cooperative attitude due to lack of external resources, which had further reduced subsidiary–parent company differentiation. SF-B Co., by contrast, had more local business controlled by the subsidiaries. Although the transaction networks were loosely centred on the Chinese headquarters, each subsidiary could be seen as a functional centre with extensive yet overlapping resources. With such extensive transaction networks, the companies at different levels of this network developed different degrees of reliance on the parent company resources. The variation in implementation of HR policies also depended on the position of the subsidiaries in the inter- and intra-corporate networks in which they were embedded.

Apart from the strategic differences between the companies in terms of the Chinese market strategy, I also found that the *managerial networks* helped to reveal the direct involvement of the parent company with HR policy implementation in the subsidiaries. A major structural difference between the sample companies was the parent company and the Chinese headquarters' involvement in the subsidiary HR management. In WG-A Co., where substantial subsidiary–parent company differentiation was observed, the Japanese parent company remained

quite remote from day-to-day HR management activities. Local managers were responsible for drawing up HR policies in the subsidiaries and decision-making was delegated to the local deputy general
manager with consent from the general manager. For WG-B Co. and
SF-B Co., the Chinese headquarters assumed a major strategic role
and acted as an administrative centre. Judging from the integration of
local managers, companies with a Chinese headquarters had clarified
the career development policies applied to the local managers and had
endorsed the HR practice of internal promotion to senior managerial positions. For WG-B Co., the Chinese headquarters assumed the
function of designing the overall HR policies and practices and were
involved in many aspects of management of subsidiaries. In SF-B Co.'s
case, most of the expatriates had been recalled to the Chinese headquarters and the business operation was largely left in the hands of
SF-B Co. The section controlled by the Chinese headquarters showed
more similarities to the parent companies than the section controlled
by the local managers. Finally, SF-A Co. showed the highest level of
similarity to the parent company HR practices. The parent company
personnel experts were directly involved in subsidiary HR management. Although the strategic importance of SF-A Co. had been dwin-
dling over the years, the subsidiary was very keen on developing HR
practices on the basis of the parent model. Personnel experts were
dispatched for both short-term and long-term expatriation. These personnel experts controlled the design and supervised the implementation of subsidiary HR management policies. The managerial networks
were thus centralized to the headquarters.

Observing that MNCs tend to keep the core functions in the home
country and relocate the peripheral functions overseas, some scholars
suggest the relationship between the parent plants and the overseas
subsidiaries reflects a core–periphery division of labour at international level (Dedoussis and Littler, 1994; Wilkinson et al., 2001).
But what are the core activities? And, if the markets shift and production needs to follow the markets, will the core activities be relocated as
well? What is observed here is that China has become more important
as a potential market as well as a low-cost production base. All four
companies were in the process of restructuring in order to effectively
coordinate technological upgrading, business expansion and managerial administration. One cannot deny that subsidiaries' functions
were directly influenced by their reliance on parent resources, their

strategic importance to the parent companies and the structure of corporate networks. All these are critical to subsidiary HRM. However, parent company dominance does not rule out subsidiary initiatives (Birkinshaw and Ridderstrale, 1999), especially when the MNCs are faced with major strategic reorientations. In my case studies, subsidiary managers constantly reassessed their functions in relation to the parent companies' changing China strategy. They also endeavoured to project their position in the new corporate networks. Subsidiary HR policies and practices were designed and developed in favour of the projected subsidiary functions.

7.3 Power struggles: control and resistance in developing local HR practices

The power struggle within the management team was most apparent from the distribution of expatriate managers. Here, I use *expatriate distribution* to refer to the functional divisions/departments that were led by the expatriate managers. *Expatriate distribution* reveals the level and forms of parent control, which thus leads to differentiation in HR policy implementation. WG-A Co., which was the subsidiary that implemented the fewest parent company HR practices, had the lowest level of expatriate distribution. Expatriate managers consisted of the general manager, the head of the accounting division, the head of the production division and the head of the quality control division. The other four expatriate managers worked in the accounting and the general manager's office, indicating that the Japanese parent company chose financial control over personnel control for this subsidiary. HR management of local managers was delegated to the deputy general managers and carried out by the HR department, led by a locally recruited manager. In SF-B Co., a moderate level of parent company HR practices was observed, and four expatriates were leading six departments. This left the HR and sales divisions in the hands of local managers. The HR division was responsible for HR management of the local managers, but the Chinese headquarters drafted and disseminated general guidelines, and an expatriate from the HR division of the Japanese parent company was assigned as the head of the Chinese HR division. Expatriates in the Chinese headquarters exerted considerable influence on the HR process, which was an important device for realizing parent control. In WG-B Co.'s case, expatriate managers were

found in both top managerial positions and some subordinate positions. The Chinese headquarters also played a central role in recruiting
young managers but their influence in deciding subsidiary HR policies
was comparatively limited. Last but not least, SF-A Co.'s HR practices
most closely resembled those of the Japanese parent. The expatriates
there were more widely distributed and control extended to all of the
functional divisions. For WG-B Co. and SF-A Co., the Japanese parent companies tended to exert their influence through personnel control, as suggested by other empirical studies of management control in
Japanese MNCs (Harzing, 1999).

Apart from the functional division between expatriates and local
managers, I also investigated the resources that subsidiary managers
deployed to influence HR policy formation and development of management practices. Formation of HR policies and development of
subsidiary HR practices was never a straightforward process. The
expatriate managers and local managers were involved in evaluating,
negotiating, applying and reviewing the outcomes. HR policy is normally an abstract principle and managers needed to decode the policy
with reference to the HR practices exercised in parent companies, host
country and possibly third countries.

Furthermore, the outlook of the managers extended beyond the
constraints of either the parent company or the host-country environment. A significant observation was the use of "third-country" practice
to resist the dominance of the parent company practices. As discussed
earlier, Chinese companies are in transition and there is no national
business system to generate management models as durable as those
in many other countries, especially Japan. The parent companies were
thus in a dominant position in terms of transferring management
expertise to the host country. Not only did the local managers' resistance to this parent company dominance come from the locality with
the institutional constraints, but they also strategically utilized management practices from other countries. More importantly, the presence
of third-country MNCs in the local area was significant and managers
gained knowledge about different management practices through both
formal channels, such as professional training, and informal channels,
such as the media and their social networks. An expatriate manager
from WG-B Co. thought that the local managers' perception of an
"American way" was the major cause of difficulty in implementing the
Japanese parent-company-based management practices.

Our local managers seem to believe that they are more individual oriented like the Americans. They want to be assessed based on the individual performance results. They want to take responsibility for their own work and not to get advice and suggestions from the senior member or their peers. I once asked one of our local managers what he will do if his plan failed? He went "I will resign". I laughed and said that was not what taking responsibility meant, neither in our company nor elsewhere, because leaving the company helps nothing with the loss to the company and everyone. (Sales Manager, WG-B Co., Japanese, 47, male)

In this sense, sometimes what contributed to the differentiation in parent–subsidiary management was not the actual practices employed by other companies, but the stereotyping of an alternative way of management.

Tensions and conflicts in the management team often extended beyond decisions on management issues. We see many examples of such tension and power struggles between managers. One example was found at WG-A Co. Employees believed that having an employees' canteen was a result of the local managers winning the "battles" against the expatriate managers' intention to make expatriates a prioritized group. While the employees agreed that the company intended to promote an egalitarian community, they saw more effort from the local managers than from the expatriates. The former expatriate general manager decided to build a raised stage in the canteen for expatriates' use, which upset many locals. The deputy general manager insisted that the stage should only be used for the end-of-year company performance, not as a secluded space for expatriate managers at lunchtime. Also, the canteen served the same food to all members of the company, regardless of their position, which was a decision initiated and promoted by the local managers. In this sense, the local managers actually utilized the concept of an "egalitarian community" against the expatriate managers' dominance in corporate management. SF-A Co. provided another example. While the food offered in the canteen was free of charge, senior managers were served with more variety of food. This produced a feeling of managers' authority rather than "transferring an egalitarian ideology" as explained by the managers. This seemed to be consistent with the company's intention of extending control over the employees. SF-B Co.'s canteen seemed to have very little to do with transferring any parent company practice. It was the only canteen among the four subsidiaries where employees paid for their food (in common with many local companies). The local employees interpreted the differences between parent company practices and those implemented in the subsidiaries as "the management made less effort to improve employee welfare than they do in the parent company" or "Japanese companies take a pragmatic approach in managing employees in a foreign country", which reflected the ambiguous and contingent nature of the company's policy concerning HR practices applied to the majority of employees.

7.4 Subsidiary managers' choices: the institutional, structural and corporate pressures filtered by the management teams

Differentiation of management practices between parent companies and subsidiaries mirrors the continuous pressures that shape subsidiary management and managers' choices in the face of these pressures. The continuing internationalization of large-scale Japanese companies and increasing deregulation of FDI in the Japanese domestic market have massively changed the exposure of Japanese companies to different management practices. At the same time, the economic downturn in the home country, the decline of the textiles and electronics industries, and the consequent financial pressures impinging on both the Japanese companies and their subsidiaries are the various reasons that drive the strategic review of their global business networks and organizational restructuring. The Japanese parent companies of all the sample subsidiaries featured in this study have reviewed their HR management at both domestic and international level. The impact of downsizing and restructuring in Japan was reflected in both the changing portfolios of subsidiary management teams and the subsidiary managers' perceptions of the parent HR practices as a successful model for subsidiaries to follow.

The Japanese parent companies' restructuring has strongly influenced expatriation. While the weight of tenure in deciding the Japanese managers' pay, promotion and expatriation has decreased, long-term employment relations among the core employee groups still show some resilience (Whitley, 2005). Expatriation to subsidiaries was often a way to maintain a long-term employment relationship with some home-country employees and reduce the parent company's HR costs. In all four subsidiaries studied, there were expatriate managers who were on two- or three-year contracts for "technical support". These expatriates were generally close to retirement age or had accepted this assignment as part of their early retirement package. For the parent company, the aim of the assignment to the subsidiaries was largely an extension of expatriate managers' "lifetime employment" with the parent companies.

Not being able to find competent local managers has been cited as a possible reason for parent companies continuing expatriation (Harzing, 2001b). In all four subsidiaries reported in this study, how-ever, parent companies' preference to promote internally trained man-agers has strongly influenced the HR policies and practices applied to the local managers. All the subsidiaries adopted HR policies to train and integrate competent local managers into the senior management team. Some companies, such as WG-B Co. and SF-B Co., had adopted a regional HR strategy and incorporated some presumed best practices in their subsidiary HR management. WG-B Co. launched a fast-track promotion policy back in the parent company and this policy was expected to be implemented in the subsidiaries in the future. SF-B Co. expanded promotion opportunities from internal positions to inter-national positions. While SF-A Co.'s and WG-A Co.'s parent compan-ies did not launch a specific regional HR strategy, restructuring in the home country did affect many aspects of subsidiary HR practices. The management trainee programme in SF-A Co. was similar to a fast-track promotion policy that encouraged development of potential young managers. WG-A Co.'s adoption of an "inpatriation-repatriation" pro-gramme was a sign that it aimed to integrate locals into the subsidiary management team.

The decline of the Japanese HRM model strongly influenced expatri-ate and local managers' understanding of the "Japanese management system" and their critical assessment of what constituted effective HR policies and practices. For instance, local managers from all four sub-sidiaries commented on the similarity between the key elements of the Japanese management system and the old "iron rice bowl". The local managers were very critical about these elements, since they were per-ceived as the cause of inefficiency in the old SOEs. This was consistent with China's departure from the Japanese influence in restructuring the local enterprises and reshaping local HRM (Zhu and Warner, 2000). However, the Japanese managers saw the influence of the "iron rice bowl" as far from having faded away. This is revealed in their

comments on how a Japanese style of management would continue
to characterize their parent companies. The general manager of SF-A
Co., for example, commented that the Chinese managers were intoler-
ant toward individual behaviours or corporate policies that "break the
hierarchical order". This was echoed by the less experienced Japanese
expatriate in SF-A Co., who found himself in a difficult situation as
his promotion gave him a higher position than more experienced local
managers.

At the same time, the presence of MNCs from different countries
of origin provided some reference point for the local managers to
assess the effectiveness of their HR policies and practices. The influence of these "third-country experiences" came from both internal and
external sources. The assessment decisions made by a small number
of managers reflected the paternalist decision-making which is commonly observed in many Korean, Taiwanese and Hong Kong invested
companies and has been sometimes generalized as the "Asian people
management system" (Zhu et al., 2007). Meanwhile, individual companies learned from their global experience. All four companies were
large-scale multinational corporations and had operations on a global
level. Management practice developed in sister plants could influence
the subsidiary, though sometimes the origin of such practices was not
clearly recorded or even remembered. While not many of the companies had expatriated third-country managers to the subsidiary management team as SF-B Co. did, managers agreed that the subsidiaries
had adopted management practices from their sister plants in other
countries.

The impact of the industry sector was reflected mainly in the HR
policies and practices applied to the local employees. As explained in
Chapters 5 and 6, companies within the same sector showed considerable differences in terms of the level of centralization of HR planning,
the way managerial knowledge and skills were acquired and career
development. However, there were some management practices that
showed characteristics of the industry. The high proportion of temporary workers employed by the household white goods manufacturers was just one example, though the two companies chose different
ways to source this group of employees. The subsidiaries occasionally
selected employees from the temporary group, which was also a practice employed by other Japanese companies in the electronics sector.
The choice of subsidiary location was related to the companies' target

of securing a low-cost labour force. As the Shanghai and Nantong areas have experienced fast transition, like other coastal areas of China, all subsidiaries found it impractical to maintain long-term employment relationships among all employee groups. Although the subsidiary managers still set out to achieve workforce stability and used some of the local institutions to encourage long-term employment relations (such as making the maximum contribution to employees' social insurance accounts), the HR practices which had actually evolved demonstrated some individual variations on the templates "intended" by management. The company preferred to recruit inexperienced graduates, who were offered a higher than average starting salary, training opportunities and career development plans. This preference made the subsidiaries attractive to fresh graduates and new immigrants to the cities. None of the subsidiaries reported difficulty in sourcing and recruiting employees. In fact, applications received largely outnumbered the vacancies and some subsidiaries chose to outsource the first round selection to the local employment agencies or schools. The concern of subsidiaries, as explained by some senior managers, was more about losing competent employees and managers to major competitors. However, none of the subsidiaries had developed sophisticated retention policies. Current HR practices offered limited internal promotion chances, lower salary for more experienced employees and an intensive workload and pressure. Neither had any of the subsidiaries developed locally oriented dismissal policies. Overall, the subsidiaries' HR practices allowed them to control overall HR costs, maintain a relatively stable senior management team, secure a pool of less experienced employees and junior managers and retain flexibility when the subsidiaries faced redundancy.

In summary, parent company dominance, locality and structural constraints all exerted considerable pressure on the management team. The subsidiary HR practices varied considerably and differentiation of subsidiary HR practices was commonly found. More importantly, I also observed that the transfer of parent company HR practices was not necessarily followed by the transfer of a parent organizational context, as has been suggested by the knowledge transfer literature (Hong et al., 2006). Rather, the meanings of the management practices evolved as subsidiaries coped with local labour market conditions and institutions, their industry characteristics, and wider corporate strategy. HR practices implemented at subsidiary level were likely to facilitate further differentiation between subsidiaries and the parent companies.

7.5 Key learning points

The study raised the question of how HR strategy was implemented in the subsidiaries and the subsidiary managers' input into strategic HR practice development. My study initially assumed that industrial sector would be an important indicator of parent company–subsidiary management differentiation. I found that the competitive strategy of the companies in the host country does have important implications for HR policy implementation. The research findings concur with the existing hybridization argument of trajectory differentiation (Boyer, 1998) that characterizes the subsidiary management formation process. The findings agree that the Japanese production regime dominates the emerging economy, where the subsidiaries assume functional positions within the corporate network. While studying forces that shape subsidiary HR practices, I uncovered the collective scenario of institutional, structural and corporate forces and the subsidiary managers' actions that mediate the impact of these forces. The number of expatriate managers alone did not sufficiently explain the cause of trajectory differentiation. In addition, more corporate-level factors were found to be relevant to trajectory differentiation and subsidiary diversity in terms of the HR practices developed.

More importantly, this research found differentiation in the connotations of some seemingly common practices, which is a result of the complex process of subsidiary policy implementation. HR policy implementation in the subsidiaries entailed a learning cycle in the subsidiaries, where the expatriate managers and the local managers enact the coded policies. In this process, it appeared that the composition of the management team affects many factors, such as the control from the parent companies and knowledge flow between the parent companies, the regional headquarters, if any, and the subsidiaries. The research findings also extend current research in knowledge transfer by adding the "process" dimension in relation to the companies' internal and external learning cycles. Corporate HR strategy is mediated by the subsidiary managers in relation to the embeddedness of their knowledge of existing HR practices internally and externally. The subsidiary's role in the corporate networks and local business networks also matters. The subsidiary's functional position in its technical, transactional and managerial networks is an indication of the relationships between subsidiary and parent company, the regional headquarters, sister plants, suppliers and clients. The networks form a wider power source, and subsidiary managers seek support to influence the direction of subsidiary HR practice development.

In terms of the HR outcomes observed, the research findings offered counter-evidence to such "single trajectory" arguments as the "race to the bottom" or "progressive transfer" within the HRM transfer literature. Subsidiary HR development is one of the key issues that concern the parent company, though the exact strategy and policies vary. Subsidiaries employ different levels of parent practices, in which some practices are implemented at subsidiary set-up, some are newly implemented, and some make a comeback as the initial adoption of the practice proves to be unsuccessful. These parent company practices are differentiated in many ways and consequently some still serve the same functions as they do in the parent company, whereas others are given new meanings and functions in the context of the subsidiary.

If I had to generalize a model of subsidiary HR practice development, I would say that the subsidiaries performed massive recruitment and offered a better starting salary to attract competent job-seekers. Training and development programmes were part of the internal selection process, in which the candidates were given opportunities for intensive on-the-job and off-the-job training. Very limited promotion opportunities were given to senior managers. Internal competition for junior and middle-level management positions was a motivator for young employees. Ambiguous retention and dismissal policies were a result of the limited promotion opportunities in subsidiaries. Turnover among the managers could lead to the intended result of screening out those employees who were "not suited to the company", but at the same time, the employees who left the subsidiary could well be the highly competent ones whom the subsidiaries intended to retain. These HR practices differ significantly from the parent practices as well as from practices prevalent in local companies. The emergence of these practices reflects the institutional, structural and corporate pressures facing the subsidiaries and subsidiary managers' interpretation, negotiation and construction of subsidiary HR practices under these competing pressures.

8 | Conclusion

This book reveals the complexity of human resource management in MNCs in China. It starts with a review of existing international HRM literature and argues that the dominant dual-pressure approach (global integration and local responsiveness) has constrained our understanding of subsidiary HR development. By moving the research focus from headquarters to the subsidiary level, the findings of this book highlight subsidiary managers' choices and actions in shaping the re-institutionalization of parent HR practices as well as the emergence of subsidiary-specific HR practices. The book therefore adds the subsidiary's perspective to the existing international HRM literature, which sees the social and institutional arrangements of the home and host countries, industry sector, formal organizational structure and informal corporate norms, and the international orientation of senior management as key determinants of subsidiary management practices. Research results based on four intensive case studies offer important evidence to address some long-established debates in international HRM literature.

Findings in this book suggest that the developmental nature of HR practices in the subsidiaries does not simply reflect a progressive transfer of parent HR practices controlled by a large number of expatriates (Harzing, 1999; Yoshihara, 2004). The quantitative assumption that a larger number of expatriates suggests more headquarters' control and therefore more intensive management transfer from the parent company (Rosenzweig and Nohria, 1994; Björkman et al., 2008a) did not prove to be the case. Rather, different subsidiary HR practices have emerged despite the fact that the number of expatriates in the subsidiaries remained constant for years. Neither did the local managers take full control of subsidiary HR and manage the local workforce with rudimentary personnel techniques (Taylor, 1999, 2001). Subsidiary managers' interests in upgrading the subsidiary's position in the MNC's global production network meant the emergence of some sophisticated HR practices at subsidiary level.

Another debate that the book has addressed is the *space* for subsidiary managers to decide HR practices. The dominant neo-institutionalist approach argues that institutions create pressures on managers to adopt management practices that are perceived to be legitimate in a given institutional setting. However, findings here suggest that subsidiary managers, strategically or through force, often filter the institutional pressures faced by subsidiaries. They also have the capacity to redirect institutional pressure in favour of the subsidiary's interests. For example, the "Americanization" pressure was often used in resistance to the parent company's influence. This result lends support to the political economy approach's argument that the power struggles among managers often shape the development of HR practices. The power struggle, as suggested by this study, is often reflected in the loci of control over subsidiary HR, the construction of functional networks, as well as the role of subsidiaries within the MNCs' chain of production and service provision.

Last but not least, the book also offers critique to the contingency approach in understanding international HRM. Contrasting subsidiary HR practices are significant within the pairs of subsidiaries where industry factors such as scale of investment, company size, age, entry model, ownership, product range, production and sales scale, market orientation and location in the host country were matched. In addition to *subsidiary differentiation* in terms of the level of parent management practices adopted by the subsidiaries, analysis of the function of parent practices in subsidiary management shows that they have different connotations in the respective subsidiaries. This clearly indicates considerable *parent practice differentiation*. I argue that such diversity is an important competence for subsidiaries and differs from the competence identified by headquarters, such as ownership of superb technological or managerial know-how, a locality with particular resource or cost advantages, or transaction cost advantage achieved through internalizing operations (Dunning, 1980, 1993; Dunning and Lundan, 2008). Subsidiary diversity therefore distinguishes subsidiaries from their parent and sister plants, indicating the future direction of subsidiary HRM development.

The actor-centred approach is supported by highlighting subsidiary managers' strategic repositioning within the MNCs, the power struggle between subsidiaries and internal and external resource holders, and progressive learning from past experiences. Below I will summarize the major research findings of the study and discuss its contributions and limitations. The first section offers a summary of key arguments developed throughout the book. The second considers problems encountered in studying the subsidiary level, which may limit the applicability and generalizability of the research results. The chapter ends by making suggestions for future research.

8.1 Generalizing the theoretical contributions from empirical findings

This study has revealed the importance of significant diversity in subsidiary HR practices which served the purpose of developing *subsidiary-specific advantages*. I challenged the approach adopted by some IHRM researchers, who study HR transfer by comparing subsidiary HR practices per se merely with the parent company practices. Whilst I have identified some similarities in HR practices across the subsidiaries, interpreted either as common practices in the specific industrial sector or the companies' response to China's particular institutional settings, subsidiary differentiation was found to be highly *firm specific*. I also showed how subsidiary managers deploy internal and external resources in order to mitigate the impact of the institutional, industrial sector and corporate forces that affect subsidiary HR practices. I have therefore argued that studies of subsidiary HR practices need to reflect the dynamics involved in subsidiary managers' choices of strategies, the power struggle in the MNC networks and the learning cycle in developing HR practices at subsidiaries.

In order to examine the moderating influence of subsidiary managers' actions and choices on the development of subsidiary HR practices, I illustrate the actor-centred approach in understanding subsidiaries' HRM in Figure 8.1, which links subsidiary managers' actions with the development of subsidiary-specific advantages and development of subsidiary HR practices.

The existing literature has identified an array of environmental, structural and organizational forces that influence subsidiary HR management practices (see review in Chapter 2). The research findings here indicate that the management team filters and manages these forces most of the time (Smith et al., 1990) and confirms that moderating actions by subsidiary management are significant in connecting the impact of these environmental, structural and organizational

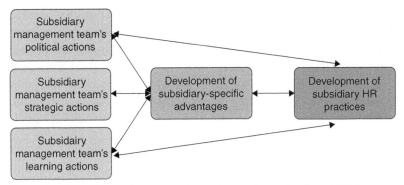

Figure 8.1 Actor-centred approach in understanding subsidiary HRM

forces. By advocating an actor-centred approach, I do not mean to deny the impact of forces such as economic booms and busts, financial crises, technological changes and legal changes that are part of the systemic features of capitalism as a political economy and are beyond the control of any one firm to manage or resist. In fact, the findings of this study did indicate such direct impact, as subsidiary HR practices have to be designed according to the local legal requirements (for example, local trade union rules), industry characteristics (such as home electrical white goods manufacturers using a large number of temporary workers during the peak season), and reorientation of corporate global strategies (for example, the centralization of HR control in the Chinese headquarters). However, the extent to which these forces influence specific HR practices varies, leading to considerable subsidiary diversity. For instance, although both WG-A Co. and WG-B Co. employ temporary workers, the source of these workers and the management practice followed by the two subsidiaries differ significantly. These results show that the connection between external forces and management practices is at firms' discretion.

Likewise, relational networks of subsidiaries are often mediated by subsidiary actors. Subsidiaries' relationships with their business partners have to be filtered through the actions, goals, power interests and perceptions of internal actors. In other words, the embeddedness of subsidiaries in their business networks is subject to subsidiary actors' mediation to create different relational networks. The impact of such relational networks on subsidiary HR practice is also filtered by the subsidiary managers and hence varies. Contrary to the idea that local embeddedness indicates more localized subsidiary HR, my research findings suggest that subsidiary actors manage their relational networks in such a way as to either invite or resist parent influence in subsidiary HR practice development. And finally, members of the subsidiary management team are responsible for deciding subsidiary HR practices. Subsidiary actors' learning capacity, the power relations of the management team and the actions of managers are all equally critical to subsidiary HR development: they moderate the impact of environmental constraints and relational networks on the way subsidiary and parent HR practices develop and diversify. Managers see the environment differently because they have their own perceptions and reasons for taking particular actions. These perceptions are not uniform, and each firm usually has its own intrinsic or tacit sets of inherited assumptions and legacies, which are filters or mediators of external factors. The following section will summarize how such factors shape and are mediated by the action of subsidiary managers to bring about subsidiary-specific advantages and diversity of subsidiary HR practices.

8.1.1 Home-country effect, host-country effect, industry sectors and the presence of third-country competition

Previous studies have revealed the critical environmental forces, such as global economic structure, industry sector, national institutions and international competition, that will influence HR practice development at subsidiary level. As discussed earlier, these forces, alone or collectively, cannot adequately explain the diversity I observed in the subsidiaries.

Global economic structure is often cited as a key to understanding the transfer of established HR practices across countries. Globalization of MNCs redefines world economic structure and affects production throughout the world. Countries show different comparative advantages at different stages of economic development. From parent companies' perspective, production will have to be located in countries where such comparative advantage meets their global competitive strategy. To some extent, my findings reflect this global economic structure, as all the case studies chose to relocate in China as a means of reducing production costs. In terms of production, however, these subsidiaries have generally adopted semi-automated technology and mainly recruited a non-skilled and semi-skilled workforce. The companies are alike in the sense that subsidiaries are responsible for routinized production, whereas the parent companies or the regional headquarters retain strategic functions. Despite a few signs of production technology being upgraded, subsidiaries' HR practices are far from converging to repertoires designed by the parent companies or to standardized low-cost routines.

Industry sector is suggested as a differentiator in understanding the HR practices adopted by subsidiaries of MNCs. In general, subsidiary HRM practices have displayed specific industry characteristics. For instance, due to product life-cycle, the household white goods manufacturers have moved to target short-term employees as their core shop-floor workforce, whereas the synthetic fibre manufacturers are more inclined to focus on retention and the long-term employment relationship. However, the study does not support the argument that companies in capital-intensive sectors are more likely to transfer HR practices from the parent companies than those in labour-intensive sectors (Kenney, 2001). This theory suggests that industry sector is a *sufficient* predictor of HRM practice. My findings, however, suggest that industry sector itself has limited implications for the diversity of subsidiary HR, due to subsidiary managers' pursuit of subsidiary-specific advantages. Although subsidiaries in the same industry sector may share some rationale for adopting (or not adopting) certain HR practices, the sector itself is less relevant to the actual process of subsidiary diversity development.

National institutions are a key factor driving cross-country management differences and are also one of the most frequently discussed factors affecting management transfer. Based on the assumption that Chinese and Japanese societies share similar cultural backgrounds, transfer of parent practices is sometimes perceived to be "straightforward" (Li et al., 2002) or "progressive" (Ma, 1998; Guan and Fan, 2003). My findings offer counter-arguments to such cultural affinity thinking, which assumes management practices embedded in one society can be transplanted to another society. I did observe that transfer of parent HR practices was often legitimized as it supported production flow, stock management and quality control systems, which were generally considered advantageous to parent companies and were seen as a prerequisite for product upgrading when subsidiaries pursued repositioning of their functions within corporate networks.

However, subsidiaries did not follow a progressive route in transferring parent HR practices. Some new forms of HR practices emerged (for example, subsidiaries prioritized the development of attraction policies over retention policies to control overall HR costs). Some existing parent company practices were employed for different HR purposes (for example, job rotation was often used to facilitate dismissal). Some standardized management practices were also adopted (such as clarification of individual job responsibilities and merit-based appraisal).

Differences in the labour markets of China and Japan cannot be ignored, and these influence emerging subsidiary diversity. Given the different stages of development, parent HR practices encountered strong resistance from local employees. Even though previous studies have identified some similarities between China's SOEs and Japan's large-scale "community firms", the implications of such similarities for HR practice transfer remain controversial (Goodall and Warner, 1997; Ding and Akhtar, 2001; Li et al., 2002). In fact, I found that local managers were more critical of HR practices that resembled the old "iron rice bowl" practices such as long-term group-based performance appraisal, and these were eventually marginalized in all subsidiaries. Although seniority-based promotion seemed to be strong, this practice was largely due to subsidiaries not having effective measures to retain competitive young managers, and was not a direct transfer of parent HR practice.

A major HR issue discussed in the study is the conflict between parent companies' preference for employing an internally promoted management team and local employees' short-term career development orientation. Labour mobility is a major feature of China's newly developed labour market. In Japan, however, most large-scale companies preserved an implicit long-term relationship with employees until substantial reform took place in the mid 1990s. My findings suggest that the relevance of parent HR practices depends on how subsidiaries assess their key local competence and the way they intend to achieve such local competence. SF-A Co.'s product quality centred on its competitive strategy, so developing an internally trained management team was of increasing importance. In contrast, SF-B Co.'s new product-based competitive strategy made it important for local managers and engineers to contribute different expertise and perspectives. In terms of HR practices, I therefore observed that SF-A

Co. used local institutions to maintain long-term employment relationships, whereas in SF-B Co., there were few measures to control mobility and retention proved to be an individual matter. Likewise, in the household white goods sector, WG-A Co. employed fewer parent practices due to its subsidiary-directed functions and reliance on the ex-SOE managers to control the local workforce. However, WG-B Co.'s key competence came from an efficient alliance with the parent-company-controlled networks; hence the parent HR practices became more relevant.

In addition to labour market conditions, prevalent local management practices are often believed to inhibit MNCs' transfer of established HR practices. In this book, I observed companies employing very different management models in China's transition. Although a large number of SOEs were restructuring as a result of central government-led structural reform, many personnel control measures (such as collective residential status), appraisal processes and welfare packages (such as subsidized housing) have remained in post-reform SOEs (see Ding et al., 2000, for a review). Privately owned companies are emerging and the HR practices employed by this group of companies range from very rudimentary personnel techniques to strategic HR planning at various levels (Benson and Zhu, 1999). In fact, I found that expatriates and local managers could not agree on what the "Chinese HRM model" was but often referred to different forms of local management practices as having "Chinese characteristics" (Warner, 2005). Nevertheless, the absence of strong local practices did not make parent practice transfer straightforward or progressive. For example, I found that all subsidiaries employed strong direct personnel control over local employees, especially where formal control and socialization measures did not work out as expected. At the same time, the presence of foreign-invested enterprises (FIEs) adds to the diversity of local management practices. Their power in the Chinese economy has made FIEs important actors in shaping institutional and social transition in China (Wu, 2000; Zhou et al., 2002; Child and Tsai, 2005). FIEs' HR practices, particularly those exercised by leading MNCs, influence subsidiary managers' interpretation of the relevance of parent practices. This point links to the final stream of external forces – the influence of management practices performed in a leading economy or leading companies, or the "dominant effects" suggested by the system, society and dominance effects framework (Smith, 2008).

The findings of this study confirm that the presence of third-country management repertoires significantly influences developing sub-sidiary HR practices. The continuous arrival of FIEs has increased demand for skilled and managerial personnel as well as the pres-sure of attracting and retaining competent people. As shown in the cases of SF-A Co. and SF-B Co., the arrival of a new rival company in the local area significantly challenged existing retention policies. Many of the managers interviewed expressed their frustration that local people would move around companies for different reasons, including promotion opportunities, personal development or even slightly better pay. Competing management practices often trigger questions on the effectiveness of the parent management repertoire and encourage subsidiary managers to initiate a review of existing HR practices. For this reason, these were often used by subsidiary managers to resist parent company dominance. Given the absence of a strong local HR management system, local managers were some-times involved in constructing an *ideal* management model, bor-rowed from leading companies' management practices and expected to fit the local conditions better. I also found that industry sector constrains the scope of relevant third-country practices. The sub-sidiaries were frequently asked to learn from the "German model" of household electrical white goods manufacturers, whereas the "American way" was found to be more relevant for managers of the synthetic fibre manufacturing units.

These findings, again, suggest that institutions are often filtered by subsidiary actors, as suggested by Elger and Smith (2005). My research findings reflect the wider trend of Japanese MNCs open-ing themselves up to other management systems and practices as their indigenous model came under the performance microscope in the long Japanese recession which started in the late 1980s. In Japan, the economic downturn stimulated many Japanese compan-ies to explore the features of alternative management systems (such as those practised by American companies). They were encouraged to consider restructuring management within an existing manage-ment framework (Inagami and Whittaker, 2005; JETRO, 2007). The Japanese parent companies of all four sample companies have been continuously reviewing and reforming their HR practices, which has then affected their overall corporate international HR strategy. As I observed, subsidiaries had implemented policies to reduce personnel costs, delegate more autonomy to the local managers, impose short-term financial performance criteria on subsidiary assessment and increase the merit weighting in individual performance appraisals. Furthermore, my findings indicate that the extent to which subsidiaries implemented such standardized HR practices differed, and this reflected subsidiaries' own internal dynamics. The influence of leading companies in the industry sector and of the "American way" was mostly perceived as a pressure. SF-A Co.'s revision of the pay-for-job grade practice, WG-A Co.'s choice of recruiting mid-career managers to middle-level managerial positions, SF-B Co.'s drive to implement standard HR practices and WG-B Co.'s maintenance of the practices performed by the parent company prior to HR restructuring are just a few examples of such subsidiary-moderated dominance effects (see Chapters 5 and 6).

8.1.2 The relational networks

The second type of force assessed in this study is the "relational networks". Parent company dominance has been elaborated in terms of subsidiaries' reliance on the parent companies for resources such as financial, technical and managerial support (Bartlett and Ghoshal, 1989). Subsidiaries relying more heavily on the Japanese parent company resources are more likely to take on the management practices promoted by the parent companies, and are expected to develop HRM that resembles the management practices of the headquarters (Beechler and Yang, 1994). This study has criticized this static view of the parent company–subsidiary interdependence. My findings indicate that the reliance of subsidiaries on parent companies for direct financial, technical, business or managerial support was weakening over the years, partly because subsidiaries continued to manufacture standardized products and partly due to the parent companies' overall regional restructuring. The Chinese headquarters, the R&D centres, sister plants in subsidiary local business networks, all offer support which was used to centralize policies in the headquarters. Subsidiaries with stronger local connections did not turn out to be more localized in terms of the HR practices employed.

Contrary to the resource-dependence view, I found it useful to view business networks as power bases (Andersson et al., 2007) where subsidiaries and parent companies (and sometimes sister plants) try to influence the development of subsidiary HR practices. Subsidiaries work in a heterarchical administrative and business network. Subsidiary diversity can be explained by the way a particular subsidiary's local business networks are incorporated into the parent company's local business networks. In this sense, direct involvement of the parent company in constructing subsidiary local networks is one way parent companies exert their influence, whereas parent companies' knowledge of the local business network can also be an important source of power (Andersson et al., 2007). Having stated this, the impact of relational networks on subsidiary HR practices is mediated by subsidiary actors. As described in Chapter 5, WG-A Co.'s decision to incorporate a parent-owned trade agent to handle sales of some of their products was a step the subsidiary took to negotiate further autonomy and control over some strategic functions. For WG-B Co., however, involving a parent-owned trade agent in their business networks was more a symbol of tightened parent control following the broader corporate regional restructure.

The role of subsidiaries in wider corporate business strategy is also critical to the development of local HR practices. Within the organizational networks, we see parent companies redirecting production from one country to another in the search for more cost-effective production locations. While the initial function allocated by the parent companies at the time of subsidiary incorporation remained a constraint on the current functions undertaken by each subsidiary, how the subsidiary was repositioned in the corporate-level restructuring became a strategic concern when subsidiary managers designed local HR policies and practices. When they were first set up in the mid 1990s, the Chinese subsidiaries in this study generally served as a supplementary production base to their Asian sister plants. Until the early 2000s, these subsidiaries were more competitive and some had replaced their sister plants' position in the corporate networks. For these subsidiaries, development of local HR practices was related to the role they played in the corporate networks. Comparing the two household white goods manufacturers, WG-A Co. aimed to become a strategic centre rather than a manufacturing centre in the Chinese market. Subsidiary managers' struggles for control in this process led to separate HR practices governing different employee groups. WG-B Co.'s pursuit of domestic and international expansion through the parent companies' business networks necessitated transfer of parent practices in order to maintain consistent quality standards. Similar results were found in the synthetic fibre sector. To achieve the ambition of replacing the Indonesian sister plant and becoming *the* Asian manufacturing centre, SF-A Co. actively invited the influence of the parent company, which somehow eased the tension associated with parent dominance. In SF-B Co.'s case, the Chinese subsidiaries were considered a regional centre and they were under less pressure to compete with the sister plants in Southeast Asian countries. This facilitated the development of local roles as well as HR practices different from those of the parent company.

Finally, the subsidiary's local embeddedness was also moderated by the subsidiary managers, and hence the impact on subsidiary HR practice development varies. As subsidiaries played a wide role in the local economy, subsidiary actors were allowed to negotiate with local agents to influence the direction of policy-making. Growing unemployment put pressure on the local government to create job opportunities and upgrade local workers' skills by attracting FDI. This had been the case since the early 1990s. Against this background, foreign-invested companies, especially large-scale companies like the ones in this study, were able to negotiate employment issues with various local agencies. For example, I observed that all subsidiaries had some level of collaboration with local universities as a source of new recruits. Subsidiaries could recruit predominantly inexperienced employees and select managers from an internally trained team, which WG-B Co. and SF-A Co. had chosen to do. However, as discussed previously, a major challenge to the internal selection policy was the mobility of local employees. As a local employer in Shanghai, WG-B Co. was in a strong position to negotiate with different technical schools, colleges and universities. Setting up training centres in collaboration with local educational institutions allowed WG-B Co. to conduct pre-entry selection, which reduced the overall labour turnover. Located in a rural economic development zone, SF-A Co. was in a weaker position to secure a large candidate base for careful screening and selection. A critical issue for SF-A Co. was thus the development of stronger retention policies to maintain long-term employment relationships. The complex nature of subsidiary embeddedness brings us back to subsidiary actors who play power games with agents outside the subsidiary.

8.1.3 *The management team*

Going against the formalistic thinking that the number of expatriates indicates the level of parent company dominance, I explored the impact of subsidiary management team composition and power plays in the development of local HR practices, and the influence of firm-specific learning cycles in developing their HR practices.

Looking back at the composition of the subsidiary management team extended my view of subsidiary managers as a group. In all subsidiaries, parent companies have reduced the number of expatriates since the early 2000s, partly due to corporate policies of reducing overall personnel costs. I have to note here that the number of expatriates was not decided merely by the parent company. Often subsidiary managers negotiated over particular cases to influence the choice of candidates and the number of expatriates. WG-A Co.'s refusal to accept an expatriate was an exceptional case, but subsidiary managers are active in negotiating the tenure, type and frequency of expatriate employment, which are signs of expatriate control. Parent company influence can be achieved through extending the tenure of expatriate managers, dispatching more frequent project-based missions or flex-patriates or assigning expatriates to multiple managerial roles. Also, following the restructuring of corporate regional policies, expatriates in other strategic functions within the same region were generally involved in the decision-making process. In particular, HRM executives in the regional headquarters were among the key actors that the subsidiary management team had to deal with.

The subsidiaries also showed considerable diversity in terms of the background of local managers. The educational background and experience of local managers can be very homogeneous, as in the cases of SF-A Co. (young graduates promoted internally) and WG-A Co. (experienced ex-SOE managers). In general, local managers who joined the company at an early stage in their career and developed managerial skills within the subsidiaries tended to show more recognition of parent company practices. WG-B Co. is an example where the locals shared a common educational background and work experience within the particular subsidiary. By contrast, managers with previous work experience, especially if gained in SOEs, often questioned the effectiveness of the parent practices by drawing an analogy between "conglomerate illness [*dai kigyou byou*]" and the "iron rice bowl [*tie fan wan]*". In subsidiaries where the management team was formed by people from more diverse backgrounds, third-country practices were frequently found to be used to resist parent dominance. But the influence of "Chinese characteristics" in shaping managers' thought and behaviour never receded.

To sum up, the management teams were composed of individual actors, not numbers. It would be naïve to believe that a reduction in the number of expatriates indicates that Japanese companies are moving away from an ethnocentric international staffing approach (Beamish and Inkpen, 1998). In fact, I found that the ethnocentric staffing approach could well persist unless localization could massively reduce HR costs or significantly increase local productivity. Neither of these seems to be achievable in the foreseeable future. More importantly, headquarters' international orientation was merely one factor that affected the internal dynamics of subsidiary HR practice development. The relational networks, diversity of team members and activities of the subsidiary actors all mediate the impact of the forces on the outcome of subsidiary HR practices.

8.1.4 Subsidiary-specific advantages and diversity of subsidiary HR

My study has shown the internal dynamics at subsidiary level and the contentious, incremental and political process of subsidiary HR practice development. There is persistent diversity in subsidiary management experiences. While I agree that tension between parent companies' desire to transfer their existing management repertoire and subsidiary resistance to parent dominance has characterized subsidiary HR practice development, the resulting HR practices are far more than simply hybrid. The research findings highlight that subsidiary management team capacity, configured by expatriation and localization policies, informs how the existing management repertoire will be used in an adaptive (Abo, 1994, 1998), formalistic (Taylor, 2001) or innovative (Hong et al., 2006) way, and this was the source of subsidiary advantage. Based on comparable cases, I have shown complexity and diversity in subsidiary HR practice development, which any simple model outlined in the "progressive transfer" and "race to the bottom line" literature will not be able to explain easily. I wanted to link subsidiary moderation with subsidiary diversity, and have thus tried to portray the process through which subsidiary HR practices came into being. I found an emergent and dyadic process, in which any existing management repertoire was evaluated, negotiated, tested, modified and re-evaluated based on the particular circumstances of a subsidiary and the internal and external contexts it inhabited. Some new forms of HR practice have evolved in this process. These new forms may be specific to a firm and different from existing management practices, local or parent. They may also be developed on the basis of existing management practices, which may take on different connotations or functions in the subsidiary context.

These findings are significant because the contingent factors were controlled in my sampling process. I can therefore confidently conclude that it was the subsidiary level that mattered. Actions and decisions of subsidiary managers are able to moderate the impact of contextual and contingent forces, and hence generate a persistently differentiated set of HR practices across subsidiaries. New forms of subsidiary HR practice distinguished subsidiaries from the parent companies, their sister plants and their key competitors, and therefore created subsidiary competence in terms of attracting, developing and retaining competent local employees. These subsidiary competences differed from those predicted in Dunning's eclectic paradigm (1980), which explained MNCs' existence from the headquarters' perspective. In other words, understanding the development of subsidiary management helps us to better explain the existence of MNCs from a subsidiary perspective.

8.2 Limitations of the study

The research study is largely based on a qualitative method conducted at a limited number of subsidiaries. While the sample selection process ensured that cases included in the study reflect a larger population of subsidiaries, some methodological issues may still undermine the generalizability of the research findings. First of all, the research design is intended to compare subsidiaries from a single country of origin, Japan, located in the same area of a single host country. One cannot simply ignore some peculiarities of the country-of-origin and host-country effects. Japanese companies, as discussed in previous chapters, are more inclined to conduct management transfer to their overseas plants. China's emerging economy has experienced systemic transitions in its society, which will not be observed in developed countries where institutions are more embedded and therefore more resilient to change. Another relevant issue in using Japanese subsidiaries in China is that these subsidiaries share the definition of "reproductive factories" (Kenney et al., 1998), which means generally being engaged in delivering home-country designed and developed products rather than acting as centres for innovation and learning. This might be the reason why limited signs of innovative management practices were found in some subsidiaries. I have to admit that my findings may need to be qualified when applied in different country contexts or industry sectors. However, the research results and arguments conform to the main findings generated by empirical research on Japanese-invested manufacturing plants in North America and the UK, namely that the subsidiary level gains control over transferring features of the home-country management overseas (Beechler et al., 1998; Boyer, 1998; Elger and Smith, 2005; Hong et al., 2006).

The second methodological constraint associated with the multiple case studies method is that the information gathered may be uneven across different units of the organizations studied. I collected information mainly from the subsidiaries, especially the managers within these factories. Some key informants at local strategic units such as the regional headquarters were also visited, but contacts with these units were less intensive compared to the fieldwork at the subsidiaries. Due to limitations of time and funding available for the study, travel to the corporate headquarters was not feasible and headquarters are thus excluded from the fieldwork. In order to gain different perspectives, the key informants were those who have been working in both the parent companies and the subsidiaries for more than two years. To compensate for the possible negative effect of writing this book based on a single source of information, I have integrated secondary sources of information and company documentation into the research.

Finally, fieldwork at the sample subsidiaries was conducted in sequence, which means I finalized studies at one subsidiary before moving on to visit the next case. The nature of semi-structured interviews and on-site observation allows research questions to emerge during the process of the study, and some issues were added to my original research questions during the progress of the fieldwork. However, limitations of resources and time in completing the study meant that I was not able to revisit each site after completion of the major fieldwork. To gain supplementary information, key informants, mainly the general managers and HR managers, were contacted again by telephone and email. Such a method may limit the view I obtained from these companies. This data was therefore used with considerable caution and constantly compared with data collected in the major fieldwork.   ·

8.3 Some theoretical issues arising from the study which require further investigation

As pointed out in Chapter 2, there is no consensus on how a firm's international HR strategy can generate competitive advantage overseas. The body of strategic IHRM research lacks a holistic theoretical model to link various issues such as expatriate activities and subsidiary performance. Expatriate well-being, subsidiary operational objectives and the overall performance of MNCs have been treated in a rather segmented manner in the existing strategic IHRM literature. This study is an attempt to identify connections between the issues by looking at the subsidiary HR practice development process, which turned out to provide important implications linking expatriation, subsidiary HR management practice and development of subsidiary competence.

As far as future research is concerned, a two-phase approach is suggested. For the first stage, the research method used in this study could be repeated in different institutional and organizational contexts. Comparative case studies of MNCs from different countries of origin, engaged in various industry sectors, competing internationally and operating in various host countries will enrich our understanding of what subsidiaries enact and what management transfers. A further step requires the incorporation of quantitative methods to operationalize the environmental forces, relational networks and management team activities identified in this chapter. Some hypotheses could be developed to test the correlation between intra-firm forces and management transfer, with environmental constraints and relational networks as the control variables. At the same time, it is equally important to test the correlation between different management transfer outcomes and company performance in terms of turnover, financial performance and long-term development. By doing so, we would be able to add statistical confidence to the research framework, benefiting strategic IHRM literature in particular and organization theory in general.

Bibliography

Abo, T. (ed.) 1994. *Hybrid Factory: The Japanese Production System in the United States*. New York: Oxford University Press.

Abo T. 1998. 'Hybridization of the Japanese production system in North America, newly industrializing economies, south-east Asia and Europe: contrasted configurations', in Boyer, R., Charron, E., Jurgens, U. and Tolliday, S. (eds.) *Between Imitation and Innovation: The Transfer and Hybridization of Productive Models in the International Automobile Industry*. Oxford University Press, pp. 216–30.

Adler, N. J. and Ghadar, F. 1990. 'International strategy from the perspective of people and culture: the North American context', in Rugman, A. M. (ed.) *Research in Global Strategic Management: International Business Research for the Twenty-first Century–Canada's New Research Agenda*. Greenwich, CT: JAI Press, pp. 179–205.

Allen, D. and Alvarez, S. 1998. 'Empowering expatriates and organizations to improve repatriation effectiveness', *Human Resource Planning* 21(1): 29–39.

Andersson, U. 2003. 'Managing the transfer of capabilities within multinational corporations: the dual role of the subsidiary', *Scandinavian Journal of Management* 19(4): 425–42.

Andersson, U., Forsgren, M. and Holm, U. 2007. 'Balancing subsidiary influence in the federative MNC: a business network view', *Journal of International Business Studies* 38(5): 802–18.

Archibugi, D. and Lundvall, B. (eds.) 2001. *The Globalising Learning Economy*. Oxford University Press.

Arthur, J. B. 1992. 'The link between business strategy and industrial relations systems in American steel mini-mills', *Industrial and Labour Relations Review* 45(3): 488–506.

Baird, L. and Meshoulam, I. 1988. 'Managing two fits of strategic human resource management', *Academy of Management Review* 13(1): 116–28.

Baliga, B. R. and Jaeger, A. 1984. 'Multinational corporations: control systems and delegation issues', *Journal of International Business Studies* 24(2): 233–48.

Bartlett, C. A. and Ghoshal, S. 1989. *Managing Across Borders: The Transnational Solution*. Boston, MA: Harvard Business School Press.
1993. 'Beyond the M-form: toward a managerial theory of the firm', *Strategic Management Journal* 14(Special Issue): 23–46.

Beamish, P. W. and Inkpen, A. C. 1998. 'Japanese firms and the declining of the Japanese expatriates', *Journal of World Business* 33(1): 35–50.

Beechler, S. and Yang, Z. J. 1994. 'The transfer of Japanese-style management to American subsidiaries: contingencies, constraints and competencies', *Journal of International Business Studies* 25(3): 467–91.

Beechler, S., Bird, A. and Taylor, S. 1998. 'Organisational learning in Japanese MNCs: four affiliate archetypes', in Birkinshaw, J. and Hood, N. (eds.) *Multinational Corporate Evolution and Subsidiary Development*. New York: St Martin's Press, pp. 333–66.

Beijing Zongheng Economic Research Centre (BZERC) 2007. *Report on China's Air Conditioner Market*. Beijing Zongheng Economic Research Centre.

Benson, J. and Zhu, Y. 1999. 'Market, firms and workers: the transformation of human resource management in Chinese manufacturing enterprises', *Human Resource Management Journal* 9(4): 58–74.

Birkinshaw, J. 1997. 'Entrepreneurship in multinational corporations: the characteristics of subsidiary initiatives', *Strategic Management Journal* 18(3): 207–29.

Birkinshaw, J. and Hood, N. 1998. 'Multinational subsidiary evolution: capability and charter change in foreign-owned subsidiary companies', *Academy of Management Review* 23(4): 141–54.

Birkinshaw, J. and Ridderstrale, J. 1999. 'Fighting the corporate immune system: a process study of subsidiary initiatives in multinational corporations', *International Business Review* 8(2): 149–80.

Björkman, I. 2002. 'The diffusion of human resource management practices among Chinese firms: the role of Western multinational corporations', *Asia Pacific Business Review* 9(2): 43–60.

Björkman, I. and Lu, Y. 1999. 'The management of human resources in Chinese-Western joint ventures', *Journal of World Business* 34(3): 306–24.

Björkman, I., Budhar, P., Smale, A. and Sumelius, J. 2008a. 'Human resource management in foreign-owned subsidiaries: China versus India', *International Journal of Human Resource Management* 19(5): 964–78.

Björkman, I., Smale, A., Sumelius, J., Suutari, V. and Lu, Y. 2008b. 'Changes in institutional context and MNC operations in China: subsidiary HRM practices in 1996 versus 2006', *International Business Review* 17(2): 146–58.

Black, J. S. and Gregersen, B. H. 1992. 'Serving two masters: managing the dual allegiance of expatriate employees', *Sloan Management Review* 33(4): 61–71.

Black, J. S., Gregersen, H. B., Mendenhall, M. E. and Stroh, L. K. 1999. *Globalizing People Through International Assignments*. Reading, MA: Addison-Wesley.

Boisot, M. and Child, J. 1999. 'Organizations as adaptive systems in complex environments: the case of China', *Organization Science* 10(3): 237–52.

Boyacigiller, N. 1990. 'The role of expatriates in the management of interdependence, complexity and risk in multinational corporations', *Journal of International Business Studies* 21(3): 357–81.

  1997. 'The role of expatriates in the management of interdependence, complexity and risk in multinational corporations', in Beechler, S. and Stucker, K. (eds.) *Japanese Business IV*. London and New York: Routledge, pp. 51–77.

Boyer, R. 1998. 'Hybridization and models of production: geography, history, and theory', in Boyer, J., Charron, E., Jurgens, U. and Tolliday, S. (eds.) *Between Imitation and Innovation: The Transfer and Hybridization of Productive Models in the International Automobile Industry*. Oxford University Press, pp. 23–56.

Brewster, C., Wood, G. and Brooks, M. 2008. 'Similarity, isomorphism or duality? Recent survey evidence on the human resource management policies of multinational corporations', *British Journal of Management* 19(4): 320–42.

Brewster, C., Carey, L., Dowling, P., Grobler, P., Holland, P. and Warnich, S. 2003. *Contemporary Issues in Human Resource Management: Gaining a Competitive Advantage*. 2nd edition. Cape Town: Oxford University Press.

Briggs, C. L. 1986. *Learning How to Ask: A Sociolinguistic Appraisal of the Role of the Interview in Social Science Research*. Cambridge University Press.

Brooks, R. and Tao, R. 2003. *China's Labour Market Performance and Challenges*. Asia and Pacific Department: IMF Working Paper.

Brown, E. 2006. Chinese labour law reform: guaranteeing worker rights in the age of globalism. Available: www.worldpress.org/Asia/2574.cfm (accessed 10 June 2012).

Bryman, A. 1988. *Quantity and Quality in Social Research*. London: Routledge.

Buck, T. 2011. 'Case selection informed by theory', in Piekkari, R. and Welch, C. (eds.) *Rethinking the Case Study in International Business and Management Research*. Cheltenham: Edward Elgar, pp. 192–209.

Caligiuri, P., Phillips, J., Lazarova, M., Tarique, I. and Burgi, P. 2001. 'The theory of met expectations applied to expatriate adjustment: the role of cross-cultural training', *International Journal of Human Resource Management* 12(3): 357–72.

Campbell, N. 1994. 'Japan's success in China', in Shuttle, M. (ed.) *The Global Competitiveness of the Asian Firm*. Basingstoke: Macmillan, pp. 129–37.

Campbell, N. and Burton, F. 1994. *Japanese Multinationals: Strategies and Management in the Global Kaisha*. London: Routledge.

Carver, A. 1996. 'Open and secret regulations and their implication for foreign investment', in Child, J. and Yuan, L. (eds.) *Management Issues in China*. London and New York: Routledge, pp. 11–29.

Chakravarthy, B. and Perlmutter, H. V. 1985. 'Strategic planning for a global business', in Root, F. R. and Visudtibhan, K. (eds.) *International Strategic Management: Challenges and Opportunities*. New York: Taylor & Francis, pp. 29–42.

Chan, A. 2001. *China's Workers under Assault: The Exploitation of Labour in a Globalising Economy*. New York: M. E. Sharpe.

Chan, J. and Pun, N. 2010. 'Suicide as protest for the new generation of Chinese migrant workers: Foxconn, global capital, and the state', *The Asia-Pacific Journal: Japan Focus*. Available: http://japanfocus.org/-Ngai-Pun/3408 (accessed: 12th June 2012).

Chandler, A. D. 1962. *Strategy and Structure*. Cambridge, MA: Harvard University Press.

Chen, M. 2004. *Asian Management System: Chinese, Japanese and Korean Styles of Business*. 2nd edition. Singapore: Thomson.

Child, J. 1972. 'Organisational structure, environment and performance: the role of strategic choice', *Sociology* 6(1): 1–22.

  1981. 'Culture, contingency and capitalism in the cross-national study of organizations', in Cummings, L. L. and Staw, B. M. (eds.) *Research in Organizational Behaviour*, vol. III. Greenwich, CT: JAI Press, pp. 303–56.

  1994. *Management in China During the Age of Reform*. Cambridge University Press.

  1997. 'Strategic choice in the analysis of action, structure, organisations and environment: retrospect and prospect', *Organisation Studies* 18(1): 43–76.

Child, J. and Tsai, T. 2005. 'The dynamic between firms' environmental strategies and institutional constraints in emerging economies: evidence from China and Taiwan', *Journal of Management Studies* 42(1): 95–125.

Child, J. and Tse, D. K. 2001. 'China's transition and its implications for international business', *Journal of International Business Studies* 32(1): 5–21.

Child, J. and Yuan, L. 1996. 'Institutional constraints on economic reform: the case of investment decisions in China', *Organization Science* 7(1): 60–77.

Chung, H. F. and Enderwich, P. 2001. 'An investigation of market entry strategy selection: exporting vs foreign direct investment modes – a home–host country scenario', *Asia Pacific Journal of Management* 18(4): 443–60.

Clarke, S. 2005. 'Post-socialist trade unions: China and Russia', *Industrial Relations Journal* 36(1): 2–18.

Clegg, S. 1998. 'Power and institutions in organization theory', in Hassard, J. and Parker, M. (eds.) *Towards a New Theory of Organizations*. London and New York: Routledge, pp. 24–52.

Clegg, S. R., Hardy, C. and Nord, W. R. 1996. *Handbook of Organisation Studies*. London: Sage.

Coase, R. H. 1937. 'The nature of the firm', *Economica* 4(16): 386–405.

Cohen, M. and Bacdayan, P. 1994. 'Organizational routines are stored as procedural memory – evidence from a laboratory study', *Organization Science* 5(2): 554–68.

Cohen, W. M. and Levinthal, D. A. 1990. 'Absorptive capacity: a new perspective on learning and innovation', *Administrative Science Quarterly* 35(1): 128–52.

Cooke, F. L. 2003. 'Seven reforms in five decades: civil service reform and its human resource implications in China', *Journal of Asia Pacific Economy* 18(3): 381–405.

  2004. 'Foreign firms in China: modelling HRM in a toy manufacturing corporation', *Human Resource Management Journal* 14(3): 31–52.

  2005a. *HRM, Work and Employment in China*. London and New York: Routledge.

  2005b. 'Vocational and enterprise training in China: policy, practice and prospect', *Journal of the Asia Pacific Economy* 20(1): 26–55.

  2005c. 'Employment relations in small commercial businesses in China', *Industrial Relations Journal* 36(1): 19–37.

  2006. 'Acquisitions of Chinese state-owned enterprises by MNCs: driving forces, barriers and implications for HRM', *British Journal of Management* 17(1): 105–21.

  2008a. 'The changing dynamics of employment relations in China: an evaluation of the rising level of labour disputes', *Journal of Industrial Relations* 50(1): 111–38.

  2008b. 'Enterprise culture management in China: "insiders'" perspective', *Management and Organisation Review* 4(2): 291–314.

  2008c. *Competition, Strategy and Management in China*. Basingstoke: Palgrave Macmillan.

2009. 'A decade of transformation of HRM in China: a review of literature and suggestions for future studies', *Asia Pacific Journal of Human
Resources* 47(1): 6–40.

2011. 'The role of the state and emergent actors in the development
of human resource management in China', *International Journal of
Human Resource Management* 22(18): 3830–48.

2012. *Human Resource Management in China: New Trends and Practices*.
London: Routledge.

Creswell, J. 2003. *Research Design: Qualitative, Quantitative, and Mixed
Methods Approaches*. Thousand Oaks, CA: Sage.

Customs House of China, 2007. Announcement of changes in imported
goods   duty.   Available: www.china-customs.com/customs-tax/54/
(accessed 25 January 2008).

Danford, A . 1998. 'Work organisation inside Japanese firms in South Wales:
a break from Taylorism?', in Thompson, P. and Warhurst, C. (eds.)
Workplaces of the Future. London: Macmillan, pp. 40–64.

De Cieri, H. and Dowling, P. J. 2006. 'Strategic international human resource
management in multinational enterprises: developments and directions', in Stahl, G. K. and Björkman, I. (eds.) *Handbook of Research
in International Human Resource Management*. Cheltenham: Edward
Elgar, pp. 15–35.

De Cieri, H., Cox, J. W. and Fenwick, M. 2007. 'A review of international
human resource management: integration, interrogation, imitation',
International Journal of Management Reviews 9(4): 281–302.

Dedoussis, V. and Littler, C. R. 1994. 'Understanding the transfer of Japanese
management practices: the Australian case', in Elger, T. and Smith, C.
(eds.) *Global Japanization? The Transnational Transformation of the
Labour Process*. New York: Routledge, pp. 175–95.

Deeg, R. 2005. 'Path dependency, institutional complementarity, and change
in national business systems', in Glenn, M., Whitley, R. and Moen,
E. (eds.) *Changing Capitalisms? Institutional Change and Systems of
Economic Organization*. Oxford University Press, pp. 21–52.

Delbridge, R. 1998. *Life on the Line in Contemporary Manufacturing: The
Workplace Experience of Lean Production and the "Japanese" Model*.
Oxford University Press.

Delbridge, R., Hauptmeier, M. and Sengupta, S. 2011. 'Beyond the enterprise:
broadening the horizons of international HRM', *Human Relations*
64(4): 483–505.

Delery, J. E. and Doty, D. H. 1996. 'Modes of theorizing in strategic human
resource management: tests of universalistic, contingency, and configurations. Performance predictions', *The Academy of Management
Journal* 39(4): 802–35.

Delios, A. and Henisz, W. J. 2000. 'Japanese firms' investment strategies in emerging economies', *Academy of Management Journal* 43(3): 305–23.

Dicken, P. and Miyamachi, Y. 1998. 'From noodles to satellites: the changing geography of the Japanese sogo shosha', *Transactions of the Institute of British Geographers* 23(1): 55–78.

Ding, D. Z. and Akhtar, S. 2001. 'The organizational choice of human resource management practices: a study of Chinese enterprises in three cities in the PRC', *International Journal of Human Resource Management* 12(6): 946–64.

Ding, D. Z., Goodall, K. and Warner, M. 2000. 'The end of the "iron rice-bowl": whither Chinese human resource management?', *International Journal of Human Resource Management* 11(2): 217–36.

Dowling, P. J., Welch, D. E. and Schuler, R. S. 1999. *International Human Resource Management: Managing People in a Multinational Context.* Cincinnati, OH: International Thomson Publishing.

Downes, M. and Thomas, A. S. 2000. 'Knowledge transfer through expatriation: the U-curve approach to overseas staffing', *Journal of Managerial Issues* 12(2): 131–51.

Dunning, J. H. 1980. 'Toward an eclectic theory of international production: some empirical tests', *Journal of International Business Studies* 11(1): 9–31.

　　1988. 'The eclectic paradigm of international production: a restatement and some possible extensions', *Journal of International Business Studies* 19(1): 1–31.

　　1993. *The Globalization of Business: The Challenge of the 1990s.* London: Routledge.

　　1995. 'Reappraising the eclectic paradigm in an age of alliance capitalism', *Journal of International Business Studies* 26(3): 461–91.

　　1998. 'Location and the multinational enterprise: a neglected factor?', *Journal of International Business Studies* 29(1): 45–66.

　　2000. 'The eclectic paradigm as an envelope for economic and business theories of MNE activity', *International Business Review* 9(2): 163–90.

　　2003. 'The eclectic (OLI) paradigm of international production: past, present and the future', in Cantwell, J. and Narula, R. (eds.) *International Business and the Eclectic Paradigm: Developing the OLI Framework.* New York: Routledge, pp. 25–46.

Dunning, J. H. and Lundan, S. M. 2008. 'Institutions and the OLI paradigm of the multinational enterprise', *Asia Pacific Journal of Management* 25(1): 573–93.

Edwards, T. and Ferner, A. 2002. 'The renewed "American challenge": a review of employment practices in US multinationals', *Industrial Relations Journal* 33(2): 94–111.

Edwards, T. and Kuruvilla, S. 2005. 'International HRM: national business systems, organizational politics and the international division of labour in global value chains', *International Journal of Human Resource Management* 16(1): 1–21.

Edwards, T. and Zhang, M. 2008. 'Multinationals and national systems of employment relations: innovators or adapters?', *Advances in International Management* 21(1): 35–58.

Edwards, T., Colling, T. and Ferner, A. 2007. 'Conceptual approaches to the transfer of employment practices in multinational companies: an integrated approach', *Human Resource Management Journal* 17(3): 201–17.

Edwards, T., Ferner, A., Marginson, P. and Tregaskis, O. 2010. 'Multinational companies and the diffusion of employment practices: explaining variation across firms', *Management International Review* 50(5): 613–34.

Egelhoff, W. G. 1988. 'Strategy and structure in multinational corporations: a revision of the Stopford and Wells model', *Strategic Management Journal* 9(1): 1–14.

Eisenhardt, K. M. 1991. 'Better stories and better constructs: the case for rigor and comparative logic', *Academy of Management Review* 16(3): 620–7.

Elbanna, S. and Child, J. 2007. 'The influence of decision, environmental and firm characteristics on the rationality of strategic decision-making', *Journal of Management Studies* 44(4): 561–91.

Elger, T. and Smith, C. 1994. *Global Japanization? The Transnational Transformation of the Labour Process*. London: Routledge.

  2005. *Assembling Work: Remaking Factory Regimes in Japanese Multinationals in Britain*. Oxford University Press.

Ferlie, E. and McNulty, T. 1997. 'Going to market: changing patterns in the organisation and character of process research', *Scandinavian Journal of Management* 13(4): 367–87.

Ferner, A. 1997. 'Country of origin effects and HRM in multinational companies', *Human Resource Management Journal* 7(1): 19–37.

Ferner, A. and Quintanilla, J. 1998. 'Multinationals, national business systems and HRM: the enduring influence of national identity or a process of "Anglo-Saxonization"', *International Journal of Human Resource Management* 9(4): 710–31.

Ferner, A., Almond, P. and Colling, T. 2005. 'Institutional theory and the cross-national drivers of HRM practices in multinational corporations', *Human Resource Management Journal* 17(4): 355–75.

Ferner, A., Edwards, T. and Tempel, A. 2012. 'Power, institutions and the cross-national transfer of employment practices in multinationals', *Human Relations* 65(1): 1–25.

Ferner, A., Quintanilla, J. and Sanchez-Runde, C. (eds.) 2006. *Multinationals, Institutions and the Construction of Transnational Practices: Convergence and Diversity in the Global Economy*. Basingstoke: Palgrave.

Fletcher, M. and Plakoyiannaki, E. 2011. 'Case selection in international business: key issues and common misconceptions', in Piekkari, R. and Welch, C. (eds.) *Rethinking the Case Study in International Business and Management Research*. Cheltenham: Edward Elgar, pp. 171–91.

Forsgren, M. and Pedersen, T. 1998. 'Centres of excellence in multinational companies: the case of Denmark', in J. Birkinshaw and N. Hood (eds.) *Multinational Corporate Evolution and Subsidiary Development*. New York: St. Martin's Press, pp. 141–61.

Forsgren, M., Holm, U. and Johanson, J. 2007. *Managing the Embedded Multinational: A Business Network View*. Cheltenham: Edward Elgar.

Franko, L., 1973. 'Who manages multinational enterprises?', *Columbia Journal of World Business* 8: 30–42.

French, W. L., Kast, F. E. and Rosenzweig, J. E. 1985. *Understanding Human Behavior in Organizations*. New York: Harper & Row.

Friedman, E. and Lee, C. K. 2010. 'Remaking the world of Chinese labour: a 30-year retrospective', *British Journal of Industrial Relations* 48(7): 507–33.

Frobel, F., Heinrichs, J. and Kreye, O. 1980. *The New International Division of Labour: Structural Unemployment in Industrialised Countries and Industrialisation in Developing Countries*. Cambridge University Press.

Fruin, W. M. 1992. *The Japanese Enterprise System: Competitive Strategies and Cooperative Structures*. Oxford: Clarendon.

Fukuda, K. 1995. 'Japanese companies in China: problems of human resource management', *Asia Pacific Business Review* 1(4): 48–62.

Gamble, J. 2000. 'Localizing management in foreign-invested enterprises in China: practical, cultural, and strategic perspectives', *International Journal of Human Resource Management* 11(5): 883–903.

2003. 'Transferring human resource practices from the United Kingdom to China: the limits and potential for convergence', *International Journal of Human Resource Management* 14(3): 369–87.

2006a. 'Introducing Western-style HRM practices to China: shop floor perceptions in a British multinational', *Journal of World Business* 41(3): 328–43.

2006b. 'Multinational retailers in China: proliferating "McJobs" or developing skills', *Journal of Management Studies* 43(7): 1463–90.

2010. 'Transferring organizational practices and the dynamics of hybridisation: Japanese retail multinationals in China', *Journal of Management Studies* 47(4): 705–32.

Gamble, J., Morris, J. and Wilkinson, B. 2004. 'Mass production is alive and well: the future of work and organization in East Asia', *International Journal of Human Resource Management* 15(2): 397–409.

Geppert, M. and Mayer, M. 2006. *Global, National and Local Practices in Multinational Companies*. Basingstoke: Palgrave Macmillan.

Geppert, M., Matten, D. and Williams, K. 2003. 'Change management in MNCs: how global convergence intertwines with national diversities', *Human Relations* 56(7): 807–38.

Gereffi, G. 1994. 'The organization of buyer-driven global commodity chains: how US retailers shape overseas production networks', in Gereffi, G. and Korzeniewicz, M. (eds.) *Commodity Chains and Global Capitalism*. Westport, CT and London: Praeger, pp. 89–122.

   1999. 'International trade and industrial upgrading in the apparel commodity chain', *Journal of International Economics* 48(1): 48–70.

Gerhart, B., Wright, P. M., McMahan, G. C. and Snell, S. A. 2000. 'Measurement error in research on human resources and firm performance: how much error is there and how does it influence effect size estimates?', *Personnel Psychology* 53(4): 855–72.

Gerlach, M. L. 1992. *Alliance Capitalism: The Social Organization of Japanese Business*. Berkeley, CA: University of California Press.

Ghoshal, S. and Bartlett, C. A. 1990. 'The multinational corporation as an interorganizational network', *Academy of Management Review* 15(4): 603–25.

   1994. 'Linking organizational context and managerial action: the dimensions of quality of management', *Strategic Management Journal* 15(2): 91–112.

Ghoshal, S. and Nohria, N. 1989. 'Internal differentiation within multinational corporations', *Strategic Management Journal* 10(4), 323–37.

Global Labour Strategies 2007. 'Undue influence: corporations gain ground in battle over China's new labor law – but human rights and labor advocates are pushing back'. Available: http://laborstrategies.blogs.com/global_labor_strategies/files/undue_influence_global_labor_strategies.pdf (accessed 10 June 2012).

Goldberg, S. L. and Kolstad, C. D. 1995. 'Foreign direct investment, exchange rate variability, and demand uncertainty', *International Economic Review* 36(4): 855–73.

Goodall, K. and Warner, M. 1997. 'Human resources in Sino-foreign joint ventures: selected case studies in Shanghai, compared with Beijing', *International Journal of Human Resource Management* 8(5): 569–94.

   1998. 'HRM dilemmas in China: the case of foreign-invested enterprises in Shanghai', *Asia Pacific Business Review* 4(4): 1–21.

Graham, L. 1995. *On the Line at Subaru-Isuzu: The Japanese Model and the American Worker*. London: ILR Press.

Greenwood, R. and Hinings, C. R. 1996. 'Understanding radical organizational change: bringing together the old and new institutionalism', *Academy of Management Review* 4(21): 1022–55.

Guan, M. and Fan, J. 2003. *Localising Japanese Companies in China* [in Japanese]. Tokyo: Shinhyouron Press.

Guillot, D. and Lincoln, J. R. 2004. 'Dyad and network: models of manufacturer-supplier collaboration in the Japanese TV manufacturing industry', in Roehl, T. and Bird, A. (eds.) *Japanese Firms in Transition: Responding to the Globalization Challenge*. London: Elsevier, pp. 159–85.

Habib, M. M. and Victor, B. 1991. 'Strategy, structure, and performance of US manufacturing and service MNCs: a comparative analysis', *Strategic Management Journal* 12(8): 589–606.

Hakansson, H. 1997. 'Organizational networks', in Sorge, A. and Warner, M. (eds.) *The IEBM Handbook of Organizational Behaviour*. London: Thomson Business Press, pp. 232–39.

Hall, P. A. and Soskice, D. W. 2001. *Varieties of Capitalism: The Institutional Foundations of Comparative Advantage*. Oxford University Press.

Hannan, M. T. and Freeman, J. 1989. *Organizational Ecology*. Cambridge, MA: Harvard University Press.

Hardy, C. and Clegg, S. 1996. 'Some dare call it power', in Clegg, S., Hardy, C. and Nord, W. R. (eds.) *Handbook of Organisation Studies*. London: Sage, pp. 622–41.

Harris, H., Brewster, C. and Sparrow, P. 2003. *International Human Resource Management*. London: CIPD.

Harvey, M., Speier, C. and Novecenic, M. M. 2001. 'A theory-based framework for strategic global human resource staffing policies and practices', *International Journal of Human Resource Management* 12(6): 898–915.

Harwit, E. 1996. 'Japanese investment in China: strategies in electronics and automobile sectors', *Asian Survey* 36(10): 978–96.

Harzing, A. 1999. *Managing the Multinationals: An International Study of Control Mechanisms*. Cheltenham: Edward Elgar.

　　2000. 'An empirical analysis and extension of the Bartlett and Ghoshal typology of multinational companies', *Journal of International Business Studies* 31(1): 101–20.

　　2001a. 'Of bears, bumble-bees, and spiders: the role of expatriates in controlling foreign subsidiaries', *Journal of World Business* 36(4): 366–79.

　　2001b. 'Who's in charge? An empirical study of executive staffing practices in foreign subsidiaries', *Human Resource Management* 40(2): 139–58.

Harzing, A. and Ruysseveldt, V. J. 2004. *International Human Resource Management*. 2nd edition. London: Sage.

Harzing, A. and Sorge, A. M. 2003. 'Societal embeddedness of internationalization strategies and corporate control in multinational enterprises: world-wide and European perspectives', *Organisation Studies* 24(2): 187–214.

Hassard, J. (ed.) 2007. *China's State Enterprise Reform: From Marx to the Market*. New York: Routledge.

Hassard, J., Morris, J., Sheehan, J. and Yuxin, X. 2006. 'Downsizing the danwei: Chinese state-enterprise reform and the surplus labour question', *International Journal of Human Resource Management* 17(8): 1441–55.

Hayes, T. and Mattimoe, R. 2004. 'To tape or not to tape: reflection on methods of data collection', in Humphrey, C. and Lee, B. (eds.) *The Real Life Guide to Accounting Research*. London: Elsevier, pp. 359–72.

Hedlund, G. 1986. 'The hypermodern MNC: a heterarchy', *Human Resource Management* 25(1): 9–35.

Heery, E. and Frege, C. 2006. 'New actors in industrial relations', *British Journal of Industrial Relations* 44(4): 601–4.

HighBeam Research 2009. *The Essential China Chemical Fiber Industry Report*. Beijing: Highbeam Research.

Hocking, J. B., Brown, M. and Harzing, A. 2004. 'A knowledge transfer perspective of strategic assignment purposes and their path-dependent outcomes', *International Journal of Human Resource Management* 15(3): 565–86.

Hoetker, G. 2004. 'Same rules, different games: variation in the outcomes of "Japanese-style" supply relationships', in Roehl T. and Bird, A. (eds.) *Japanese Firms in Transition: Responding to the Globalization Challenge*. London: Elsevier, pp. 187–212.

Hofstede, G. 1980. *Culture Consequences: International Difference in Work-related Values*. Beverly Hills, CA: Sage.

    1994. 'The business of international business is culture', *International Business Review* 3(1): 1–14.

    2001. *Culture's Consequences: Comparing Values, Behaviors, Institutions, and Organizations Across Nations*. 2nd edition. Thousand Oaks, CA: Sage.

Holdaway, S. 2000. 'Theory and method in qualitative research', in Burton, D. (ed.) *Research Training for Social Scientists: A Handbook for Postgraduate Researchers*. London: Sage, pp. 156–66.

Hong, J. F. L., Easterby-Smith, M. and Snell, R. S. 2006. 'Transferring organizational learning systems to Japanese subsidiaries in China', *Journal of Management Studies* 45(5): 1027–58.

Hoopes, D. G., Madsen, T. L. and Walker, G. 2003. 'Why is there a resource-based view? Toward a theory of competitive heterogeneity', *Strategic Management Journal* 24(10): 889–902.

Howard, A., Liu, L. Wellins, R. S. and Williams, S. 2008. 'Employee retention in China 2007: the flight of human talent', Society for Human Resource Management. Available: www.ddiworld.com/ddiworld/media/trend-research/employee-retention-in-china-2007_fullreport_ddi.pdf (accessed 10 June 2012).

Huber, G. 1991. 'Organizational learning – the contributing process and the literature', *Organization Science* 2(1): 88–155.

Hughes, J. M. C. 2002. 'HRM and universalism: is there one best way?', *International Journal of Contemporary Hospitality* 14(5): 221–8.

Huselid, M. A. 1995. 'The impact of human resource management practices on turnover, productivity, and corporate financial performance', *Academy of Management Journal* 38(3): 635–72.

Huselid, M. A., Jackson, S. E. and Schuler, R. S. 1997. 'Technical and strategic human resource management effectiveness as determinants of firm performance', *Academy of Management Journal* 40(1): 171–88.

Inagaki, K. 2003. *Map of Companies Invested in China* [in Japanese]. Tokyo: 21st Century Research Centre.

Inagami, T. and Whittaker, D. H. 2005. *The New Community Firm: Employment, Governance and Management Reform in Japan.* Cambridge University Press.

Ip, O. K. M. 1999. 'A case study of human resource management in the People's Republic of China: convergence or non-convergence?', *International Journal of Employment Studies* 7(2): 61–79.

Itagaki, H. (ed.) 1997. *The Japanese Production System: Hybrid Factories in East Asia.* Basingstoke: Macmillan.

Jackson, G. and Deeg, R. 2008. 'Comparing capitalisms: understanding institutional diversity and its implications for international business', *Journal of International Business Studies* 39(4): 540–61.

Jackson, S. E. and Schuler, R. S. 1995. 'Understanding human resource management in the context of organizations and their environments', *Annual Review of Psychology* 46(1): 237.

Jackson, S. E., Schuler, R. S. and Rivero, J. C. 1989. 'Organizational characteristics as predictors of personnel practices', *Personnel Psychology* 42(4): 727–86.

Japan Chemical Fibre Association (JCFA) 2007. Japan's chemical fibre industry. Available: www.jcfa.gr.jp/f7-stat.html (accessed: 22 January 2007).

Japan Institute for Labour Policy and Training (JILPT) 2006. *Survey on Human Resource Management of Japanese Multinational Corporations.* 4th edition. Tokyo: JILPT.

Jaussaud, J. and Liu, X. 2011. 'When in China ... The HRM practices of Chinese and foreign-owned enterprises during a global crisis', *Asia Pacific Business Review* 17(4): 473–91.

JETRO 2002. *JETRO White Paper on Foreign Direct Investment*. Tokyo: Japan External Trade Organisation.

2005. *JETRO White Paper on Foreign Direct Investment*. Tokyo: Japan External Trade Organisation.

2007. *JETRO White Paper on Foreign Direct Investment*. Tokyo: Japan External Trade Organisation.

2008. *JETRO White Paper on Foreign Direct Investment*. Tokyo: Japan External Trade Organisation.

2011. *JETRO White Paper on Foreign Direct Investment*. Tokyo: Japan External Trade Organisation.

Kalu, T. 1995. 'A framework for empirically investigating the power of functional units in organizations', *Scandinavian Journal of Management* 11(3): 251–68.

Katz, D. and Kahn, R. L. 1966. *The Social Psychology of Organizations*. New York: Wiley.

Kawakami, S. 1996. 'Local problems', *Far Eastern Economic Review* 3: 44–46.

Kawamura, M. and Hayashikawa, S. 1998. *Big Bang of the General Trading Companies* [in Japanese]. Tokyo: Toyo Keizai Press.

Keenoy, T. and Schwan, R. 1990. 'Review article human resource management: rhetoric, reality and contradiction', *International Journal of Human Resource Management* 1(3): 363–84.

Kenney, M. 2001. 'Regional clusters, venture capital and entrepreneurship: what can the social sciences tell us about Silicon Valley', in Organisation for Economic Co-Operation and Development (ed.) *Social Sciences and Innovation*. pp. 55–76.

Kenney, M. and Florida, R. 1993. *Beyond Mass Production: The Japanese System and its Transfer to the U. S.* New York: Oxford University Press.

(eds.) 2003. *Locating Global Advantage: Industry Dynamics in the International Economy*. Stanford University Press.

Kenney, M., Goe, W., Contreras, R., Romero, J. and Bustos, M. 1998. 'Learning factories or reproduction factories?: labor-management relations in the Japanese consumer electronics maquiladoras in Mexico', *Work and Occupations* 25(3): 269–304.

Kirk, J. and Miller, M. L. 1986. *Reliability and Validity in Qualitative Research*. Beverly Hills, CA and London: Sage.

Knight, J. and Song, L. 2005. *Towards a Labour Market in China*. Oxford University Press.

Koike, K. 1997. *Human Resource Development*. Tokyo: Japan Institute of Labour.

Kopp, R. 1984. 'International human resource policies and practices in Japanese European and United States multinationals', *Human Resource Management* 33(4): 581–99.

1994. *The Rice-Paper Ceiling: Breaking Through Japanese Corporate Culture*. Berkeley, CA: Stone Bridge Press.

Kristensen, P. H. and Zeitlin, J. 2005. *Local Players in Global Games: The Strategic Constitution of a Multinational Corporation*. New York: Oxford University Press.

Kumar, V. and Subramanian, V. 1997. 'A contingency framework for the mode of entry decision', *Journal World Business* 32(1): 53–72.

Kwong, J. and Qui, Y. 2003. 'China's social security reforms under market socialism', *Public Administration Quarterly* 27(2): 188–209.

Lam, A. 1997. 'Embedded firms, embedded knowledge: problems of collaboration and knowledge transfer in global cooperative ventures', *Organization Studies* 18(6): 973–96.

2000. 'Tacit knowledge, organizational learning and societal institutions: an integrated framework', *Organization Studies* 21(3): 487–513.

Lane, P. J. 2001. 'Absorptive capacity, learning, and performance in international joint ventures', *Strategic Management Journal* 22(12): 1139–61.

Lane, P. J. and Lubatkin, M. 1998. 'Relative absorptive capacity and interorganisational learning', *Strategic Management Journal* 19(5): 461–77.

Laurent, A. 1986. 'The cross-cultural puzzle of international human resource management', *Human Resource Management* 25(1): 91–102.

Lee, C. K. 1995. 'Engendering the worlds of labour: women workers, labour markets, and production politics in the south China economic miracle', *American Sociological Review* 60 (Jun): 378–97.

1999. 'From organized dependence to disorganized despotism: changing labour regimes in Chinese factories', *China Quarterly* 157(Mar): 44–71.

2007. *Against the Law: Labour Protests in China's Rustbelt and Sunbelt*. Berkeley, CA: University of California Press.

Legewie, J. 2002. 'Control and co-ordination of Japanese subsidiaries in China: problems of an expatriate-based management system', *International Journal of Human Resource Management* 13(6): 901–19.

Li, J., Karakowsky, L. and Lam, K. 2002. 'East meets east and east meets west: the case of Sino-Japanese and Sino-west joint ventures in China', *Journal of Management Studies* 39(6): 841–63.

Li, J., Lam, K., Sun, J. and Liu S. 2008. 'Strategic human resource management, institutionalization, and employment modes: an empirical study in China', *Strategic Management Journal* 29(3): 337–42.

Li, Y. and Sheldon, P. 2010. 'HRM lives inside and outside the firm: employers, skill shortages and the local labour market in China', *International Journal of Human Resource Management* 21(2): 2173–93.

Liu, M., Xu, L. and Liu, L. 2004. 'Wage-related labour standards and FDI in China: some survey findings from Guangdong province', *Pacific Economic Review* 9(3): 225–43.

Lowe, J., Morris, J. and Wilkinson, B. 2000. 'British factory, Japanese factory and Mexican factory: an international comparison of front', *Journal of Management Studies* 37(4): 541–62.

Lu, Y. and Björkman, I. 1997. 'HRM practices in China-Western joint ventures: MNC standardization versus localization', *International Journal of Human Resource Management* 8(5): 614–28.

Lucio, M. M. and Weston, S. 1994. 'New management practices in a multinational corporation: the restructuring of worker representation and rights', *Industrial Relations Journal* 25(2): 110–21.

Luo, Y. 1998. *International Investment Strategies in the People's Republic of China*. Ashgate: Aldershot & Brookfield.

Lupton, T. 1971. *Management and the Social Sciences*. London: Penguin.

Ma, Z. 1998. 'What to learn from the Japanese? The process of Japanese-style management transfer to China', in Strange, R. (ed.) *Management in China: The Experience of Foreign Businesses*. London: Cass, pp. 118–31.

March, R. M. 1992. *Working for a Japanese Company*. New York: Kodansha International.

Marchington, M. and Grugulis, I. 2000. '"Best practice" human resource management: perfect opportunity or dangerous illusion?', *International Journal of Human Resource Management* 11(6): 1104–24.

Matanle, P. and Wim, L. (eds.) 2006. *Perspectives on Work, Employment and Society in Japan*. Basingstoke: Palgrave Macmillan.

Mayo, E. 1949. 'Hawthorne and the Western Electric Company', in Pugh, D. E. (ed.) *Organizational Theory: Selected Readings*. 4th edition. London: Penguin.

McGaughey, S. L., Iverson, R. D. and Decieri, H. 1997. 'A multi-method analysis of work-related preferences in three nations: implications for inter- and intra-national human resource management', *International Journal of Human Resource Management* 8(1): 1–17.

McNulty, T. and Ferlie, E. 2002. *Reengineering Health Care: The Complexities of Organizational Transformation*. Oxford University Press.

McSweeney, B. 2002a. 'Hofstede's model of national cultural difference and their consequences: a triumph of faith a failure of analysis', *Human Relations* 55(1): 89–118.

2002b. 'The essentials of scholarship – a reply to Geert Hofstede', *Human Relations* 55(11): 1363–72.

Meyer-Ohle, H. C. and Legewie, J. 2000. 'Does nationality matter? Western and Japanese multinational corporations in Southeast Asia', *European Review* 8(4): 553–67.

Miah, M. K. and Bird, A. 2007. 'The impact of culture on HRM styles and firm performance: evidence from Japanese parents, Japanese subsidiaries/joint ventures and South Asian local companies', *International Journal of Human Resource Management* 18(5): 908–23.

Milkman, R. 1991. *Japan's California Factories: Labor Relations and Economic Globalization*. Los Angeles, CA: Institute of Industrial Relations, University of California.

Milliman, J., Von Glinow, M. A. and Nathan, M. 1991. 'Organizational life cycles and strategic international human resource management in multinational companies: implications for congruence theory', *Academy of Management Review* 16(2): 318–39.

Ministry of Economy, Trade and Industry of Japan (METI) 2006. *METI Basic Survey on Overseas Business Activities*. Tokyo: METI.

Moore, F. 2006. 'Governing the outposts? Exploring the role of expatriate managers in a multinational corporation', in Geppert, M. K. and Mayer, M. (eds.) *Global, National and Local Practices in Multinational Companies*. New York: Palgrave, pp. 167–87.

   2011. 'Holistic ethnography: studying the impact of multiple national identities on post-acquisition organisations', *Journal of International Business Studies* 42(special issue): 645–71.

Morgan, G. and Kristensen, P. H. 2006. 'The contested space of multinationals: varieties of institutionalism, varieties of capitalism', *Human Relations* 59(11): 1467–90.

Morgan, G., Whitley, R. and Moen, E. (eds.) 2005. *Changing Capitalisms? Internationalization, Institutional Change, and Systems of Economic Organization*. Oxford University Press.

Morgan, G., Kelly, B., Sharpe, D. and Whitley, R. 2003. 'Global managers and Japanese multinationals: internationalization and management in Japanese financial institutions', *International Journal of Human Resource Management* 14(3): 389–407.

Morris, J., Wilkinson, B. and Gamble, J. 2009. 'Strategic international human resource management or the "bottom line"? The cases of electronics and garments commodity chains in China', *International Journal of Human Resource Management* 20(2): 348–70.

Morris, J., Wilkinson, B. and Munday, M. 2000. 'Farewell to HRM: personnel practices in Japanese manufacturing plants in the UK', *International Journal of Human Resource Management* 11(6): 1047–60.

Myloni, B., Harzing, A. and Mirza, H. 2004. 'Host country specific factors and the transfer of human resource management practices in multinational companies', *International Journal of Manpower* 25(6): 518–34.

2007. 'The effect of corporate-level organizational factors on the transfer of human resource management practices: European and US MNCs and their Greek subsidiaries', *International Journal of Human Resource Management* 18(12): 2057–74.

Nakagane, K. 2000. *SOE Reform and Privatization in China: A Note on Several Theoretical and Empirical Issues*. University of Tokyo.

Nakos, G. and Brouthers, K. D. 2002. 'Entry mode choice of SMEs in central and Eastern Europe', *Entrepreneurship Theory and Practice* 27(1): 47–64.

National Bureau of Statistics of China (various years). *China Statistical Year Book*. Beijing: National Bureau of Statistics of China.

Neuman, L. W. 1997. *Social Research Methods: Qualitative and Quantitative Approaches*. 3rd edition. Needham Heights, MA: Allyn & Bacon.

Nohria, N. and Ghoshal, S. 1997. *The Differentiated Network: Organizing Multinational Corporations for Value Creation*. San Francisco, CA: Jossey-Bass.

Noon, M. 1992. 'Human resource management: a map, model or theory?', in Blyton, P. and Turnbull, P. (eds.) *Reassessing Human Resource Management*. London: Sage, pp. 175–90.

Oddou, G., Derr, C. B. and Black, J. S. 1995. 'Internationalizing managers: expatriation and other strategies', in Selmer, J. (ed.) *Expatriate Management: New Ideas for International Business*. Westport, CT: Quorum, pp. 3–16.

Organisation for Economic Cooperation and Development (OECD) 2002. *Foreign Direct Investment in China: Challenges and Prospects for Regional Development*. Paris: OECD.

O'Hagan, E., Gunnigle, P. and Morley, M. J. 2005. 'Issues in the management of industrial relations in international firms', in Scullion, H. and Lineham, M. (eds.) *International Human Resource Management: A Critical Text*. London: Palgrave Macmillan, pp. 156–80.

Ouchi, W. 1981. 'Theory Z: how American business can meet the Japanese challenge', *Business Horizons* 24(6): 82–3.

Paik, Y. and Teagarden, M. B. 1995. 'Strategic international human resource management approaches in the maquiladora industry: a comparison of Japanese, Korean, and US Firms', *International Journal of Human Resource Management* 6(3): 568–87.

Paterson, L. S. and Brock, M. D. 2002. 'The development of subsidiary-management research: review and theoretical analysis', *International Business Review* 11(2): 139–63.

Penga, M. W., Leea, S. and Tanb, J. 2001. 'The keiretsu in Asia: implications for multilevel theories of competitive advantage', *Journal of International Management* 7(4): 253–76.

Penrose, E. 1958. *The Theory of the Growth of the Firm*. Oxford University Press.

Perkins, S. J. and Shortland, S. M. 2006. *Strategic International Human Resource Management: Choices and Consequences in Multinational People Management*. London and Philadelphia: Kogan Page.

Perlmutter, H. V. 1969. 'The tortuous evolution of the multinational company', *Columbia Journal of World Business* 4(1): 9–18.

Perry, E. 1996. *Putting Class in Its Place: Worker Identities in East Asia*. Berkley, CA: Institute of East Asia Studies, University of California.

Perry, E. and Selden, M. 2010. *Chinese Society: Change, Conflict and Resistance*. 3rd edition. London and New York: Routledge.

Pettigrew, A. M. 1985. *The Awakening Giant: Continuity and Change in Imperial Chemical Industries*. Oxford: Blackwell.

  1992. 'The character and significance of strategy process research', *Strategic Management Journal* 13(2): 5–16.

  2003. 'Strategy as process, power and change', in Cummings, S. and Wilson, D. (eds.) *Images of Strategy*. Oxford: Blackwell, pp. 301–30.

Pfeffer, J. 1992. *Managing with Power: Politics and Influence in Organizations*. Boston, MA: Harvard Business School.

  1994. *Competitive Advantage Through People: Unleashing the Power of the Workforce*. Boston, MA: Harvard Business School Press.

  1996. 'When it comes to best practices – why do smart organisations occasionally do dumb things?', *Organisation Dynamics* 25(1): 33–44.

  1998. *The Human Equation: Building Profits by Putting People First*. Boston, MA: Harvard Business School Press.

Piore, M. J. 1992. 'Arrangements of a cognitive theory of technological change and organizational structure', in Nohria, N. and Eccles, R. G. (eds.) *Networks and Organizations: Form, Structure and Action*. Boston, MA: Harvard Business School Press, pp. 25–56.

Poole, M. S., Van de Ven, A. H. and Dooley, K. 2000. *Organizational Change and Innovation Processes: Theory and Methods for Research*. Oxford University Press.

Porter, M. E. 1986. *Competition in Global Industries*. Boston, MA: Harvard Business School.

Prahalad, C. K. and Doz, Y. L. 1987. *The Multinational Mission: Balancing Local Demands and Global Vision*. London: Collier Macmillan.

Pudelko, M. and Harzing, A. 2007a. 'Country-of-origin, localization, or dominance effect? An empirical investigation of HRM in foreign subsidiaries', *Human Resource Management* 46(4): 535–59.

2007b. 'How European is management in Europe? An analysis of past, present and future management practices in Europe', *European Journal of International Management* 1(3): 233–53.

Pun, N. and Smith, C. 2007. 'Putting transnational labour process in its place: dormitory labour regime in post-socialist China', *Work, Employment & Society* 21(1): 27–45.

Punnett, B. J. 1998. 'Culture, cross-national', in Poole, M. and Warner, M. (eds.) *The IEBM Handbook of Human Resource Management*. London: Thompson Learning, pp. 9–25.

Quintanilla, J. and Ferner, A. 2003. 'Multinationals and human resource management: between global convergence and national identity', *International Journal of Human Resource Management* 14(3): 363–8.

Reutersward, A. 2005. 'Labour protection in China: challenges facing labour offices and social insurance', *OECD Social, Employment and Migration Working Papers*. OECD.

Ritchie, J. 1998. 'Evolving China strategies: how the Japanese compare', in Strange, R. (ed.) *Management in China: The Experience of Foreign Business*. London and Portland, OR: Frank Cass, pp. 132–47.

Rosenfeld, R. H. and Wilson, D. C. 1999. *Managing Organizations: Text, Readings and Cases*. 2nd edition. London: McGraw-Hill.

Ross, A. 2007. 'Outsourcing as a way of life? Knowledge transfer in the Yangze Delta', in Lee, C. K. (ed.) *Working in China: Ethnographies of Labour and Workplace Transformation*. New York: Routledge, pp. 118–208.

Rosenzweig, P. M. 2006. 'The dual logic behind international human resource management: pressures for global integration and local responsiveness', in Stahl, G. K. and Björkman, I. (eds.) *Handbook of Research in International Human Resource Management*. Cheltenham: Edward Elgar, pp. 36–48.

Rosenzweig, P. M. and Nohria, N. 1994. 'Influences on human resource management practices in multinational corporations', *Journal of International Business Studies* 25(2): 229–51.

Rowley, C. and Cooke, F. L. 2010. *The Changing Face of Management in China*. London: Routledge.

Rowley, C. and Warner, M. 2007. 'Introduction: globalizing international human resource management', *International Journal of Human Resource Management* 18(5): 703–16.

2010. 'Chinese management at the crossroads', *Asia Pacific Business Review* 16(3): 268–80.

Rowley, C., Benson, J. and Warner, M. 2004. 'Towards an Asian model of HRM: a comparative analysis of China, Japan and Korea', *International Journal of Human Resource Management*, 15(4/5): 917–33.

Rugman, A. M. and Verbeke, A. 1992. 'A note on the transnational solution and the transaction cost theory of multinational strategic management', *Journal of International Business Studies* 23(4): 761–71.

2001. 'Subsidiary-specific advantages in multinational enterprises', *Strategic Management Journal* 22(3): 237–50.

Rugman, A. M., Verbeke, A. and Yuan, W. 2011. 'Re-conceptualizing Bartlett and Ghoshal's classification of national subsidiary roles in the multinational enterprise', *Journal of Management Studies* 48(2): 253–77.

Sako, M. 2005. *Shifting Boundaries of the Firm: Japanese Company-Japanese Labour*. Oxford University Press.

Scandura, T. A. and Williams, E. A. 2000. 'Research methodology in management: current practices, trends, and implications for future research', *Academy of Management Journal* 43(6): 1248–64.

Schneider, B. 2000. 'Why good management ideas fail: the neglected power of organizational culture', *Strategy and Leadership* 28(1): 24–29.

Schuler, R. 1989. 'Strategic human resource management and industrial relations', *Human Relations* 42(2): 157–84.

Schuler, R. S. and Jackson, S. E. 1987. 'Linking competitive strategies with human resource management practices', *Academy of Management Executive* 1(3): 207–19.

2001. 'Human resource management: past, present, and future', in Blanpain, R. and Engels, C. (eds.) *Comparative Labour Law and Industrial Relations in Industrialized Market Economies*. The Hague: Kluwer, pp. 101–31.

Schuler, R. S., Dowling, P. J. and De Cieri, H. 1993. 'An integrative framework of strategic international human resource management', *International Journal of Human Resource Management* 12(4): 717–64.

1999. 'An integrative framework of strategic international human resource management', in Schuler, R. S. and Jackson, S. E. (eds.) *Strategic Human Resource Management: A Reader*. London: Blackwell, pp. 319–355.

Schutte, H. 1998. 'Between headquarters and subsidiaries: the RHQ solution', in Birkinshaw, J. and Hood, N. (eds.) *Multinational Corporate Evolution and Subsidiary Development*. New York: St. Martin's Press, pp. 102–37.

Scott, W. R. 1995. 'Introduction: institutional theory and organizations', in Scott, W. R. (ed.) *The Institutional Construction of Organizations*. Thousand Oaks, CA: Sage, pp. xi–xxii.

2002. *Organizations: Rational, Natural, and Open Systems*. Upper Saddle River, NJ: Prentice Hall.

Scullion, H. 2001. 'International human resource management', in Storey, J. (ed.) *Human Resource Management: A Critical Text*. London: International Thomson Publishing, pp. 288–313.

Scullion, H. and Paauwe, J. 2004. 'International HRM: recent developments in theory and research', in Harzing, A. and Ruysseveldt, J. (eds.) *International Human Resource Management*. London: Sage.

Shaffer, M. A., Harrison, D. A. and Gilley, K. M. 1999. 'Dimensions, determinants, and differences in the expatriate adjustment process', *Journal of International Business Studies* 30(3): 557–81.

Sharpe, D. R. 2001. 'Globalisation and change: organisational continuity and change within a Japanese multinational in the UK', in Morgan, G., Kristensen, P. H. and Whitley, R. (eds.) *The Multinational Firm: Organizing Across Institutional and National Divides*. Oxford University Press, pp. 196–224.

   2006. 'Shop floor practices under changing forms of managerial control: a comparative ethnographic study of micro-politics, control and resistance within a Japanese multinational', *Journal of International Management* 12(3): 318–39.

Shibata, H. 2009. 'A comparison of the roles and responsibilities of manufacturing engineers in Japan and the United States', *International Journal of Human Resource Management* 20(9): 1896–1913.

Silver, B. 2003. *Forces of Labour: Workers' Movements and Globalization since 1870*. Cambridge University Press.

Silver, B. and Zhang, L. 2009. 'China as an epicentre of world labour unrest', in Hung, H. (ed.) *China and the Transformation of Global Capitalism*. Baltimore, MD: Johns Hopkins University Press, pp. 174–87.

Silverman, D. 2000. *Doing Qualitative Research*. 2nd edition. London: Sage.

Smircich, L. and Stubbart, C. 1985. 'Strategic management in an enacted world', *Academy of Management Review* 10(4): 724–38.

Smith, C. 2003. 'Living at work: management control and the dormitory labour system in China', *Asia Pacific Journal of Management* 20(3): 333–58.

   2005. 'Beyond convergence and divergence: explaining variations in organizational practices and forms', in Ackroyd, S., Batt, R. Thompson, P. and Tolbert, P. (eds.) *The Oxford Handbook of Work and Organization*. Oxford University Press.

   2008. 'Work organisation within a globalising context: a critique of national institutional analysis of the international firm and an alternative perspective', in Smith, C., McSweeney, B. and Fitzgerald, R. (eds.) *Remaking Management: Between Global and Local*. Cambridge University Press, pp. 25–60.

Smith, C. and Meiksins, P. 1995. 'System, society and dominance effects in cross-national organisational analysis', *Work Employment and Society* 9(2), 241–67.

Smith, C., Child, J. and Rowlinson, M., 1990. *Reshaping Work: The Cadbury Experience*. New York: Cambridge University Press.

Smith, C., McSweeney, B. and Fitzgerald, R. (eds.) 2008. *Remaking Management: Between Global and Local*. Cambridge University Press, pp. 1–16.

Snell, S. A. and Dean, J. W. Jr. 1992. 'Integrated manufacturing and human resource management: a human capital perspective', *Academy of Management Journal* 35(3): 467–504.

Soo, M. T. and Denisi, A. S. 2003. 'Host country national reactions to expatriate pay policies: a model and implications', *Academy of Management Review* 28(4): 606–21.

Sorge, A. and Warner, M. (eds.) 1997. *The IEBM Handbook of Organizational Behaviour*. London: Thomson International Business Press.

Stone, L. K. 1991. 'Expatriate selection and failure', *Human Resource Planning* 29(1): 9–17.

Stopford, J. M. and Wells, L. T. 1972. *Managing the Multinational Enterprise: Organization of the Firm and Ownership of the Subsidiaries*. New York: Basic Books.

Strange, R. 1998. (ed.) *Management in China: The Experience of Foreign Business*. London and Portland, OR: Frank Cass.

Strange, S. 1999. 'An international political economy perspective', in Dunning, J. H. (ed.) *Governments, Globalization, and International Business*. Oxford University Press, pp. 132–45.

Takeuchi, N., Chen, Z. and Lam, W. 2009. 'Coping with an emerging market competition through strategy-human resource alignment: case study evidence from five leading Japanese manufacturers in the People's Republic of China', *International Journal of Human Resource Management* 20(12): 2454–70.

Taylor, B. 1999. 'Patterns of control within Japanese manufacturing plants in China: doubts about Japanization in Asia', *Journal of Management Studies* 36(6): 853–73.

2001. 'Labour management in Japanese manufacturing plants in China', *International Journal of Human Resource Management* 12(4): 600–20.

Taylor, S. 2006. 'Emerging motivations for global HRM integration', in Ferner, A., Quintanilla, J. and Sanchez-Runde, C. (eds.) *Multinationals and the Construction of Transnational Practices: Convergence and Diversity in the Global Economy*. London: Palgrave, pp. 109–30.

Taylor, S., Beechler, S. and Napier, N. 1996. 'Toward an integrative model of strategic international human resource management', *Academy of Management Review* 21(4): 959–85.

Thomas, D. C. 1998. 'The expatriate experience: a critical review and synthesis', *Advances in International Comparative Management* 12(1): 237–73.

Townley, B. 1993. 'Foucault, power, knowledge and its relevance for human resource management', *Academy of Management Review* 18(3): 518–45.

Toyo Keizai, 2006. *Toyo Keizai Databank: Japanese-Invested Companies Overseas (sorted by host country)*. Tokyo: Toyo Keizai Press.

Truss, C. 2001. 'Complexities and controversies in linking HRM with organizational outcomes', *Journal of Management Studies* 38(8): 1121–49.

Tsai, W. and Ghoshal, S. 1998. 'Social capital and value creation: the role of intrafirm networks', *Academy of Management Journal* 41(4): 464–78.

Tsurumi, Y. 1976. *The Japanese Are Coming: A Multinational Interaction of Firms and Politics*. Cambridge, MA: Ballinger.

Tung, L. R. 1981. 'Selection and training of personnel for overseas assignments', *Columbia Journal of World Business* 16(1): 68–78.

  1984. 'Strategic management of human resources in the multinational enterprise', *Human Resource Management* 23(2): 129–43.

Vernon, R. 1966. 'International investment and international trade in the product cycle', *Quarterly Journal of Economics* 80(2): 190–207.

Walsh, J. and Zhu, Y. 2007. 'Local complexities and global uncertainties: a study of foreign ownership and human resource management in China', *International Journal of Human Resource Management* 18(2): 249–67.

Wang, X. and Kanungo, R. N. 2004. 'Nationality, social network and psychological well-being: expatriates in China', *International Journal of Human Resource Management* 15(5): 775–93.

Warner, M. 1993. 'Human resources management "with Chinese characteristics"', *International Journal of Human Resource Management* 4(1): 45–65.

  1995. 'Managing China's human resources', *Human Systems Management*, 14(3): 239–48.

  1997. 'China's HRM in transition: towards relative convergence?', *Asia Pacific Business Review* 3(4): 19–33.

  1999. 'Human resources and management in China's "hi-tech" revolution: a study of selected computer hardware, software and related firms in the PRC', *International Journal of Human Resource Management* 10(1): 1–20.

  2000. 'Introduction: the Asia-Pacific HRM model revisited', *International Journal of Human Resource Management* 11(2): 171–82.

  (ed.) 2003. *Culture and Management in Asia*. London and New York: Routledge.

  (ed.) 2005. *Human Resource Management in China Revisited*. New York: Routledge.

  2006. 'Globalization: a critical introduction: organizational theory and multinational corporation', *Journal of General Management* 32(2): 101–3.

2008. 'Reassessing human resource management "with Chinese characteristics": an overview', *International Journal of Human Resource Management* 19(5): 771–801.

2009. '"Making sense" of HRM in China: setting the scene', *International Journal of Human Resource Management* 20(11): 2169–93.

Warner, M. and Zhu, Y. 1998. 'Re-assessing Chinese management: the influence of indigenous versus exogenous models', *Human Systems Management*, 17(4): 245–55.

Weick, K. E. 1995. *Sensemaking in Organizations*. Thousand Oaks, CA: Sage.

2003. 'Enacting of environment: the infrastructure of organizing', in Westwood, R. and Clegg, S. (eds.) *Debating Organization: Point-Counterpoint in Organization Studies*. Malden, MA: Blackwell, pp. 183–94.

Whitley, R. 1992. 'Societies, firms and markets: the social structuring of business systems', in Whitley, R. (ed.) *European Business Systems*. London: Sage, pp. 5–45.

1996. 'The social construction of economic actors: institutions and types of firms in Europe and other market economies', in Whitley, R. and Kristensen, P. H. (eds.) *The Changing European Firm: Limits to Convergence*. London: Routledge, pp. 39–66.

1999. *Divergent Capitalisms: The Social Constructing and Change of Business Systems*. Oxford University Press.

2000. 'The institutional structuring of innovation strategies: business systems, firm types and patterns of technical change in different market economies', *Organization Studies* 21(5): 855–86.

2002. 'Introduction: the institutional structuring of market economies', in Whitley, R. (ed.) *Competing Capitalisms: Institutions and Economies*. Cheltenham: Edward Elgar, pp. ixxx–vii.

2005. 'How national are business systems? The role of states and complementary institutions in standardizing systems of economic coordination and control at the national level', in Morgan, G., Whitley, R. and Moen, E. (eds.) *Changing Capitalisms? Internationalization, Institutional Change, and Systems of Economic Organization*. Oxford University Press, pp. 190–234.

2007. *Business Systems and Organizational Capabilities: The Institutional Structuring of Competitive Competences*. Oxford University Press.

Whitley, R., Morgan, G., Kelly, W. and Sharpe, D. 2003. 'The changing Japanese multinational: application, adaptation and learning in car manufacturing and financial services', *Journal of Management Studies* 40(3): 643–72.

Wilkinson, B., Gamble, J., Humphrey, J., Morris, J. and Anthony, D. 2001. 'The new international division of labour in Asian electronics: work organization and human resources in Japan and Malaysia', *Journal of Management Studies* 38(5): 675–95.

Williamson, O. E. 1975. *Markets and Hierarchies: Analysis and Antitrust Implications*. New York: Free Press.

Wright, P. M., McMahan, G. C., Snell, S. A. and Gerhart, B. 2001. 'Comparing line and HR executives' perceptions of HR effectiveness: services, roles, and contribution', *Human Resource Management* 40(2): 111–23.

Wu, X. B. 2007. *Thirty Years of Turbulence* [in Chinese]. Beijing: CITIC Publishing.

Wu, Y. 2000. 'Is China's economic growth sustainable? A productivity analysis', *China Economic Review* 11(3): 278–96.

Yin, R. 1994. *Case Study Research: Design and Methods*. 2nd edition. Thousand Oaks, CA and London: Sage.

   2003. *Case Study Research: Design and Method*. 3rd edition. London: Penguin Books.

Yoshihara, H. 2001. 'Sogo Shosha: global organizations managed by Japanese and in Japanese', in Taggart, J. H., Berry, M. and McDermott, M. (eds.) *Multinationals in a New Era: International Strategy and Management*. Basingstoke: Palgrave, pp. 153–65.

   2004. 'Decline of Japan's predominance in Asia', in Roehl, T. and Bird, A. (eds.) *Japanese Firms in Transition: Responding to the Globalization Challenge*. London: Elsevier, pp. 159–85.

Yoshino, M. Y. 1996. *Japan's Multinational Enterprises*. Cambridge, MA: Harvard University Press.

Zahra, S. A. and George, G. 2002. 'Absorptive capacity: a review, reconceptualization, and extension', *Academy of Management Review* 27(2): 185–203.

Zhang, M. and Edwards, C. 2007. 'Diffusing "best practice" in Chinese multinationals: the motivation, facilitation and limitations', *International Journal of Human Resource Management* 18(12): 2147–65.

Zhang, M., Nyland, C. and Zhu, C. J. 2010. 'Hukou-based HRM in contemporary China: the case of Jiangsu and Shanghai', *Asia Pacific Business Review* 16(3): 377–93.

Zheng, C. and Lamond, D. 2009. 'A critical review of human resource management studies (1978–2007) in the People's Republic of China', *International Journal of Human Resource Management* 20(11): 2194–227.

Zhongzhi, 2008. *A Study of Pay Level at Foreign Invested Companies in Shanghai, China* [in Chinese]. Shangahi: Zhong Zhi Consultant Co.

Zhou, C., Delios, A. and Yang, J. Y. 2002. 'Locational determinants of Japanese foreign direct investment in China', *Asia Pacific Journal of Management* 19(1): 63–86.

Zhu, C. J. 2005. *Human Resource Management in China: Past, Current and Future HR Practices in the Industrial Sector*. London and New York: Routledge.

Zhu, C., Cooper, B., De Cieri, H. and Dowling, P. 2005. 'A problematic transition to a strategic role: human resource management in industrial enterprises in China', *International Journal of Human Resource Management* 16(4): 513–31.

Zhu, Y. and Warner, M. 2000. 'An emerging model of employment relations in China: a divergent path from the Japanese?', *International Business Review* 9(3): 345–61.

Zhu, Y., Warner, M. and Rowley, C. 2007. 'Human resource management with "Asian" characteristics: a hybrid people-management system in East Asia', *International Journal of Human Resource Management* 18(5): 745–68.

Zou, M. and Lansbury, R. D. 2009. 'Multinational corporations and employment relations in the People's Republic of China: the case of Beijing Hyundai Motor Company', *International Journal of Human Resource Management* 20(11): 2349–69.

Index